First printing: June 2000

ISBN: 0-89221-499-6
Library of Congress Catalog Card Number: 00-102661

All Scripture quotations in this book, unless otherwise noted, are
taken from the New American Standard Bible, © 1960, 1962, 1963,
1968, 1971, 1972, 1973, 1975, 1977, 1995 by the Lockman Foundation. Used by permission.

Cover illustration by Jud Guitteau from Illustration Works, Inc.

Printed in Canada.

Please visit our website for other great titles:
www.newleafpress.net

For information regarding publicity for author
interviews contact Diana Fletcher at (870) 438-5288.

Living for Christ
in the
End Times

Living for Christ
in the
End Times

Balancing Today with the Hope of Tomorrow

Dr. David Reagan

New Leaf Press

Dedicated to

Dennis Pollock, Gary Fisher, and Don Perkins

— three men who have devoted their lives
to proclaiming the Lord's soon return

Expressions of Thanks

I want to thank the exceptional staff of Lamb & Lion Ministries for all the support and encouragement they gave me during the writing of this book. The only way I can write is to go into isolation and focus totally on writing. When I do that, it puts an extra strain on all my staff members since they must cover letters, e-mail messages, and phone calls that I would normally handle.

There are two staff members in particular who deserve special thanks. One is my secretary, Kay Bien, who proofread the text. The other is the ministry's financial director, George Collich Jr., who performed the tedious job of checking all the Scripture references.

I also want to thank the trustees of Lamb & Lion Ministries who have been so supportive and encouraging. I am particularly indebted to Ya'acov Hugg of Haifa, Israel, for constantly prodding me over the years to do more writing.

I want to express appreciation to the thousands of radio listeners who have sent me a great variety of articles over the years, mainly about American society, the Church, and Israel. I have used many of these on my daily radio program "Christ in Prophecy," and I have included a few of them in this book. The only problem is that these articles are usually torn from a magazine or cut from a newspaper and often arrive without any indication of their source or their precise date. Where this proves to be the case with a reference in this book, I have indicated it in the endnotes.

I must also mention that I owe a great debt of gratitude to

Ann, my wife of 40 years. She is a gentle, loving, soft-spoken first grade teacher who knows how to deal with me when I act like a first grader! I praise God for her love and companionship and for her constant encouragement.

Most of all, I am indebted to my Lord and Savior, Jesus of Nazareth, who patiently pursued me over a period of 20 years while I ran from His call on my life. I am thankful that He never gave up on me, and that when I finally got to the end of my rope, He was still there and still willing to forgive and forget and entrust me with a ministry. What grace! I praise Him for His lovingkindness.

Contents

Preface

T his book deals with secular and spiritual paganism and how Christians should respond to both. In dealing with spiritual paganism, I have some harsh things to say regarding both Christian leaders and churches. I do not relish making such statements. I have felt compelled to make them because the stakes are so high. Souls are in peril because of widespread heresy and apostasy in the Church today. I don't think we can any longer afford the luxury of "tiptoeing through the tulips."

The Bible says that the end times will be a period of great deception (Acts 20:28–30; 1 Tim. 4:1; and 2 Tim. 4:3–4). I feel that those whom God has called to be watchmen on the walls (Isa. 62:6) must put a face on heresy and apostasy by naming names.

❖ Responses to Criticism ❖

I have discovered over the years that when someone identifies heretical or apostate leaders in the Church, they are always condemned in one of four ways. The most common response is for people to quote the verse that says, "Do not touch My anointed ones" (1 Chron. 16:22). This verse has unfortunately become a shield for all kinds of false prophets and teachers. The context of the verse makes it clear that it is addressed to political leaders who desire to murder the preachers and prophets of God. It has nothing to do with the public exposure of a false teacher. Furthermore, false teachers are not anointed of God.

A second verse that is always trotted out in response to criticism is Matthew 18:15, which states that when a brother sins against you, you should reprove him in private. This verse applies to personal wrongs. When I publicly renounce a false teacher, I am not responding to someone who has wronged me personally.

Rather, I'm dealing with a person who is publicly harming the body of Christ with false teaching. Such a person needs to be dealt with publicly, and if the person feels that is not proper, then he should keep his mouth shut. When you speak in the public arena, whether through a book, a radio program, or a TV show, you should expect to be held publicly accountable.

Paul practiced this. He publicly confronted Peter when Peter resorted to playing politics with the Judaizers in the Early Church (Gal. 2:11–14). Paul also named names when it came to dealing with false teachers. On two occasions, He warned the Church against Hymenaeus, Philetus, and Alexander who were teaching false doctrine (1 Tim. 1:20 and 2 Tim. 2:17).

❖ Arguments about Judging ❖

The third way in which people often react to the criticism of false teachers is to quote Matthew 7:1: "Do not judge lest you be judged." But this verse has to be balanced by the command of Jesus in John 7:24: "Judge with righteous judgment." We must also keep in mind that the Bible tells us repeatedly that we are to test what we are taught (Acts 17:11; 1 Thess. 5:21; 1 John 4:1; and Rev. 2:2). There is simply no way to test what we hear without drawing judgmental conclusions.

What we are not to judge is motives. Only God knows a person's motives. Also, we are not to judge based upon appearance (John 7:24). But we certainly have a right and a responsibility to judge words and actions by testing them against the Word of God.

The fourth common response to criticism is more general in nature. "We shouldn't criticize our own." This attitude is rooted in a feeling that Christians get enough criticism from the world. We should, therefore, circle the wagons and protect our own, regardless of how off-the-wall they may be. Well, the Christian leaders I criticize in this book are not "our own." A person who denies the resurrection of Jesus is not a Christian, regardless of what he calls himself and regardless of what ecclesiastical position he may hold. The same is true of a person who denies that Jesus was God in the flesh.

Paul wrote that anyone who denies the resurrection has no hope (1 Cor. 15:12–19). It doesn't make any difference if the person is a pastor, a bishop, or a seminary professor. If he or she denies the resurrection of Jesus, that person is not a Christian. As to the identity of Jesus, it is the heart of Christianity. If He was not who He said He was — God in the flesh — then we have no hope, for no one else could die for our sins.

❖ The Centrality of Jesus ❖

With regard to this issue, we must keep in mind that all truth is important, but all truth is not equally important. A person can be wrong about many things and still be saved, but if he is wrong about Jesus, there is no hope for him.

Putting your faith in a false Jesus cannot save you. This is the error of the cults. The Jesus of the Jehovah's Witnesses is the Archangel Michael. The Jesus of the Mormons is the brother of Lucifer and is considered to be one of several thousand gods created by the super-god Adam, an exalted man. The Jesus of the many spiritist groups is a medium of the sixth sphere of the astro-projection (whatever that gobbledygook means!).

The Jesus of the liberal, apostate Christian leaders is the Jesus of the theme song in the Broadway musical *Jesus Christ Superstar.* That song says over and over, "He's a man, he's just a man." He is a false savior created in their own image, full of their own faults.

Many apostate leaders today claim to believe an orthodox Jesus, but they deny that He is the only way to God. Instead, they teach that He is one of many paths to God. They argue that one can also find God through Mohammed, Buddha, the Dali Lama, or a hundred other false spiritual leaders. What we need to keep in mind is that when they take this position, they are calling Jesus a liar, for He said clearly that there is no way to the Father except through Him (John 14:6). People who call Jesus a liar are not among "our own." They are not true Christians. They are wolves in sheep's clothing (Matt. 7:15 and Acts 20:28–30).

❖ Criticism of Churches ❖

With regard to churches, I name specific denominations when I give examples of heresy and apostasy. It would have been easier and certainly more diplomatic to have simply referred to "a mainline denomination" rather than specifically name one. But again,

I feel the necessity to put a face on the apostasy that exists in the Church today. As I said before, there is too much at stake to do otherwise. Also, denominational loyalty often causes us to be blind about apostasy. We can see it in other groups but not in our own unless someone confronts us with it.

But the main thing you need to keep in mind as you read my criticisms of denominations is that heresy and apostasy exist today in all denominational groups. Doctrinal impurity is one of the signs of the end times (2 Tim. 4:1–4). I have personally experienced Methodist churches that were apostate. I have also come across Methodist churches that were orthodox but which were dead, and I have experienced Methodist churches that were alive and well. The same is true in all denominations. There are apostate Baptist churches and Baptist churches that are on fire for the Lord.

For 20 years I have had the blessing of preaching for a nondenominational ministry that goes among churches of all denominations. In the process I have discovered that you cannot judge a church by its signboard or its denominational affiliation. A church must be judged by what is happening in its pulpit. Is the Bible being preached as the Word of God and is Jesus being exalted as the only hope for mankind? If so, the church is a good one, regardless of its denominational label.

❖ Faithful Local Churches ❖

Many of our denominations today are corrupt at the top in the sense that their national leaders are apostates who deny the fundamentals of the faith. But many of the local churches affiliated with those denominations are rock-solid, standing on the Word and preaching Jesus.

I think of First Baptist Church in North East, Pennsylvania, a suburb of Erie. This church is affiliated with the Northern Baptist denomination, which is about as liberal as they come. When the pastor, Randy Elliott, called me about ten years ago and asked me to hold a meeting for his church, I was surprised.

"Aren't you a Northern Baptist church?" I asked.

"Yes," he replied. "Why do you ask?"

"Well," I responded, "do you know where I'm coming from?"

"Oh yes," he said, "I listen to your radio program daily. Our church lines up with what you preach."

"And you are still affiliated with the Northern Baptists?" I asked in surprise.

"Yes, we are hanging in there with the hope that we can have an impact on our denomination."

That story is true for many local churches in the Presbyterian, Methodist, and Lutheran denominations, as well as others like the Disciples of Christ. Many Bible-believing and Christ-exalting local churches have retained their denominational affiliations because they hope to influence their national leaders to come home to the Lord. They know they will have no influence at all if they leave and end up on the outside looking in.

❖ My Personal Heritage ❖

I feel I must add a special word concerning a group I talk about a lot in this book — the non-instrumental Churches of Christ. This is the group I was born into and grew up in. I left the group 30 years ago, but I was affiliated with them for the first 30 years of my life.

This group came out of what is called the Restoration Movement, a religious movement that began among Presbyterians in the early 1800s. The leaders, Barton W. Stone and Alexander Campbell, desired to rid themselves of denominationalism and return to the Bible as their only creed. It was one of many "Back to the Bible" movements that have characterized the American scene over the years.

The Restoration Movement ultimately spawned three groups — the liberal Disciples of Christ, the middle-of-the-road Independent Christian Churches, and the reactionary Churches of Christ. Since many of the Independent Christian Churches took the name Church of Christ, the Churches of Christ started referring to themselves as "the non-instrumental Churches of Christ." They used this designation because one of their distinguishing doctrines was a condemnation of musical instruments in worship. The non-instrumental Churches of Christ are strictly a cappella.

They are strict about a lot of other things. So strict, in fact, that they grew increasingly legalistic as the years passed. By the 1950s, there were more than 25 different Church of Christ groups who were so legalistic, sectarian, and exclusivistic that they would have nothing to do with each other! There was the non-Sunday school group, the non-human literature group, the no-kitchen-in-the-church group, the one-cuppers (who opposed the use of multiple cups for communion), the wine-before-the-bread group (who opposed those who broke the bread first), and the premillennialists (most Churches of Christ were amillennial). There was even a group that was simply known as "The Antis." They were opposed to located preachers, mission societies, orphans' homes, and a variety of other things. One wag summed them up by saying, "You name it, and they are agin' it!" There was, of course, the "mainline church" which was amillennial, multiple cup, bread-before-the-wine, and which had Sunday school, located ministers, and kitchens in their buildings.

❖ Denomination, Sect, or Cult? ❖

The Churches of Christ claimed to be non-denominational, and that claim was correct in a sense. Although they were a clearly identifiable group like the Baptists and Methodists, they did not consider themselves to be a *part* of the body of Christ, like the other denominations. No, they considered themselves to be *the* body of Christ! In other words, they considered themselves to be the one and only true church.

That's why in looking back on them, I consider them to be what I call a sect. They were not a cult because they had an orthodox view of Jesus. But they certainly were not a denomination since they did not consider themselves to be a denominated part of the body of Christ. They *were* the body of Christ.

The Churches of Christ have come a long way in the past 30 years toward being more open and accepting of other churches. This has been due primarily to the impact of Christian bookstores and Christian radio and television. You see, none of these things existed before the 1960s. When I was a kid, there were no Christian bookstores, TV didn't exist, and Christian radio consisted of church services being broadcast on Sunday morning. The result was that it was easy to keep folks isolated and ignorant.

When our preachers got up and blasted the Baptists as "heathern," we could easily shout "Amen!" After all, most of us had never read a book written by a Baptist, nor had we ever heard a sermon by a Baptist or visited a Baptist church. Christian publishers and Christian media have opened up all aspects of Christendom to be experienced by everyone, and with this openness has come the realization that the body of Christ cannot be confined to any one group.

There have always been small groups within the Churches of Christ who were grace-oriented, in particular the non-Sunday school group and the premillennialists. But today the mainline churches are moving more in the direction of openness as exemplified by Max Lucado, one of the most popular Christian writers in America today. He is the preaching minister of a Church of Christ in San Antonio, Texas (Churches of Christ do not believe in using the term pastor).

❖ Heresy and Apostasy ❖

I talk a lot in this book about apostasy, so I think I need to define what I am referring to. I see a difference in heresy and apostasy. To me, heresy consists of unbiblical doctrines that do not threaten one's salvation. They impede your sanctification (your development into the image of Jesus), but they do not impact your justification (your legal standing before God as born-again and thus forgiven of all your sins).

Prophecy is a good example. What you believe about Bible prophecy will impact the way you live here and now, and so it is important. But it will not impact where you spend eternity, so lines of fellowship should not be drawn over differences in prophetic viewpoints. Heaven is going to contain amillennialists, premillennialists, postmillennialists, and people who never knew the difference in a millennium and a millepede!

Apostasy is a more serious matter. Apostasy consists of a denial of the fundamentals of the faith — matters that relate to the identity of Jesus and the efficacy of His sacrifice on the Cross. These are issues that relate to salvation and thus to one's eternal destiny.

An example of apostasy would be a denial of the virgin birth, because if Jesus was not virgin born then He was not God in the flesh. The same is true of the Resurrection. If Jesus was not resurrected, then He was not divine, and He is not our Savior.

This book is not just about apostasy and heresy. It is primarily about how to develop a deep and meaningful relationship with God that will, in turn, protect you from spiritual deception and sustain you in the midst of secular persecution. It is my hope that your reading of this book will draw you into a deeper relationship with the Lord than you have ever known before.

Part One

The Descent into Paganism

Chapter 1

❖ ❖ ❖

The Decay of Society

An American sports legend, Magic Johnson, reveals that he has AIDS. Rumors begin to fly that he is bi-sexual. He is confronted on national television about the rumors. Instead of simply denying them, he begins to boast about how macho he is, claiming to have been to bed with as many as six women at one time! Is America outraged? No. President Bush appoints him to serve on a national AIDS commission.[1]

❖ ❖ ❖

The actress Suzanne Somers appears on the TV program *Good Morning, America.* She is trying to jump-start her flagging career. The appearance is prompted by her agreement to pose nude for *Playboy* magazine. The interviewer asks, "Why would you pose nude for *Playboy* now, when you sued them several years ago for publishing nude photos of you?"

Ms. Somers explains that the previous photos were taken by an amateur photographer and were published without her consent. "I decided that since there were bad nude photos of me that had already been published, I might as well get some good ones published." She goes on to say that she laid down two conditions for the new photo spread in *Playboy.* "First, they had to let me select the photographer. And second, they had to let me select the photos to be used." She then makes the announcement that she decided to get her son (who was 19 at the time) involved in the project. "I spread out the photos on the floor and let him select the ones to be used in the magazine."

"Oh, that was so thoughtful of you," replies the interviewer.[2]

❖ ❖ ❖

The movie star Dustin Hoffman is to be interviewed on television for the first time in his home. The interviewer is a young woman in her mid-twenties. After a few introductory comments, she presents her first question to Mr. Hoffman: "Could you tell us about your first sexual experience?"

For a fleeting moment I hope Mr. Hoffman will express outrage and ask her to leave. But, no, he just giggles with glee and proceeds to tell her in lurid detail about how his older brother arranged for him to go to bed with a prostitute when he was 15 years old.[3]

❖ ❖ ❖

The president of the United States, Bill Clinton, decides to begin a sexual dalliance with a White House intern the age of his daughter. Eventually, when the affair becomes public, it is revealed that on one occasion she performed oral sex on the president while he was talking to a congressman on the phone. On another occasion, the president inserted a cigar in her vagina, then placed it in his mouth and said, "It tastes good."

Is America outraged over these revelations? No. The president's popularity rating soars to new heights.[4]

❖ ❖ ❖

What's the point? A nation that once honored God has plunged into a moral abyss. And the decay has reached the point where, in the words of the prophet Jeremiah, the nation does "not even know how to blush" (Jer. 6:15).

The descent has been swift. When I was born in 1938:

Abortionists were considered the scum of the earth and were sent to prison.

Pregnancy out of wedlock was thought of as scandalous, and "living together" was unthinkable.

Drugs were something you bought at a pharmacy (or "drug store").

Alcoholism was considered a sin, not a disease.

Popular music was free of demonic beats and words.

Movies were devoid of nudity, passionate love scenes, mindless violence, and filthy language.

Eastern religion was still in the East.

The corrupting influence of television was non-existent.

Pornography was something that circulated underground.

Public school students prayed in their classes and read the Bible, and creation could still be taught as an alternative to evolution.

High school graduates could read their diplomas.

The Ten Commandments were still legal.

AIDS was a gift of the Spirit (1 Cor. 12:28 refers to the gift of aids or helps, depending on the translation).

Our governments — local, state, and national — still promoted Judeo-Christian values rather than lotteries, horse racing, and casino gambling.

Christian teaching focused on sacrificing for Christ rather than confessing materialistic success.

Governmental authority was respected. Police were held in high esteem.

Houses and cars were never locked.

Social security was a job. Living on welfare was considered a disgrace.

Language was civil. Manners still prevailed. Women were treated with dignity and respect.

Looking back over the last 60 years, the old Virginia Slims cigarette ad seems to sum it up best: "We've come a long way, baby!" Yes, we have, and it has been in the wrong direction.

Today, we are murdering 4,000 babies a day in the name of "freedom of choice" for women.

We spend more on gambling each year than we do on food.

We are assaulted by a glut of pornography in books and movies and on the Internet.

We are consuming 55 percent of all the illegal drugs in the world, even though we constitute only 5 percent of the world's population.

Our families are being destroyed by an epidemic of spousal violence, child abuse, and divorce.

Our prisons are overflowing because of a breakdown of law and order.

Our cities are jungles of violence where people dare not venture out at night.

Our homes are fortresses with bars on the windows, guns in the cabinets, and electronic security systems monitoring the doors and windows.

Our schools are filled with drugs, rebellion, and violence.

Our governing bodies are shot full of corruption.

Our churches are apathetic and compromised by worldliness.

Our entertainment industry has become a purveyor of violence and immorality, and as we export its products abroad, we serve as the moral polluter of planet Earth.

❖   Our Schools as a Mirror of Society   ❖

The best way I can think of to summarize the decay of American society is to consider the results of a public school survey that was conducted in the mid-1940s and again in the mid-1980s. The survey was taken by the Fullerton, California, Police Department in conjunction with the California Department of Education. The purpose was to determine the major disciplinary problems in the schools. The comparative results speak volumes (see Table 1).

Table 1
Leading Public School Disciplinary Problems[5]

1940s	1980s
1. Talking	1. Drug abuse
2. Chewing gum	2. Alcohol abuse
3. Making noise	3. Pregnancy
4. Running in hallways	4. Suicide
5. Getting out of place in line	5. Rape
6. Wearing improper clothing	6. Robbery
7. Not putting paper in wastebaskets	7. Assault

In January 1993, *Time* magazine reported some sobering statistics from the National Education Association that affirms the deterioration of our schools. According to the NEA report, every school day:

100,000 students tote guns to school

160,000 skip classes because they fear physical harm

40 are hurt or killed by firearms

6,250 teachers are threatened with bodily injury

260 teachers are actually assaulted[6]

That's *every day!*

An insightful commentary about what has happened to the children of America was posted on the Internet recently:

What a Concept!

Whoa! What in the world is happening with our kids today? Let's see . . . I think it started when Madelyn Murray O'Hair complained that she didn't want any prayer in our schools, and we said, "Okay."

Then someone said you had better not read the Bible in school. After all, it says, "Thou shalt not kill, thou shalt not steal, and love your neighbor as yourself." And we said, "Okay."

Then the Supreme Court said that we could no longer post the Ten Commandments in our classrooms because they might influence our children, in violation of the concept called "separation of church and state." And we said, "OK."

Remember Dr. Benjamin Spock, who said we shouldn't spank our children when they misbehave, because their little personalities would be warped and we might damage their self-esteem? And we said, "Okay."

Then someone said that teachers and principals better not discipline our children when they misbehave. And our administrators said, "Whoa, no one in this school better touch a student when they misbehave because we don't want any bad publicity, and we surely don't want to be sued."

Then someone said, "Let's let our daughters have abortions if they want, and we won't even tell their parents." And we said, "Okay."

Then someone else said, "Let's give our sons all the condoms they want so they can have all the 'fun' they desire, and we won't tell their parents." And we said, "That's another great idea!"

And then some of our top officials said, "It doesn't matter what we do in private as long as we do our jobs." And we said, "As long as I have a job and the economy is good, it doesn't matter to me what anyone does in private."

So now we're asking ourselves why our children have no conscience, why they don't know right from wrong, and why it doesn't bother them to kill.

Probably, if we think about it long and hard enough, we can figure it out. I think it has a great deal to do with "we reap what we sow."

Whoa! What a concept![7]

❖ Rejecting the Ten Commandments ❖

In 1980 in the case of *Stone v. Graham,* the United States Supreme Court ruled that it is unconstitutional to hang the Ten Commandments on the wall of a school room.[8]

Think about that for a moment. The Ten Commandments are the foundation of Western Civilization. Our entire legal system is rooted in them.

The reasoning of the Court was right out of the "Twilight Zone." The Court stated that "if the posted copies of the Ten Commandments are to have any effect at all, it will be to induce the school children to read, meditate upon, perhaps to venerate and obey, the Commandments." The Court then proceeded to state that these were not "permissible objectives."[9] Is it any wonder that so many of our schools have become jungles of drugs and violence?

❖ Modernizing the Commandments ❖

A man by the name of Ken Matto has revised the Ten Commandments to reflect current values. He calls his revision "The Ten Replacements."[10]

1. Thou shalt create gods in man's image to confirm the deity of man and the evolution of intelligence. Your gods may be created according to self-revelation.

2. Thou shalt make unto thyself images and symbols of your beliefs. If your image is a cow or a rock star or a pentagram, that is fine. All things are relative in the evolution of the species.

3. Thou shalt take the name of God and Jesus in vain since Jesus was not God, and God is anything you care to make him — or her.

4. Thou shalt profane the Sabbath Day because you get double time on Sunday, and your family need not be in church since it is full of hypocrites. And furthermore, isn't making money the important thing?

5. Thou shalt dishonor thy father and mother because they are only good to bail you out of jail or put a roof over your head. Too bad they don't possess the wisdom and knowledge of the years like you do, being a 13 year old.

6. Thou shalt kill since you will only be acting on pent-up rage because your father disciplined you one time when you were five.

7. Thou shalt commit adultery. After all, we have a free-thinking and open society, and since your faith is in science, you know they will soon come up with a cure for AIDS or Herpes Simplex II.

8. Thou shalt steal, for isn't everybody doing it? When you get out into the workplace you can steal time, pencils, products, and anything else you deserve. After all, didn't you have a deprived childhood because daddy and mommy refused to buy you $90 attitude pants with the crotch down to your knees?

9. Thou shalt bear false witness. After all, it really isn't false witness; it is just looking out for number one. If a good lie saves your hide, come on, why not?

10. Thou shalt always covet your neighbor's things because if you outdo them, your self-esteem will sky-rocket, and you will finally be someone special. Remember, your pride is the most important thing.

The amazing thing is that in the midst of all this moral depravity, we have the audacity to call ourselves a "Christian nation"! The fact of the matter is that we are a post-Christian nation that is now wallowing in secularism and paganism. Steve Allen has summed it up well in a remark he often makes about the American entertainment industry: "We have vulgarians entertaining barbarians."[11] Where did America get off course? How have we managed to move so quickly from a God-fearing nation to one that thumbs its nose at God?

❖ The Road to Depravity ❖

An outline of our course to depravity can be found in the writings of the apostle Paul. In Romans chapter one he states that the road to destruction for a nation begins when its institutions decide to "suppress the truth in unrighteousness," an action that will ultimately lead to people worshiping the creation rather than the Creator (Rom. 1:18, 25).

The decade of the 1960s proved to be the turning point for America. But the cultural revolution against God that characterized that decade was rooted in developments that occurred early in the 20th century. The two most influential were intellectual tides that swept into America from Europe. They arrived almost simultaneously.

One was Darwinism with its atheistic attack on the very concept of God. The origin and purpose of man was called into question. Man was reduced to a mere animal, a product of chance with no particular purpose.

The other was the German School of Higher Criticism which challenged the Bible as the infallible revelation of God. The Bible was viewed instead as man's search for God and was therefore considered to be full of myth, legend, and superstition.

The Christian world view suddenly came under attack from without and within the Church. The faith of many was shattered.

❖ Embracing Moral Relativism ❖

As the authority of God's Word was undermined, and man's purpose became meaningless, moral relativism gradually took center stage. People began to challenge traditional concepts of right and wrong. As in the days of the judges of Israel, people began to do what was right in their own eyes (Judg. 21:25). They called it "different strokes for different folks." Each man became a god unto himself, able to determine for himself his own values and ethics, if any. And anyone who would dare judge someone else's actions was declared "intolerant."

By the 1980s America had reached the point referred to in Judges 2:10 — we had produced a whole generation "who did not know the Lord."

We had "suppressed the truth in unrighteousness" by banning prayer from public schools, prohibiting the posting of the Ten Commandments, and declaring that evolution was the only theory that could be taught about the origin of the universe.

Suddenly government was actively promoting all sorts of

abominable activity such as gambling, abortion, and homosexuality. Eastern religions and mystical intellectual philosophies like the New Age movement began to displace Christianity.

Earth Day became a national celebration. People gathered to worship "Mother Earth" rather than the Father God who created the earth. They joined hands and hummed to get synchronized with the rhythm of "Mother Earth." They further celebrated their new religion by hugging a tree or stroking a salmon.

Millions of people paid hundreds of dollars each to attend self-discovery seminars of various types. What they all had in common was the teaching that God resides in each of us, and that we must learn how to release our "god power."

❖ Wallowing in Despair ❖

By the 1990s America had fulfilled another prophecy of the apostle Paul about the end times. It is found in 2 Timothy 3:1–5:

> But realize this, that in the last days difficult times will come. For men will be lovers of self, lovers of money, boastful, arrogant, revilers, disobedient to parents, ungrateful, unholy, unloving, irreconcilable, malicious gossips, without self-control, brutal, haters of good, treacherous, reckless, conceited, lovers of pleasure rather than lovers of God, holding to a form of godliness, although they have denied its power.

Notice that this prophecy predicts that the society of the end times will love three things: self, money, and pleasure. The love of self is humanism, the religion of America today. The love of money is materialism, America's god.

When your religion is focused on self, and your god is money, the result is always a lifestyle based on the love of pleasure, which is hedonism. Needless to say, that is the lifestyle of the "liberated" American as he enters the 21st century.

But God cannot be mocked (Gal. 6:7). Humanism, materialism and hedonism constitute a deadly combination. They always produce the same payoff. It is what philosophers call nihilism, which is a $64 word for despair.

Look again at 2 Timothy 3:1–5. The passage describes a society wallowing in despair. The description reads like the news that we witness on TV every evening. The news reports are full of boastful, arrogant revilers who are ungrateful and unholy — as well as stories about rebellious children and reckless, conceited haters of good. And we are constantly bombarded with the opinions of those "professing to be wise" but who in reality are fools (Rom. 1:22).

❖ God's Discipline for Nations ❖

In Romans, Paul tells us how God dealt with people in rebellious nations. He says that God "gave them over in the lusts of their hearts to impurity" (Rom. 1:24). In other words, God steps back, lowers His hedge of protection around the nation, and allows sin to multiply as a judgment upon the nation.

The first consequence is a sexual revolution like the one that occurred in America in the 1960s. Paul refers to it as the dishonoring of their bodies (Rom. 1:24).

Paul says that if this judgment does not produce repentance, God will take another step back and lower His hedge of protection even further. In this second stage, He will deliver the nation to "degrading passions" (Rom. 1:26). Paul explains that this judgment will be manifested in a plague of homosexuality. He says women will exchange the natural function for that which is unnatural, and men will abandon the natural function of the woman and burn in their desire toward one another: "Men with men committing indecent acts" (Rom. 1:27). Paul even mentions that those who participate in such evil will receive "in their own persons the due penalty of their error" (Rom. 1:27). Thus, the modern-day AIDS epidemic is portrayed clearly as a judgment of God.

Nor is that the end of the process. Again, Paul notes that if the society persists in its rebellion, God will take another step back and lower His hedge of protection even further, giving them over "to a depraved mind" (Rom. 1:28). At that point Paul says the society will become like the one he describes in 2 Timothy 3 — "filled with all unrighteousness, wickedness, greed, evil; full of envy, murder, strife, deceit, malice; they are gossips, slanderers, haters of God, insolent, arrogant, boastful, inventors of evil, disobedient to parents, without understanding, untrustworthy, unloving, unmerciful" (Rom. 1:29–31). He then adds a sobering thought: "We know that the judgment of God rightly falls upon those who practice such things" (Rom. 2:2).

❖   Teetering on the Edge of Destruction   ❖

America has reached the third and final stage that leads from judgment to destruction. God has placed judgment after judgment on our nation in an attempt to call us to repentance — judgments like the war in Vietnam, the drug epidemic, the AIDS plague, the disintegration of the family, civil riots, violence in the schools, and natural disasters.

But we have refused to repent. We have, in fact, set our jaw against God, determined to go our own way and do our own thing. This attitude was recently manifested in the incredible proclamation issued by President Bill Clinton in June of 1999 when he called for Americans to "celebrate" homosexuality. He declared June 1999 to be Gay and Lesbian Pride Month.[12] I responded by sending him an e-mail message in which I asked, "What will you ask us to 'celebrate' next? Will you proclaim Adultery Pride Month? What about a month honoring prostitutes or pedophiles?"

The interesting thing is that despite our continuing rebellion, God has not yet touched our false god — the Almighty Dollar. I suspect He is still patiently waiting for us to repent, and if we fail to do so He will destroy our god with the greatest economic collapse in recorded history — one that will reduce us to Third World status and remove us from our position as the world's only superpower.

God brought the Soviet Union down overnight, and He can do the same to us, just as He did to the superpower Babylon in ancient history. At the time He touched the Soviet Union, it was the world's greatest military power. But all its nuclear weapons and missiles could not protect it from the hand of God. Overnight the Soviet Union was reduced to political and economic chaos.

❖   Begging for Judgment   ❖

The destruction that will fall upon us will be much worse. That's because of the biblical principle that says, "From everyone who has been given much shall much be required" (Luke 12:48). The Russian people can say, "We did not know." But what can Americans say? We have been blessed like no other nation since ancient Israel. In addition to our political and economic blessings, we have been blessed spiritually with a saturation of the gospel. We have an average of five Bibles in each home, we have radio and television evangelists, and we have an over-abundance of churches. We have no excuse before God.

The Bible teaches that God never pours out His wrath without warning. He has been warning America for three decades through His judgments and His prophets. He has raised up prophetic voices throughout the land to warn the people of impending judgment — voices like Dave Wilkerson in New York City, whom I consider to be God's Jeremiah to America.

Non-Christians have understandably mocked these warnings as "millennial madness." What is tragic is that many Christian leaders have also responded with ridicule. Many Christians seem to believe that God sits on His throne draped in an American flag, and that He would never touch His "anointed nation." After all, isn't He dependent on the wealth and influence and technology of America to spread the gospel all over the world?

❖ A Biblical Example of National Arrogance ❖

It has happened before. When God got ready to pour out His wrath on ancient Judah, He raised up prophets like Micah and Jeremiah to warn the people of their impending doom. And what was their response? They pointed to the Lord's temple and assured the prophets that God would never allow anything to happen to it (Jer. 7:1–4). They were safe, they thought, because the Shekinah glory of God resided in their temple. The prophets were "full of wind," they argued, because God would protect His temple and the nation to which He had entrusted it (Jer. 5:13). Their attitude was arrogance gone to seed.

And so it is in America today. We are a proud nation. After all, we are "number one." In our pride we have turned our back on God. Like the Jews of biblical times, we want the blessings of God but not the God of the blessings.

Our pride has also prompted us to become an imperialist nation. We wander pell-mell around the earth like a giant in a drunken stupor, throwing our weight around, trying to run the affairs of everyone else. One day it's Somalia, the next day, Haiti, and then Kosovo and Indonesia. The irony of it is that while we are trying to solve the problems of other nations, we can't even keep the peace in the streets of our own major cities. What hubris!

❖ A Biblical Type of America ❖

Our prophetic type in the Bible is the nation of Judah. If you want to read about America in Bible prophecy, read Isaiah 5 and Jeremiah 5 and 6. These two prophets list the sins that motivated God to destroy that nation. The sobering reality is that they are the same sins that characterize America today.

Isaiah speaks of injustice, greed, pleasure seeking, blasphemy, moral perversion, intellectual pride, intemperance, and political corruption. Regarding moral perversion, Isaiah says people were "calling evil good, and good evil" (Isa. 5:20). That's precisely what we are doing in America today regarding abortion, homosexuality, and gambling. Isaiah sums up the root of his nation's decay (and America's) by asserting, "They have rejected the law of the Lord of hosts, and despised the word of the Holy One of Israel" (Isa. 5:24).

Jeremiah, writing about 75 years later (God is so patient!), lists the same sins as still prevailing in the land. But he adds some new ones to the list: immorality and religious corruption. His summary statements are very revealing:

They have made their faces harder than rock (Jer. 5:3).

They have refused to repent (Jer. 5:3).

This people has a stubborn and rebellious heart (Jer. 5:23).

They do not even know how to blush (Jer. 6:15).

God destroyed this nation. Why would He deal any differently with a modern day clone? God "is the same yesterday and today, yes and forever" (Heb. 13:8). Or, as it is stated in Malachi 3:6, "I, the Lord do not change."

❖ Christianity under Attack ❖

As America descends further into a moral abyss, Christians are going to come under increasing attack. Already society has written off evangelical Christians as "intolerant bigots" because they are the only ones speaking out today in behalf of righteousness. The media have declared open season on Christians. Christianity, the Bible, and Jesus are openly mocked in movies, books, television programs, and the arts. Similar attacks on blacks, homosexuals, Jews, or even Muslims would not be tolerated. But everything sacred to Christians can be trampled. There is no escaping the fact that we are in the midst of a culture war in America. The forces of paganism, secularism, atheism, and humanism have launched an all-out attack on Judeo-Christian values.

The two sides in this war were well represented in the responses to the Columbine High School massacre in the spring of 1999.

Speaking from a Judeo-Christian perspective, Billy Graham said:

> I agree with those who have remarked that the problem is not guns. Rather, it is the hearts of people which need to be changed. I would add that only God can change our hearts. That is the reason Jesus said, "You must be born again." Only God can give us a new nature that is demonstrated by love.[13]

Speaking from the pagan perspective, Howard Stern, the radio "shock-jock" said:

> There were some really good-looking girls running out with their hands over their heads. Did those kids [the killers] try to have sex with any of the good-looking girls? They didn't even do that? At least if you're going to kill yourself and kill all the kids, why wouldn't you have some sex?[14]

❖ A Double Standard ❖

As the culture war intensifies, the press is practicing a double standard. For example, when reporting acts of violence against blacks, homosexuals, or Jews, the deeds are instantly categorized as "hate crimes." But with regard to the acts of violence specifically aimed at Christians — as in the schools in Paducah, Kentucky, and Littleton, Colorado, or at the church in Fort Worth — these are written off as "random acts of violence."

Nationwide, people are being discriminated against in job hirings and promotions simply because they are Christians, something that would have been unthinkable in this country just a few years ago. Churches are being harassed as never before by zoning boards and building inspectors.

The situation is going to get worse rather than better. Jesus told His disciples that the world would hate them just as it hated Him (John 15:18–19). Jesus also prophesied that in the end times, right before His return, all true believers would be hated on account of His name and would be persecuted (Matt. 24:9). The only reason more professing Christians are not being persecuted today is because most have become so compromised by the world that it would be hard to find enough evidence to convict them of being Christians!

❖   The Prospect of Suffering   ❖

In addition to specific persecution, we as Christians face the suffering that is going to engulf our nation if Jesus tarries and delays His return until after America is judged for its rebellion. When God judges a nation, the rain falls on the just and the unjust. Believers are not immune to the suffering, but they are promised that God will walk with them through the suffering and sustain them. As God got ready to destroy Judah, He spoke reassuring words to the true believers in the land:

> When you pass through the waters, I will be with you;
> And through the rivers, they will not overflow you.
> When you walk through the fire, you will not be
> scorched, Nor will the flame burn you. For I am the
> Lord your God, The Holy One of Israel, Your Savior
> (Isa. 43:2–3).

Many of the believers who heard these words suffered terribly from the long siege of Jerusalem. Many were carried into captivity. But the Lord was always there to encourage them and to see to it that their basic needs were met.

❖ **Crucial Questions** ❖

As those of us who are Christians face both focused persecution and generalized suffering, how then should we live? How can we live victorious lives in the midst of societal chaos? How can we endure persecution and suffering? How can we remain faithful to the Lord? Are we to withdraw from the world? Are we to arm ourselves, flee to the wilderness, and hunker down in bunkers?

Before we consider the answers to these questions, let's look at another aspect of the challenge we face as Christians living in the end times. Let's consider the condition of the Church.

Endnotes

1 Interview of Magic Johnson by Roger Mudd on the program *20/20*, produced by ABC Television, 1992. Exact date of the broadcast is unknown. The interview was witnessed by the author.

2 Interview of Suzanne Somers on the program *Good Morning America*, produced by ABC Television, 1984. Exact date of the broadcast is unknown. The interview was witnessed by the author. The *Playboy* spread of her photos was published in the December 1984 issue.

3 Interview of Dustin Hoffman on the program *CBS This Morning*, produced by CBS Television and broadcast on March 3, 1992. The interview was witnessed by the author.

4 *The Starr Report: Report of the Office of the Independent Counsel to the United States House of Representatives*, September 9, 1998. Available on the Internet at http://www.fednet.net/starr/1cover.htm. See Section III F: "March 31 Sexual Encounter." The report is available in several different editions in printed form. See, for example, *The Starr Report: The Official Report of the Independent Counsel's Investigation of the President* (Roseville, CA: Prima Publishing, 1998).

5 "The Week, January 10–16, 1993," *Time*, January 25, 1993, p. 23. *Time* cites the source of the statistics as the National Education Association.

6 Ezra Brown, "Getting Tough: New Jersey Principal Joe Clark Kicks Up a Storm about Discipline in City Schools," *Time*, February 1, 1988, p. 54.

7 An item taken from the Internet in the summer of 1999. Widely circulated, with no date or author indicated.

8 *Stone v. Graham*, 449, U.S. 39 (1980). For a good survey of court decisions that have impacted America's schools in a negative way, see David Barton's book *America: To Pray or Not to Pray,* (Aledo, TX: WallBuilder Press, 1991).

9 Ibid.

10 Mailed to the author in 1997 by Ken Matto. Ken lives in Edison, New Jersey, where he works as a production planner in a coffee company. He holds a Doctor of Ministry degree from Bethany Theological Seminary.

11 Steve Allen and Shirley Jones serve as honorary co-chairpersons of the Parents Television Council which is fighting to clean up television in the United States. The materials of this organization can be obtained by writing to 600 Wilshire Blvd., Suite 700, Los Angeles, CA 90017.

12 Bill Clinton, "Gay and Lesbian Pride Month, 1999," June 11, 1999. A proclamation by the President of the United States of America. Presidential proclamations are available on the Internet at http://www.whitehouse.gov

13 *The Lamplighter,* magazine published by Lamb & Lion Ministries, June–July 1999, p.13.

14 "Stern Blasted for Comments about Colorado Tragedy," *AFA Journal*, June 1999, http://www.afajournal.org/archives/23060000005.asp.

Chapter 2

❖   ❖   ❖

The Apostasy in the Church

T he man's title was Regional Minister. He was the equivalent of a bishop, overseeing more than 400 churches in his particular denomination, The Disciples of Christ.

He had called and invited me to come to his office in Fort Worth to get acquainted. When I entered, he asked me to sit down, and then he said something peculiar — "Excuse me while I find a witness."

He returned a few minutes later with a secretary. He told her to have a seat and to start taking notes. I asked him why he needed a witness.

"Because I'm going to read you the riot act," he responded. He then proceeded to do just that. "I want you to get out of my churches and stay out of them!"

"Why?" I asked.

"Because I don't want any of my people hearing your message."

"But my message is right out of the Bible," I protested. "All I'm doing is preaching the soon return of Jesus."

"I know," he said, "and that's the message I don't want my people to hear."

I was dumbfounded. "Don't you believe in the Second Coming?" I asked.

"Not what you call the Second Coming," he replied. "I believe the Second Coming occurs when a person accepts Jesus. He becomes alive in that person's heart. That's all there is to the Second Coming."

Before I could reply, he quickly added, "And there's another reason I don't want you preaching to my people. You are a salvationist!"

I had been called a lot of names in my life, but never that one. "What do you mean by that term?" I asked.

"Oh. You are one of those guys who believes a fellow can hear a sermon and come under conviction about sin, and that conviction will ultimately lead him to repent and experience what you call being 'born again.' "

"I plead guilty," I replied. "What are you?"

"Well, I'm not a salvationist!" he snapped. "I believe that any person in the world who is growing more mature is in the process of being saved."

"Does that apply to Hindus, Buddhists, and Muslims?" I asked.

"Yes," he replied.

"Whether they ever accept Jesus or not?"

"That's right."

One of the most curious things about this whole experience is that on the wall behind this man's desk was a framed quotation that read: "I speak where the Bible speaks, and I am silent where the Bible is silent."

Welcome to the bizarre world of Christian apostasy.

❖ Apostasy in Prophecy ❖

The Bible clearly prophesies that the Church of the end times will be characterized by apostasy. Paul said that the Antichrist will not be revealed until "the apostasy comes first" (2 Thess. 2:3). Jesus prophesied that "many will fall away" and "most people's love will grow cold" (Matt. 24:10, 12).

In the Book of Revelation, chapters 2 and 3, the apostle John records seven letters of Jesus to seven churches in the area of modern-day Turkey. Among other things, these letters present a panoramic prophetic survey of the Church in history. The last of the churches mentioned, the one that represents the Church of the end times, is the church at Laodicea. It is pictured as a church that is neither hot (healing) nor cold (refreshing), but rather is lukewarm or tepid (Rev. 3:15–16). In short, it is a church that is apathetic. Jesus also pictures it as a worldly church enamored with its wealth (Rev. 3:17). The Lord is so dissatisfied with this church that He declares, "Because you are lukewarm, and neither hot nor cold, I will spit you out of My mouth" (Rev. 3:16).

Paul supplies us with some strong clues as to why the end-times Church will be weak, vacillating, and full of apostasy. One of those clues can be found in Paul's famous prophecy about end-time society, the one in 2 Timothy 3. After describing in graphic detail how society will fall apart in the end times, Paul adds that the basic reason will be due to people "holding to a form of godliness, although they have denied its power" (2 Tim. 3:5). There will be no lack of religion, says Paul, but people will deny the true power that is able to transform society for the good, producing peace, righteousness, and justice.

Another clue is located in Paul's famous proiphecy about end-time society, this one in 2 Timothy 4:3–4 which says that "the time will come when they [Christians] will not endure sound doctrine; but wanting to have their ears tickled, they will accumulate for themselves teachers in accordance to their own desires; and will turn away their ears from the truth, and will turn aside to myths."

What is that power? First and foremost it is the power of the blood of Jesus — the very power that was blasphemed by the regional minister who confronted me, claiming that salvation can be achieved apart from Jesus. It is also the power that comes from accepting the Bible as the infallible Word of God. It is the power of believing in a Creator God with whom all things are possible. And certainly it includes a belief in the power of the Holy Spirit.

Today, these essential beliefs, which constitute the power of Christianity, are being subjected to an unparalleled assault from within the Church itself. The Bible says that in the end times people will mock the promise of the Lord's return (1 Pet. 3:2–3). What is so shocking is that most of the mockery is coming from within the Church!

❖ The Root of Apostasy ❖

How have we reached this crisis point in the Church? It is rooted in something I mentioned in the previous chapter — the German School of Higher Criticism which invaded this country big time in the 1920s. According to the "scientific approach" of this school of skeptics, the Bible is not the revealed Word of God.

Rather, it is man's search for God, and therefore it is filled with myth, legend, and superstition.

Today this viewpoint dominates the seminaries of America. The Bible is studied not to be believed and obeyed but to be analyzed, dissected, and criticized. The result is that the Scriptures have lost their authority.

Accordingly, so what if the Scriptures condemn homosexuality? The relevant verses were written thousands of years ago by men who knew nothing about modern physiology or psychology, and who certainly did not understand that homosexuality is "natural" or genetically determined. Paul was simply a victim of his own prejudices and probably was a homosexual himself who was simply engaged in self-loathing. Absurd? Yes, but not from the viewpoint of those Christian leaders who have rejected the authority of the Scriptures.

❖ Apostate Leaders ❖

John Spong, the recently retired Episcopal bishop of New Jersey, has written books in which he denies the virgin birth, denies the miracles of Jesus, denies the resurrection, denies the Second Coming, and argues that Paul and Timothy were homosexual lovers. Bishop Spong has become so enamored with other religions that he has announced he will no longer witness to those caught up in the spiritual darkness of pagan faiths![1]

Similar apostate thoughts were mouthed by Norman Vincent Peale in 1984 on the Phil Donahue program. Peale announced, "It's not necessary to be born again. You have your way to God; I have mine. I found eternal peace in a Shinto shrine. . . . I've been to Shinto shrines, and God is everywhere."[2]

Phil Donahue was so shocked that he actually came to the defense of Christianity. "But you're a Christian minister," he retorted, "and you're supposed to tell me that Christ is the way and the truth and the life, aren't you?"

Peale replied, "Christ is one of the ways. God is everywhere."

Look again at Peale's incredible statement: "It's not necessary to be born again." What did Jesus say? "Truly, truly, I say to you, unless one is born again, he cannot see the kingdom of God" (John 3:3). Whom are we to believe?

Rick Miesel of Biblical Discernment Ministries points out

that Peale was a thorough-going modern day exponent of the Fourth Century apostasy called Pelagianism — that is, he was "someone who believed that human nature is essentially good and that human beings are saved by developing their inner potential."[3]

❖ Schuller's Apostate Gospel ❖

Peale's leading disciple, Robert Schuller, has outdone his teacher with the development of his "gospel of possibility thinking." In his book *Self-Esteem: The New Reformation,* Schuller states that the leaders of the Reformation Movement made a mistake in centering their theology around God instead of man![4]

Schuller teaches that the essence of man's problem is low self-esteem.[5] The Bible teaches that it is pride. Schuller says that when Jesus referred in John 7:38 to "rivers of living water" flowing out of believers, He was speaking of self-esteem.[6] The very next verse says He was speaking of the Holy Spirit. Schuller argues that sin is anything that robs us of our "divine dignity" (our "divine dignity"?).[7] The Bible says sin is rebellion against God.

Like Spong and Peale, Schuller redefines the meaning of being born again. He says it means being "changed from a negative to a positive self-image — from inferiority to self-esteem, from fear to love, and from doubt to trust."[8] The Bible denies that being born again is the result of changes in attitude. Rather, the Bible teaches that being born again relates to coming alive spiritually through faith in Jesus as Lord and Savior. Being born again is a spiritual phenomenon, not a psychological one. The experience will certainly result in changes in attitude, but it is not produced by them. Schuller confuses cause and effect.

❖ The Response of Christendom ❖

Schuller's book calling for a "new reformation" caused a firestorm of controversy. The editors of *Christianity Today* decided to send a team to California to interview him. The meeting produced three articles which were published in August of 1984.[9] The first article was entitled, "Hard Questions for Robert Schuller about Sin and Self-esteem." It consisted of a transcript of a taped interview. The second article was a brief one in which Schuller defined his concept of sin and tried to make it appear biblical.

The third article was an evaluation of Schuller's theology by two of the magazine's editors. They concluded cautiously that he was orthodox.

The editors were obviously snookered by Schuller's engaging personality and his mastery of double-speak. He knew his audience, and he sang to them. They hit him with anything but "hard questions." In fact, they threw him softballs. He responded with exactly what he knew they wanted to hear. They proceeded to ignore the fact that what he said to them was contrary to what he had written in his book and to what he was preaching (and still is).

But this fact was not overlooked by the readers. *Christianity Today* was deluged with critical mail. A person from Buena Park, California, wrote:

> The crux of the matter is simple — in print he [Schuller] affirms one thing; in private, cornered by evangelical theologians, he affirms another. Until Dr. Schuller says what he means and means what he says, *in print,* his private recanting only serves to further inflame the already infected wounds.[10]

A reader in Kirkland, Washington, wrote, "Your tough-questioned interview with Robert Schuller revealed even a tougher, hardened man whose gospel of secular shammanism has seduced some of the very elect of Christendom."[11] Another letter writer referred to Schuller as "a modern-day apostle of humanism."[12] The most insightful letter read as follows:

> Schuller is so downright likeable. One wants to agree with him. Nevertheless, I still have to side with C.S. Lewis who said: "The greatest barrier I have met [when presenting the Christian faith to modern unbelievers] is the almost total absence from the minds of my audience of any sense of sin. . . . The ancient man approached God (or even the gods) as the accused person approaches a judge. For the modern man, the roles are reversed. He is the judge; God is in the dock." Schuller's basic problem is that he's willing to accept the switch.[13]

The letters continued to pour in for weeks, and they were so critical that Dr. Schuller decided to respond to them. In a long letter published in the October 5, 1984, issue of *Christianity Today,* he made an incredible comment that has haunted him to this day:

> I don't think anything has been done in the name of Christ and under the banner of Christianity that has proven more destructive to human personality and, hence, counterproductive to the evangelism enterprise than the often crude, uncouth, and unchristian strategy of attempting to make people aware of their lost and sinful condition.[14]

As a writer for *Time* put it in an article in 1985, "For Schuller, an acknowledgment of self-worth, more than a confession of sinfulness, is the path to God."[15]

❖ Further Evidence of Schuller's Apostasy ❖

In an appearance on the Phil Donahue show in 1980, Schuller tried, incredibly, to portray Jesus as an egotist! Here's what he said:

> The Cross sanctifies the ego trip. That's very significant. In other words, Jesus had an ego. He said, "I, if I be lifted up, will draw all men to me." Wow! What an ego trip He was on![16]

What blatant blasphemy — to accuse the One who was the very essence of humility of being an egotist!

Schuller also seems to teach universalism — the apostate idea that all men will ultimately be saved. In the summer 1986 issue of his magazine *Possibilities,* Schuller declared, "The Christ Spirit dwells in every human being whether the person knows it or not."[17]

Schuller gave a speech at the headquarters of the Unity Church in Lees Summit, Missouri, and shared with their pastors his church growth principles. This is a cult that denies the deity of Jesus and which teaches reincarnation! He also dedicated a new Unity Temple in Warren, Michigan, in spite of warnings from a local Baptist pastor not to do so because of the errors of this cult.[18] In a recent speech honoring an Islamic spiritual leader named Alfred Mohammed, Schuller said that if he were to come back in 100 years and find his descendants to be Muslims, it wouldn't bother him![19] Dave Hunt responded to this statement by saying, "Apparently, Schuller is unconcerned that Islam denies that Jesus is God and that He died for our sins" and that Islam "offers a gospel of good works salvation, and death in jihad [holy war] as the only sure way to the Muslim 'heaven' where the faithful are rewarded with rivers of wine . . . and harems of beautiful women."[20]

❖ Apostasy in Canada ❖

Another modern day apostate is the Reverend Bill Phipps who was elected moderator of the United Church of Canada in 1998. This is the largest Protestant group in the nation. At a press conference following his election, Phipps proceeded to deny all the fundamentals of the Christian faith, including the deity of Jesus. "I don't believe Jesus was God," he said. He added, "I don't believe Jesus is the only way to God. I don't believe He rose from the dead . . . I don't know whether these things happened. It's an irrelevant question."[21]

Note the gross apostasy in this man's statements. When he denies that Jesus is the only way to God, he makes Jesus out to be a liar, for Jesus said, "I am the way, and the truth, and the life; no one comes to the Father, but through Me" (John 14:6). When he states that the truth regarding the resurrection is "irrelevant," he makes a liar of the apostle Paul who wrote, "If Christ has not been raised, then our preaching is vain. . . . and if Christ has not been raised, your faith is worthless" (1 Cor. 15:14–17).

Of course, these men would probably respond to any quotation of Scripture with contempt, arguing that Scripture is unreliable. That's exactly what the so-called "scholars" of the highly touted "Jesus Seminar" concluded.

❖ An Apostate Seminar ❖

The Jesus Seminar was formed in 1985 by Robert Funk, a New Testament scholar at the University of Montana. The avowed purpose of the seminar was "to renew the quest for the historical

Jesus."[22] The seminar conducted this quest in a very unusual way. Meeting twice a year for six years, the group voted on each of the sayings of Jesus recorded in the Gospels. They voted by dropping colored beads in a box. A black bead meant Jesus definitely did not make the statement in question. A gray bead meant he did not say it, but it might have represented His thinking. A pink bead meant He probably said something like this, but not in the words recorded. A red bead meant He definitely made the statement.[23]

As you can see, the very approach expressed contempt for the veracity of the Gospel accounts. What a spectacle this must have been to the Lord as He watched these so-called scholars vote on passages from His Word. "Professing to be wise, they became fools" (Rom. 1:22).

The seminar began with 30 scholars. Over the following six years, more than 200 persons participated in the deliberation. But only 74 hung in to the end. Most of those who dropped out did so because of their disgust with the process and their discomfort with the fact that the radical fringe element of New Testament scholarship in America was disproportionately represented.[24]

The final product of the seminar, published in 1993, was a blasphemy of God's Word. It was titled *The Five Gospels.*[25] The title comes from the fact that the seminar decided to grant the apocryphal Gospel of Thomas equal standing with the four traditional Gospels.

Only 15 sayings of Jesus made it into *The Five Gospels* in red! In Matthew's account of the Lord's Prayer, the only words that made it in red were, "Our Father." Only one saying in the entire Book of Mark was colored red. It is the statement of Jesus in Mark 12:17 where He told His disciples to "Render to Caesar the things that are Caesar's, and to God the things that are God's." Likewise, only one statement from the Gospel of John qualified for the red coloring: "A prophet has no honor in his own country" (John 4:44).

The chilling thing to keep in mind is that the men who produced this spiritual pornography are professors at seminaries across America. They are the ones who are training the current generation of pastors and teachers.

❖ **Apostasy in the Denominations** ❖

The apostasy is not confined to the seminaries. It is pervasive. It can be found in all denominations. Consider the following examples.

In 1997 on the eve of Lent, the Right Reverend Alan Smithson, the Bishop of Jarrow (Anglican Church in England), held a press conference in London. He announced that it was traditional for Christians to give up something during the 40 days of Lent. He then dramatically announced that he had decided to give up Bible reading! He went on to explain that he was going to devote his time during Lent to reading the Koran, because he felt like the Muslim scriptures would make him "more understanding, more compassionate, and more fully human."[26]

R. Kirby Godsey, president of Mercer University, a school heavily supported by the Georgia Baptist Convention, "denies the infallibility of the Bible, the unique power and authority of God, the validity of the Gospel's account of the life and teachings of Jesus, the efficacy of Christ's atonement, and the uniqueness of Christ as the only Savior."[27]

In 1997 the General Board of Global Ministries of the United Methodist Church sponsored a meeting in Kansas City that attracted 4,000 participants from all over the world. Called, "Global Gathering III," the conference featured a parade of speakers who attacked the fundamentals of the Christian faith. One speaker declared that the crucifixion of Jesus reveals an "abusive Heavenly Father who is not fit for Christian worship." The speaker urged instead that the Church revere all the world's children as little messiahs equal to Jesus.[28]

The most revolutionary speaker at that conference was Nancy Pereira, a Methodist theologian from Brazil. She specifically rejected the atonement of Jesus in words that dripped with blasphemy:

> We have to stop praising Abraham's knife. We have to stop praising Solomon's sword. We have to stop praising Jesus' cross. . . . We have to find other expressions of salvation and liberation. . . .
>
> We have developed a Christology with a tradition of a

cross. That is a sacrificial Christology. It's a mechanism of salvation that heeds guilt, pain, whipping and death. We have to look at Jesus' cross as a tragedy, a human episode without any sense of meaning.[29]

United Methodists teamed up with Presbyterians and Lutherans in 1993 to stage a feminist "Re-Imagining Conference." The conference sent shock waves through Christendom as the speakers denigrated Jesus and called for the participants to focus their adoration instead on a female deity called Sophia.[30]

Five years later, a second conference called "Re-Imagining Revival" was held in Minneapolis. The participants were subjected to an endless stream of New Age gobbledygook. The program opened in a darkened room, with lanterns and drums, and a welcome that included the words, "We call upon spirits, we call upon you from the past." When gospel hymns were sung, the words were rewritten to remove all references to the blood of Christ, the Cross, and the Second Coming. The divinity and sinlessness of Jesus, as well as His substitutionary death on the cross and His resurrection from the dead were all explicitly denied. Great pains were taken to repudiate the God of Scripture in favor of pagan goddesses like Sophia, Isis, Aphrodite, and Brigid. Regarding sexual morality, a speaker named Delores Williams said, "No sexuality is unclean in the context of the sacred. In the eyes of deity, it doesn't matter who you are sleeping with."[31]

Significantly, the conference concluded with a Sunday morning worship service where each woman took a bite from an apple "to show her solidarity with Eve's quest for wisdom and her 'resistance' to the boundaries set by God's Word."[32]

❖ Apostasy in Local Churches ❖

The spreading cancer of apostasy in the Church is not confined to theologians and church conferences. It can be found at the grassroots level, in local churches.

Consider the following advertisement that appeared in a newspaper in Wichita, Kansas. It was run by the College Hill United Methodist Church to promote their Sunday worship services. The ad was illustrated with a photo of sheet music burning on a music stand.

This Sunday Morning
Our Sanctuary Will Be
Hotter Than Hell.

This week's worship service will be positively smokin.' But it won't be fire and brimstone in the air. Instead, prepare yourself for some wickedly divine, white-hot jazz.

We'll heat things up with the heavenly sounds of renowned jazz torch singer Donna Tucker. Then, if the church is still standing, we'll burn the place down with the red, hot, and blue jazz of piano recording artist Frank Mantooth.

Both services will include a moving musical tribute to the late, great Newt Graber. Lisa Hittle will lead the Jazz Friends Combo at the 8:30 service and the Jazz Friends Community Big Band at 11 a.m.

It all promises to be a severely swingin' religious experience. So be there or be square. And, oh yeah, don't forget. Dress cool.[33]

The Episcopal New Church Center in Walkersville, Maryland, hired a public relations firm to develop a print and television advertising campaign. One of the first ads in this campaign carried a banner headline that read, "To Hell With Church!" It showed a man thinking, "If I want to feel guilty, I'll eat some cheese fries." Another ad in the series showed a painting of Christ nailed on the cross. Scrawled over the painting were the words, "Of course people with pierced body parts are welcome in our church."[34]

Do you remember the furor that was caused when an artist, supported by the National Endowment for the Arts, placed a crucifix in a bottle of his urine and called his artistic creation, "Piss Christ"? Well, it is one thing for a pagan to ridicule the crucifixion of Jesus, but it is entirely something else for a church to do so.

The Maryland church really went wacky when it moved to producing TV ads. They hired a fellow known for the kinky cartoons he produces for *Saturday Night Live*. His first ad for the church opened with a father and son tossing a baseball to each other in the front yard.

"Guess what, Timmy?" the father asks. "Tomorrow your mother and I are going to take you to church." The father continues, "Not only will you be able to learn about the wages of sin and eternal damnation, but you can play fun games like 'Bible Sword Drill' and sing inspirational songs like 'Kumbaya' and 'I've Got Joy, Joy, Joy Down in My Heart.'"

Dejected by this prospect, little Timmy walks into the middle of the road and holds out his hands in surrender as a semi-truck blows its horn and bears down on him.[35]

Not only apostate, but sick.

❖ Inter-Faith Apostasy ❖

The big move at the grassroots level these days is interfaith worship services. I'm not talking about inter-denominational — rather, the emphasis is on inter-*faith*. Christians are inviting Muslims, Jews, Hindus, American Indian practitioners of "native religion," and others to join in worshiping "the one true god, regardless of the name you may give to him or her." A radio listener of mine who was a member of a Friends Church wrote a description of one of these services that she attended in Newport, Rhode Island.

Last year I attended a National Day of Prayer service at a local Catholic church.

A man opened the service with some off-the-wall remarks. Then a Unitarian offered an Iroquois Indian prayer to the sun and moon. They were followed by a Bahai leader who boldly proclaimed, "Contrary to what the Bible says, the world was not created in seven days, but in fact, creation is still going on."

I went home with a heavy heart. I prayed and sought the Lord concerning my attending such meetings in the future, and, instantly, the scripture came to me, "What fellowship hath light with darkness, or the Spirit of Christ with Belial?"

I had my answer, and shall never go again.[36]

The dear lady who wrote that letter showed more spiritual discernment than did Pope John Paul II when, in October 1986, he invited the leaders of the world's religions to come to Assisi, Italy, to join him in praying for world peace.[37] One hundred sixty representatives came, including the Dali Lama (who considers himself to be a god). Each representative prayed to his own god at the pope's request! Did the pope believe their gods were real? Or did he believe that they were all praying to the same god, but under different names?

❖ The Most Popular Apostasy ❖

These questions bring us to the most popular apostasy in Christendom today. It is the teaching that God has revealed himself in many different ways to different cultures and that, therefore, all religions worship the same god, but just use different names. From this viewpoint, the Allah of Islam is the same as the Yahweh of Judaism. The natural conclusion that is drawn from this apostate idea is that there are many different paths to God, Jesus being only one of them. This has led liberal leaders of groups like The National Council of Churches in the United States and the World Council to condemn missionary activity as "arrogant" and "anti-cultural."[38]

The Bible teaches that these apostate Christian leaders are eventually going to succeed, at least temporarily. Their triumph will occur when the Antichrist forms his one world religion (Rev. 13:12).

❖ The Apostate One-World Religion ❖

Major steps have already been taken to establish a unified world religion. In June of 1997 over 200 delegates from religious groups all over the world gathered at Stanford University to begin drafting a charter for an international interfaith institution to be called The Organization of United Religions.[39]

The meeting was convened and presided over by Reverend William Swing, the Episcopal Bishop of San Francisco. Since 1993 he has been traveling worldwide to set up a network of religious leaders interested in a one world religious organization. The Bishop told the *San Francisco Chronicle*:

I've spent a lot of time praying with Brahmins, meditating with Hindus, and chanting with Buddhists. I feel I've been enormously enriched inwardly by exposure to these folks. I've gone back and read our own scriptures, and it's amazing how they begin to read differently when you're exposed to more truth from more people in other parts of the world.[40]

This statement is the epitome of the new tolerance that is being evidenced by Christendom's apostate leaders. (Incidentally, I wonder what "new truth" he found outside the Bible!)

The group hopes to have their charter ready for ratification by June of 2000, and their goal is to have the new organization fully operable by 2005. They intend for the headquarters to be located at the Presidio, the former military base in San Francisco. As one conference leader put it, "The UR is meant to be for religions what the UN is for nations."[41]

❖ Continuing Apostasy in Melbourne ❖

A month later many of the same people gathered in Melbourne, Australia, for a conference on religion and cultural diversity. The Archbishop of Canterbury (the leader of the Church of England) was present, and the pope sent one of his highest-ranking cardinals, Francis Arinze.[42]

At the opening banquet, the lights were dimmed and people were told to focus on the candle on their table while the following prayer was offered:

Let us focus on the candle, the small quivering fire, the light in the darkness, the call to evening prayer, the call to thanksgiving . . . for our togetherness, for our unity as sons and daughters of the earth in this vast and ancient land, this sacred soil of the Dreamtime.

In the presence of the Ineffable Other, the Holy Being of Infinity, the Numinous Beyond, the One and the Ultimate, the Alpha and the Omega, the Unknown and the Unknowable, Lord of the Cosmos, Center of Creation . . . we pray to you. . . .[43]

Can you imagine any Christian leader praying such clap-trap? Since when, from a Christian viewpoint, has our Creator God become "unknown and unknowable"? Only a professing Christian captivated and deceived by the new tolerance could pray such a blasphemous prayer.

Understandably, the conference concluded that the one cardinal sin is absolutism. Belief that one's religion contains absolute truth was decried as pride.[44]

The conference's most popular workshop was on "Religious Fundamentalism." The featured speaker was an ordained Christian minister who, until recently, was the full-time chaplain at the University of Melbourne. He denounced Christians who believe in the Bible and embrace creationism as "mean-spirited." He also called them "authoritarian and dictatorial," "violent," "aggressive," "pathological," and "dangerous." He characterized them as people who are incapable of independent thinking and who "brandish their floppy Bibles like weapons."[45]

Talk about paving the way for the Antichrist! I can hear him speaking now:

> It makes no difference what you call your god. He can be Yahweh or Baal or Allah or Krishna or Mother Earth or Self. Just give me your allegiance as your god's Messiah, and I will guarantee your freedom to worship as you please.

❖ The Challenge ❖

Englishman William Booth (1829–1912), who founded the Salvation Army, was a man with a great zeal for the Lord and a passion for lost souls. He was also a man of vision. On the eve of the 20th century, when Christendom was caught up in euphoria about how the Church would soon take the world for Christ, Booth predicted that the Gospel would not fare well in the new century. Specifically, he prophesied that by the end of the 20th century, much of the Church would be preaching the following:[46]

> Christianity without Christ
> Forgiveness without repentance

Salvation without regeneration
Heaven without hell

That's exactly where we are today. Because of it, as we begin the 21st century, Christians are faced with unparalleled challenges from the decay of society and the apostatizing of the Church. Increasingly, many are going to give up hope. Some will express this hopelessness by withdrawing from society and assuming a siege mentality. Others will throw in the towel and adopt the attitude, "If you can't lick them, join them."

Considering the magnitude of the challenge, is there any hope for triumphant Christian living? And if so, how then shall we live?

Endnotes

1 John Shelby Spong, *Rescuing the Bible from Fundamentalism: A Bishop Rethinks the Meaning of Scripture* (San Francisco, CA: Harper, 1992). Another revealing book by Bishop Spong is *Why Christianity Must Change or Die: A Bishop Speaks to Believers in Exile* (San Francisco, CA: Harper, 1999). A good summary of Bishop Spong's views can be found on the Internet in his "Call for a New Reformation," http://www.dioceseofnewark.org/jsspong/reform.htm.

2 Dave Hunt, "Revival or Apostasy," *The Berean Call,* October 1997, p. 2.

3 Rick Miesel, "Robert Schuller: General Teachings/Activities," Computer Discernment Notebook of Biblical Discernment Ministries, January 1999, http://www.rapidnet.com/~jbeard/bdm/exposes/schuller/general.htm, p. 8. See also his article on Norman Vincent Peale at the same website: http://www.rapidnet.com/~jbeard/bdm/Psychology/guidepo/peale.htm.

4 Robert Schuller, *Self Esteem: The New Reformation,* (Waco, TX: Word Books, 1982), p. 39. An insightful review of Schuller's writings can be found in an article by Joseph P. Gudel entitled "A New Reformation?" It was published in *Passport Magazine*, January–February 1988. It is available on the Internet at http://www.issuesetc.org/resource/archives/guide12.htm. There are other excellent summaries of Schuller's thought that can be found on the Internet. One is an article by David W. Cloud entitled "Evangelicals and Modernist Robert Schuller" (http://cnview.com/on_line_resources/evangelicals_and_modernist_robert_schuller.htm).

Another good analysis is entitled, "The God of the Bible Versus the God of Multi-level Marketing: Positive Thinking," (http://www.users.fast.net/~gospeltruth/positive.htm).

5 Ibid., p. 19.

6 Ibid., p. 80.

7 Ibid., p. 14.

8 Ibid., p. 68.

9 *Christianity Today,* August 10, 1984. The three articles were: Robert Schuller, "Hard Questions for Robert Schuller about Sin and Self-esteem," p. 14–20; Robert Schuller, "Schuller Clarifies His View of Sin," p. 21; and Kenneth S. Kantzer and Paul W. Fromer, "A Theologian Looks at Schuller," p. 22–24.

10 Kim Riddlebarger, "The Enigma of Robert Schuller," (letter to the editor), *Christianity Today,* September 21, 1984, p. 6.

11 William Cantelon, "More on Schuller," (letter to the editor), *Christianity Today,* October 19, 1984, p. 11.

12 Hugh Cantelon, "More on Schuller," (letter to the editor), *Christianity Today,* October 19, 1984, p. 11.

13 James Kiefer, "Schuller's Critics Comment," (letter to the editor), *Christianity Today,* October 5, 1984, p. 12.

14 Robert Schuller, "Dr. Schuller Comments," (letter to the editor), *Christianity Today,* October 5, 1984, pp. 12–13.

15 Richard Stengel, "Apostle of Sunny Thoughts," *Time,* March 18, 1985, p. 70.

16 *The Phil Donahue Show,* transcript 08120, August 12, 1980, p. 10.

17 Robert Schuller, *Possibilities* Magazine, Summer 1986, p. 12.

18 Miesel, "Robert Schuller: General Teachings/Activities," p. 5. Schuller's support of the Unity Church is also documented in an article by Dave Hunt published in the *CIB Bulletin,* January 1988. In a letter to the author dated January 24, 2000, Dave Hunt states that he has a tape recording of the speech that Schuller delivered to the Unity pastors about church growth principles.

19 Dave Hunt, "What's Happening to the Faith?" *The Berean Call,* May 1998, p. 1.

20 Ibid.

21 R. Albert, "The Immoderator," *World Magazine*, March 1998, p. 18.

22 "The Jesus Seminar: The Search for Authenticity," http://home.fireplug.net/~rshand/reflections/messiah/seminar.htm.

23 In April 1996, *Time* featured the Jesus Seminar on its cover under the title "The Search for Jesus." The cover article presented a comprehensive survey of the seminar's organization, methodology, and

conclusions. See David Van Biema, "The Gospel Truth? — The Iconoclastic and Provocative Jesus Seminar Argues That Not Much of the New Testament Can Be Trusted. If So, What Are Christians to Believe?" *Time,* April 8, 1996.

24 Craig L. Blomberg, "The Seventy-Four 'Scholars': Who Does the Jesus Seminar Really Speak For?" *Christian Research Journal,* Fall 1994, p. 32. Also available on the Internet at http://www.rim.org/muslim/jesusseminar.htm.

25 Robert W. Funk and Roy W. Hoover, *The Five Gospels* (San Francisco, CA: Harper, reprint edition, 1997). A good review of this book can be found in an article by D.A. Carson entitled "Five Gospels, No Christ." The article appeared in *Christianity Today,* April 25, 1994, p. 30–33.

26 "Bishop Gives Up Bible for Lent," unsigned article, *Daily Mail,* London, England, February 14, 1997, p. 31.

27 Dave Hunt, "What's Happening to the Faith?" *The Berean Call,* May 1998, p. 1. Dr. Godsey's views can be found in the book *When We Talk About God, Let's Be Honest,* (Macon, GA: Smyth & Helwys Publishing Co., 1996). The Georgia Baptist Convention adopted a resolution of censure in November 1996 in which it asked the trustees of Mercer University to consider whether Dr. Godsey should be continued as president of the institution. The trustees voted to affirm his presidency.

28 Mark Tooley, "Church Gathering Features Radical Speakers," *AFA Journal,* June 1997, p.19.

29 Ibid.

30 Jackie Alnor, "Invasion of the Sophia Women," *Christian Sentinel,* Spring 1999, p. 24–25. An excellent summary of the 1993 Re-Imagining Conference can be found on the Internet in an article by Craig Branch entitled, "Re-imagining God." The article is located at http://watchman.texan.com/search/watchman...watchman%20 fellowship%5C%5Creimagin%2E.htm.

31 "Gays, Radical Feminists Despise Scripture, Continue Assault in Mainline Churches," unsigned article in the *AFA Journal,* June 1998, p. 9.

32 Ibid.

33 A copy of the advertisement, which appeared in the *Wichita Eagle,* Wichita, Kansas, was cut from the newspaper and sent to the author by one of his radio listeners. No date appeared on the ad.

34 John Kirkpatrick, "Ads Fish for Churchgoers with Irreverent Approach," *Dallas Morning News,* April 18, 1998, p. 1F.

35 Ibid., p. 11F.

36 Jeannine Vaillancourt of Middletown, Rhode Island, in a letter to the author dated January 29, 1997.

37 Richard N. Ostling, "A Summit for Peace in Assisi," *Time,* November 10, 1986, p. 78–79.

38 A good summary of the apostasy of the World Council of Churches can be found on the Internet at http://cnview.com/on_line_resources/world_council_of_churches.htm. The article, written by M.H. Reynolds, is entitled "The Truth about the WCC."

39 William Norman Gregg, "Pagans of the World, Unite!" *PropheZine,* issue #46, August 15, 1997, http://www.best.com/~ray673/search/database/is46.2.htm.

40 Ibid., p. 2.

41 W.B. Howard, "The First Religion and Cultural Diversity Conference, Melbourne, July 1997," *PropheZine*, issue #46, August 15, 1997, http://www.prophezine.com/search/database/is46.3.htm, p. 15.

42 Ibid., p. 1.

43 Ibid., p. 3.

44 Ibid.

45 Ibid., p. 4–7.

46 Joseph Revell, "The Salvation Army Revisited," *Report from the Wall,* (an Internet daily devotional message sent from yosef@gulf.net), December 18, 1998, p. 2.

Part Two

The Christian Response to Paganism

❖ ❖ ❖

Chapter 3

❖   ❖   ❖

Standing on the Word of God

I t was the early 1980s and I had been invited to speak at a Presbyterian church located in the mid-cities area between Dallas and Fort Worth.

The invitation came through the efforts of a radio listener who called and asked if I would be willing to present a lesson on Bible prophecy at his church on a Sunday evening. I responded that I would be happy to do so.

"Well," he said, "start praying for me."

"What do you mean?" I asked.

"I mean it's going to be hard to get you invited," he replied. "You see, our pastor doesn't like Bible studies, so on Sunday nights we normally just have secular entertainment — like a folk singer. In fact, to get you invited, I'm going to need a jazzy title."

"A jazzy title?" As I repeated the words, an unusual and catchy title suddenly popped into my mind. "How about, 'The Future of the Late Great Planet Earth'?"

"That's jazzy!" he replied. "I'll see what I can do."

The next day he called back. He was so excited you could have heard him shouting across Dallas. "He agreed, he agreed! I didn't even have to argue with him. Our pastor said for me to call you and invite you."

❖ A Memorable Evening ❖

The evening arrived, and I did not sense anything wrong until the pastor began his introduction: "We are so glad to have an expert on Bible prophecy here with us this evening. He is going to prove to us that there is no prophecy in the Bible, and in the process, he is going to show us how ridiculous it is to take seriously the books on prophecy like those written by Hal Lindsey."

I don't know what else he said because his second sentence had put me in a state of shock. Was he introducing me? Or was he introducing someone else that he expected me to debate? As my mind was racing with these questions, I suddenly heard my name. It was me he was talking about!

I motioned him aside, and in front of about 50 people we had a whispered conference.

"I think there has been a big misunderstanding," I told him.

"What do you mean?" he asked.

"Well, you see, I happen to believe in the validity of Bible prophecy, and I also believe Hal Lindsey's books are very good guides to understanding prophecy." I paused for a moment to let my words sink in, then I asked, "Do you want me to go home?"

The pastor looked stunned. He thought for a moment, and then he whispered, "No, you can stay, but keep it short."

I walked to the pulpit not knowing where to begin or what to say. I suddenly thought about the first gospel sermon ever preached, the one presented by Peter on the Day of Pentecost. I thought that might be a good place to start since it contains one quotation of prophecy after another from start to finish.

"Please turn in your Bibles to Acts chapter two," I announced.

Now, I'm the type of preacher who likes to hear the pages rustle when I announce a Scripture. As I turned to the passage, I noticed that my pages were the only ones rustling.

"How many of you have your Bibles with you this evening?" I asked. Not a single person raised a hand.

"Well, then, please look in your pew Bibles."

A man yelled out, "We don't have any pew Bibles in this church."

I thought for a moment and then said, "It's going to be difficult to teach you a Bible lesson without Bibles. Would several of you men go through the education wing of the building and gather up the Bibles? I'll lead some songs while you're doing so."

Several men jumped up and headed for the classrooms. I started leading some hymns.

About five minutes later, the men returned empty-handed. "We couldn't find any Bibles," one of them announced.

I immediately thought of the time when King Josiah of Judah ordered the temple to be purged of idols, and the priests found the Word of God in a dark corner behind an idol. They had lost God's Word, and so had this church.

At that point, the pastor jumped up. "I think I have some Bibles in my office," he said.

He returned with about five Bibles. We organized the people into groups and gave each group a Bible.

❖ A Disruptive Bible Study ❖

"Now," I said triumphantly, "let's turn to Acts chapter two."

The pages began to rustle. And they rustled and rustled! People were looking for the Book of Acts at both the beginning and the end of the Bible. I was astounded.

I decided to quickly shift gears and conduct a Bible drill. During the next ten minutes, I introduced them to the Bible, telling them the difference in the Old and New Testaments, and showing them the types of literature — historical, prophetic, wisdom, apocalyptic, etc. They were delighted. I finally got them to the Book of Acts and made my point. I then asked them to turn to Daniel. The moment I did, the pastor sprang out of his seat.

"I'm sorry," he shouted, "but we do not allow the Book of Daniel to be read in this church!"

"Why not?" I asked.

"Because it is a fraudulent piece of literature that pretends to be prophecy but really isn't. It claims to have been written 500 years before Christ, when it was really written about the time of Christ." He paused for a moment, and then he pointed his finger at me in an accusatory way. "You obviously are not a seminary graduate, or else you would know better than to quote the Book of Daniel."

I decided to take him on. (Keep in mind that all this was going on in front of his congregation!) "How," I asked, "can you claim the Book of Daniel was written at the time of Christ when it was included in the Septuagint translation of the Hebrew Scriptures?"

"What do you mean?" he replied.

"I mean, the Septuagint was translated about 280 years before Christ."

"Well, I don't believe that is when it was translated," he snapped.

"I have another question for you," I quickly added. "How do you explain the fact that when Alexander the Great came to destroy Jerusalem in 333 B.C., he was confronted by the high priest who showed him where he was prophesied in the Book of Daniel. He was so impressed that he spared the city from destruction."

"Where did you get that story?" he asked.

"You will find it in the writings of Josephus," I replied.[1]

"You can't believe anything Josephus says," he retorted in disgust. "All he ever did was write old wives' tales."

"Do you want me to go home?" I asked again.

"No, I just don't want you to quote from Daniel."

"Okay," I said, "let's consider the very first messianic prophecy in the Bible. Please turn to Genesis 3:15."

Again, the pastor sprang to his feet. "I don't want you to read that passage," he said.

"Why?"

"Because I know what you are going to do with it. You're going to use it to teach about the virgin birth."

"Is there something wrong with that?"

"Yes," he replied. "We don't believe in the virgin birth at this church."

❖ God's Mysterious Ways ❖

And so it went all evening — the pastor trying to protect his people from the Word of God. I found out later how I got invited, and the story impressed upon me both the sovereignty of God and His sense of humor.

I found out that when the radio listener went to his pastor's office to see if I could be invited, the pastor was reading a book entitled *The Future of the Late Great Planet Earth.* It was a book I had never heard of. It was a book that attacked Bible prophecy and attempted to refute the writings of Hal Lindsey in his book *The Late Great Planet Earth.* Because I had proposed that exact title for my presentation, the pastor thought I was going to present that book's viewpoint, so he authorized my invitation. The Lord truly does work in strange and mysterious ways!

❖ The Need for God's Word ❖

That jolting experience emphasized to me the importance of God's Word. It has impressed upon me to this day that the first key to a triumphant Christian life in the end times is to get back to the Bible as the source of all authority, respecting it as the Word of God. It is the drift from the Bible that has weakened the Church and undermined its impact on society.

All across America today, and all around the world, there is a "famine of the Word" (Amos 8:11 and Jer. 6:10). The wisdom of man has replaced the Word of God in many pulpits. Too often sermons are nothing more than warmed-over, inspirational ditties drawn from sources like the *Reader's Digest.*

This lack of respect for God's Word is not just a problem confined to liberals. It is easy to take potshots at them because their apostasy is so gross. But often, in doing so, we overlook the fact that those of us who claim to stand on the Word are often guilty of ignoring it or manipulating it.

❖ Ignoring the Word ❖

With regard to ignoring the Word, public opinion polls consistently show that even Evangelicals rarely read their Bibles. A Gallup poll a few years ago showed that the average evangelical home in America has five Bibles. Yet, it also revealed that only 12 percent of Evangelicals read the Bible daily. Billy Graham responded to the poll by observing, "The Bible is the least read best seller of all time."[2] The tragic result is that at most evangelical churches today, you could ask people to turn to Hezekiah 4:1, and most would be embarrassed to discover there is no such book!

How many Christians do you know who spend as much time daily reading the Bible as they do reading the newspaper? How about you?

Ignorance of the Word paves the way for heresy and apostasy because people do not know how to use the Bible to test what they are taught. The apostle Paul commended the people of the city of Berea for testing everything he taught by the Scriptures (Acts 17:10–11). How much more so should we test what is taught by those who are not Apostles.

This is particularly true today, in this time of Christian super-stars who have been created by the media. Christians often become slavish followers of some media personality, willing to accept anything that he or she may teach, regardless of how off-the-wall it may be. The mentality becomes one of saying, "It has to be true because Brother So-and-So said so." Well, in the words of the Gershwin song, "It ain't necessarily so!"

❖ Manipulation of the Word ❖

Another way people abuse the Bible is through manipulation. The process is one that reminds me of a story recorded in Jeremiah 36. The king of Judah, Jehoiakim, heard that Jeremiah the prophet had written a new scroll with words from the Lord. He sent for the scroll and asked that it be read to him. Every time a portion was read that the king did not like, he took a knife, cut the passage from the scroll, and threw it into a fireplace that was blazing next to him (Jer. 36:20–26).

The Lord was enraged with the contempt that the king showed toward His Word. He directed Jeremiah to rewrite the scroll, and then He told Jeremiah to speak some prophetic words to the king. He told the king that none of his descendants would sit on the throne of David. He also told the king that his dead body would be cast out to rot in the heat of the day and frost of the night (Jer. 36:30).

The message of this story is very clear. God takes His Word seriously, and anyone is foolish to mess with it.

Evangelicals recoil in horror to such a story, but the truth is that there are "Bible-believing" people who are daily involved in putting a knife to Scripture.

❖ Editing the Word ❖

Take my heritage, for example. I grew up in the non-instrumental Churches of Christ, a conservative, Bible-honoring group of people. Yet we played games with God's Word all the time.

We took a razor blade to Hebrews 6:1–2 where one of the fundamentals of the faith is defined as "instruction about baptisms."[3] We cut the "s" off the end of the word, baptisms, because we believed only in water baptism. We denied Spirit baptism and we ignored the baptism of fire.

We used that same razor blade to cut out the next phrase which refers to the "laying on of hands" (Heb. 6:2). We didn't believe in doing that because it was something the Pentecostals did. So, we wrote it off as a "first century practice" that no longer had any relevance. In doing so, we closed our eyes to a fundamental biblical truth.

We took a pocketknife to James 5:13–15. This is the passage that says a person who is ill should call the elders to anoint them with oil and pray for them. We also wrote it off as "first century" and argued it was no longer applicable.

We did the same thing with 1 Timothy 2:8 which says, "I want men in every place to pray, lifting up holy hands." The very thought was horrifying to us because, again, that was the kind of emotional thing that only Pentecostals did. It's interesting in looking back on it. We loved 1 Timothy 2:11 — "Let a woman quietly receive instruction." But we took a pocketknife to 1 Timothy 2:8 because we were not going to tolerate anyone lifting their hands.

Sometimes the passages we wanted to discard were so large that we had to resort to a bigger cutting instrument. Accordingly, we applied a hunting knife to Revelation 20. We were militantly amillennial (meaning we did not believe in a future earthly reign of Jesus), so we simply had to ignore this passage that so clearly teaches that Jesus is returning to reign for a thousand years as King of kings.

Scissors were applied to 1 Corinthians 12 and 14. We delighted in Paul's great love poem in 1 Corinthians 13, but we could not tolerate the chapters on each side of it because they discussed in detail something we didn't believe in — namely, spiritual gifts.

We had to use pinking shears to get rid of a very thick passage that drove us batty. That was Romans 9 through 11. We couldn't stand these chapters because they taught that God still has a purpose for the Jewish people, and that part of that purpose is to bring a great remnant to salvation in their Messiah.

And, believe it or not, we took an axe to the Old Testament. Our preachers argued that it had been "nailed to the Cross" and was thus no longer valid for Christians. Some of the stories, like Noah and the ark, might be appropriate for children, but the New Testament alone was the only Scripture appropriate for mature Christians. We were a "New Testament people," and we took that so literally, that many of us did not even own a complete Bible.

❖ Spiritualizing the Word ❖

Sometimes, we would leave a passage in the Bible, but we would manipulate it by spiritualizing it. We particularly took that approach in regard to prophecies about the Second Coming. Our position was a very peculiar one: "The Bible means exactly what it says unless it is talking about the Second Coming; then it never means what it says."

I remember one day discovering Zechariah 14:1–9. I was only 12 at the time, but I could clearly understand what this passage said, and it disturbed me deeply. Again, our church took the position that Jesus was never coming back to reign on this earth. Accordingly, I had heard our preacher say many times, "There is not one verse in the Bible that even implies that Jesus will ever put His feet on this earth again."

Well, Zechariah 14 does more than imply. It states point blank that the Messiah will return to the Mount of Olives and that when His feet touch the ground, the mount will split apart (Zech. 14:4). It concludes by asserting that on that day the Lord will become "king over all the earth" (Zech. 14:9).

What could be clearer? I decided to confront the minister of my church with it. I did so in fear and trembling. He read the passage and then re-read it several times. I don't think he had ever seen it before. As he continued to re-read it, I began to wonder if he was ever going to say anything. Finally, he did. He stuck his finger in my face and said, "Son, I don't know what this passage means, but I'll guarantee you one thing, it doesn't mean what it says!"

Well, my name is Reagan, and that means I'm Irish, so I am naturally stubborn. I was not willing to accept that answer. Furthermore, that very minister had taught me that "the Bible means what it says."

From that time on, every time a preacher would come to town and proclaim, "There is not a verse in the Bible that even implies . . ." I would confront him with Zechariah 14. Always the response was the same: "It doesn't mean what it says."

Finally, when I was about 19, a preacher came who was a seminary graduate, something that was rare in our church in the 1950s. When he made the same claim, I confronted him. He did not hesitate for a moment in giving me an answer. He knew the passage, and he was ready. "It's apocalyptic!" he asserted with great authority. I had no idea what that meant. For all I knew, it was some sort of disease! But it sounded good to me. And, after all, he was a seminary graduate.

So, when I started preaching, I did what most young preachers do — I parroted what I had heard. I would declare confidently, "There is not one verse in the Bible that even implies that Jesus will ever put His feet on this earth again." When some little old lady would come up and challenge me with Zechariah 14, I would shout, "Apocalyptic!" She would run for the door, and I would smile. The tragic thing is that I didn't have the slightest idea what I was talking about.

Then, one day, I did something I had never done before — I read the entire Book of Zechariah. I discovered that it is full of prophecies about the First Coming. It prophesies that the Messiah will come on a donkey, be hailed as a king, and be betrayed by a friend for 30 pieces of silver. It also says He will be lifted up and pierced in the hands.

As I read these prophecies, a simple truth suddenly jumped out at me. It dawned on me that every one of those prophecies meant exactly what they said! That discovery immediately led me to a conclusion that changed my life. I decided that if the First Coming prophecies meant what they said, then the Second Coming prophecies must also mean what they say. It doesn't take a rocket scientist to figure this out.

That day I decided to stop playing games with God's Word. I decided to accept its plain-sense meaning regardless of whether or not the meaning lined up with all my traditional doctrines. That was the day the Bible started coming alive for me. Ever since that time I have followed what I call the "golden rule" of biblical interpretation: "If the plain sense makes sense, don't look for any other sense, lest you end up with nonsense."

❖ Proof-Texting the Word ❖

I also had to discard my proof text approach to the Bible. My spiritual heritage treated the Bible like it was the Texas Code Annotated. In our viewpoint, the Old Law had been replaced by the New, and the New Law was the New Testament. So, we treated it like a law book rather than a collection of biographies and love letters.

The result was that I never read the Word just to let it minister to me. Rather, I searched it for proof texts that I could use to nail a Baptist to the wall or to cut the legs out from underneath a Presbyterian. I used proof texts like they were hand grenades.

I was in my twenties before I ever sat down and read the Bible for the sheer joy of reading it. The occasion was a Christmas gift from my parents. They gave me a copy of the J.B. Phillips paraphrase of the New Testament.[4] Up to that time I had never really enjoyed reading the Bible because the only version available was the King James, and it read like Shakespeare to me. The language was too stilted, and I had difficulty understanding it.

The Phillips paraphrase had a transforming affect upon me. I started reading it and couldn't put it down. I was captivated by it. For the first time in my life, I read God's Word with an open heart and not just mentally, looking for proof texts.

❖ Receiving the Word ❖

The Holy Spirit began to minister to me as I read. The first thing I noticed is that I had never heard any sermons like those recorded in the Book of Acts. The sermons I had heard all my life were about the "plan of salvation." I couldn't find a single sermon in Acts about such a thing. All the sermons in Acts were about a Man, not a plan. The Apostles preached Jesus. They preached His death, burial, and resurrection and especially emphasized His resurrection as proof that He was God in the flesh. I discovered that I had been converted to a plan rather than the Man, Jesus. That crucial discovery came from simply reading God's Word with an open heart, allowing the Holy Spirit to be my teacher.

The toughest lesson I had to learn was the importance of exalting God's Word over the traditions of my heritage. This proved painful because my heritage, like most conservative groups, did not allow much latitude in opinion. We had a saying: "In faith, unity; in opinion, liberty; in all things, love." It sounded good, but the problem for us was that nothing fell into the realm of opinion!

Tradition was sacred to us. It was exalted over the Word. To violate it meant condemnation (what we called "the left foot of fellowship"). But as I learned to follow God's Word wherever it might lead, I discovered that the benefits far outweighed the pain.

❖ Discoveries about the Word ❖

In John 8:31–32 Jesus said, "If you abide in My word, then you are truly disciples of Mine; and you shall know the truth, and the truth shall set you free." Notice the qualifier. It is a big "if." To be set free, we must abide in His Word, even if it violates our sacred traditions. On another occasion, Jesus told the scribes and Pharisees that they were hypocrites because, "Neglecting the commandment of God, you hold to the tradition of men" (Mark 7:8).

For my spiritual life to turn around and take on power, I had to come to the realization that the Scriptures were not written for intellectuals and that I did not have to have a Ph.D. in hermeneutics to understand what they said. They were written for the common person.

I had to come to the realization that the Scriptures were not written to be analyzed like a Shakespearean play. They were written to convict people of sin and draw them to salvation in Jesus.

I had to come to the realization that the Scriptures are not hard to understand if you rely on the Holy Spirit and accept them for their plain sense meaning. God knows how to communicate.

I had to come to the realization that the Scriptures were not given as a legal code to put mankind into a legalistic straitjacket. Rather, they were given as a love letter from God to draw us into a deep, personal relationship with Him.

I had to come to the realization that the Scriptures are far more sacred than the traditions of men — that the Scriptures will liberate whereas tradition will enslave.

I had to come to the realization that the Scriptures have supernatural power, the power to penetrate people's souls and change their lives — that God's Word is "living and active and sharper than any two-edged sword, and piercing as far as the division of soul and spirit, of both joints and marrow, and able to judge the thoughts and intentions of the heart" (Heb. 4:12).

❖ The Validity of the Word ❖

All these realizations that brought the Bible alive to me run contrary to the thinking of modern man, even to the thinking of many professing Christians. Why should anyone believe that this book called the Bible is different from all other books? What sets it apart? How do we know it came from God?

A good place to start is the fact that the Bible itself claims to be divinely inspired. More than 3,000 times the biblical writers claim to be speaking the words of God. Over and over, the writers say, "Thus says the Lord," or "The Lord said." These are the most common phrases in the Bible.

The writers also repeatedly refer to the Scriptures as "the Word of God" (1 Sam. 9:27 and Acts 6:2), and they affirm that it is inspired by God (2 Tim. 3:16).

Most importantly, Jesus affirmed the Scriptures as the inspired Word of God. On one occasion, as Jesus was teaching, He was interrupted by a woman who yelled, "Blessed is the womb that bore You," to which Jesus replied, "On the contrary, blessed are those who hear the word of God, and observe it" (Luke 11:27–28).

In His Sermon on the Mount, delivered early in His ministry, Jesus affirmed that He had come to fulfill the Scriptures. He asserted that heaven and earth would pass away before one jot (the smallest letter) or tittle (the smallest stroke) of God's Word would pass away — thus affirming the verbal inspiration of the Scriptures (Matt. 5:18). At the end of His ministry, in the last prayer He prayed with His disciples, Jesus referred to the Scriptures as the Word of God and then added, "Thy word is truth" (John 17:14–17).

Jesus' life is a testimony to His belief in the divine authority of the Scriptures. At age 12 He confounded the spiritual leaders of Israel with His knowledge of God's Word (Luke 2:41–51). He used the Scriptures to justify His messianic claims (Luke 4:16–21). He used Scripture to teach the fundamentals of kingdom living (Matt. 5–7). He used Scripture to confront and confound Satan (Matt. 4:1–11). He used Scripture to teach His disciples after His resurrection (Luke 24:27, 44–45).

Jesus quoted Moses, the Psalms, and the prophets. And yes, He quoted the two Old Testament books that modern day liberals despise the most — Jonah and Daniel.

The disciples of Jesus evidenced the same respect for the Scriptures. The Gospel of Matthew quotes Old Testament passages repeatedly from beginning to end, attempting to prove to

Jewish readers that Jesus fulfilled messianic prophecy. Paul refers to the Scriptures as "inspired by God" (2 Tim. 3:16). Peter refers to the Hebrew prophets as men who were guided in what they said by "the Spirit of Christ within them" (1 Pet. 1:11). The apostle John asserted that the one who loves the Lord is the one who "keeps His word" (1 John 2:5).

❖ The Unique Nature of the Word ❖

Now, having said all of this, I want to pause to point out that I am aware of the fact that I am using the Bible to prove the Bible. I could thus be accused of circular reasoning: "The Bible is the Word of God because the Bible says so."

Therefore, I must take a moment to point out that you do not commit the error of circular reasoning when you use the Bible to prove the Bible. The reason is very simple. You see, the Bible is not one book! It is a collection of 66 books written by more than 40 authors over a period of 1,600 years.

Therefore, if you quote Jeremiah or Isaiah to substantiate Daniel, or if you quote Daniel to verify Revelation, you are not involved in circular reasoning. Instead, you are quoting altogether independent sources who happen to be bound together between the covers of the same book. Yet the paradox is that the more you read these books, the more you realize that the sources are not all that independent.

Here's my point — the authors of those 66 books came from every walk of life, including kings, peasants, philosophers, fishermen, poets, statesmen, scholars, tax collectors, farmers, and medical doctors. They wrote in every conceivable place — palaces, dungeons, prisons, on islands, in the wilderness, in cities, and in the midst of wars. They wrote in different moods, ranging from the heights of ecstasy to the depths of despair and sorrow.

They spoke on hundreds of controversial subjects. They wrote in three different languages. They utilized every conceivable literary style — history, law, poetry, biography, memoirs, letters, sermons, drama, parables, prophecy — you name it!

Yet, despite all this diversity, their writings interlock with a harmony and continuity from Genesis to Revelation that can only be explained by pointing to divine inspiration.

I could present a lot of other evidence that the Bible is the authoritative Word of God, but space does not permit it. I will just mention a few points in passing. One is the wisdom of the Bible's message and the life-changing impact of that message upon millions of lives throughout history. Another is the detail of its historical records and their accuracy, as confirmed by archeology. And then, of course, there is the remarkable survival of the Bible despite the efforts of so many to destroy it. The permanence of God's Word was attested by Isaiah when he wrote, "The grass withers, the flower fades, but the word of our God stands forever" (Isa. 40:8).

❖   Prophetic Verification of the Word   ❖

Some of the most convincing evidence of the Bible's divine inspiration is to be found in its prophecies. More than one-fourth of the Bible is prophetic in nature. In addition to the well-known messianic prophecies, there are hundreds of secular prophecies about people, cities, and nations, many of which have already been fulfilled in history.

Take, for example, Micah's prophecy that Jerusalem and its temple would be destroyed (Mic. 3:11–12). This prophecy was written over 150 years before the Babylonians conquered Jerusalem and destroyed the temple. Micah's contemporary, Isaiah, prophesied that the children of Israel would be taken into captivity, but they would ultimately be released by a man named Cyrus (Isa. 44:28). This prophecy was written 150 years before the reign of Cyrus who issued the order for the Jews to return home (Ezra 1:1–4). Jeremiah prophesied that the Babylonian captivity would last exactly 70 years (Jer. 29:10). Years later, when Daniel discovered Jeremiah's prophecy (Dan. 9:2), he calculated that the Jews were in their 69th year of captivity. Believing that Jeremiah was a prophet of God and that his words were inspired of God, Daniel dropped to his knees and prayed for the fulfillment of Jeremiah's prophecy (Dan. 9:4–19). The next year, the prophecy was fulfilled when the first group of Jews were sent back to Jerusalem by Cyrus (Ezra 1:1–4).

Are these remarkable prophecies and their fulfillment a matter of coincidence? I think not. Such prophetic fulfillment is beyond the realm of possibility. It carries the handprint of God.

The New Testament contains similar prophecies that have been accurately fulfilled in history. Consider the prophecy Jesus made the last time He left the Galilee for Jerusalem. He put a curse upon three towns where He had focused His ministry because they had refused to repent (Matt. 11:20–24). Those towns were Capernaum, Chorazin, and Bethsaida. About 150 years later, a great earthquake destroyed all three. In fact, they were so completely destroyed, that by 1800 critics of the Bible were using these three towns as proof positive that the Bible is full of error. They claimed the towns never existed! Today, you can go visit all three because they have since been discovered by modern archeologists.

In like manner, Jesus prophesied that the city of Jerusalem and its temple would be completely destroyed. As He put it, "There will not be left one stone upon another" (Luke 21:6). Those words were spoken in about A.D. 30. Forty years later, the Romans conquered the city and totally destroyed the temple.

Prophecy is one of the most unique features of the Bible. No other book that forms the basis of a religion contains prophecy. There are no prophecies in the Koran, the Book of Mormon, the Hindu Vedras, or the sayings of Confucius or Buddha. It is no wonder that the Bible's prophetic books set the teeth of liberals on edge, for the Bible's prophetic passages mark it as a book of supernatural origin.

❖ Crucial Questions about the Word ❖

What is your relationship with the Bible? Is it nothing more than a decoration for your coffee table? Do you read it occasionally, when there is a crisis, or when you need a verse to prove something? Maybe you are a regular reader but you do so out of a sense of duty rather than passion.

Do you really consider the Bible to be the Word of God? Really? If so, then why don't you treat it as such?

Let me put it this way — if you were to receive a letter from the White House in a beautiful gold embossed envelope with your name and address engraved on it, what would you do with it? Would you put it on your coffee table and show it off to all your friends? Or would you open it and read it?

The Bible is a personal letter to you from your Creator. It's designed to feed your soul by encouraging you, enlightening you, guiding you, empowering you, and pointing you to Jesus — the only true hope for your life.

Commit yourself to read it daily. It will nourish your soul and enable you to live a victorious Christian life in the midst of an increasingly pagan world.

Endnotes

1 Paul L. Maier, translator and editor, *Josephus: The Essential Works* (Grand Rapids, MI: Kregel Publications, 1988), p. 201–202.
2 Bruce Wilkinson, "Is There Something You Can't Live Without?" *Moody Monthly,* undated article, p.8.
3 *King James Version* of the Bible. Other versions refer either to baptisms or washings.
4 J.B. Phillips, *The New Testament in Modern English* (New York: The Macmillan Company, 1958).

Chapter 4

❖ ❖ ❖

Believing in the Power of God

GOD DOES NOT HEAL!" This headline blared across the top of a full-page advertisement in the *Fort Worth Star Telegram* in the mid-1980s. It was signed by about 20 ministers from the non-instrumental Churches of Christ.

The ad proclaimed that God had not healed anyone in the last 2,000 years, and, if Jesus were to delay His return for another 2,000 years, God would not heal anyone during that time period either. The ad then challenged anyone to prove they had been miraculously healed, and it offered a $10,000 reward to anyone who could do so.

The ad was so outlandish that it made the evening news on several of the Dallas-Fort Worth television stations. One station in particular gave it detailed coverage. A reporter was shown interviewing one of the ministers who had signed the ad. Incredibly, he was a hospital chaplain! The minister affirmed that he did not believe in supernatural healing.

"Then why are you here in this hospital?" the reporter asked.

"I am here to comfort those who are suffering," the minister replied.

I thought, *You're going to comfort them by assuring them that God no longer heals? What kind of comfort is that?*

In the next segment of the news report the reporter was shown interviewing an Assembly of God preacher who was pastor of a church in Fort Worth. The pastor's face was terribly deformed, including the fact that he did not have any ears.

The reporter asked him if he had ever experienced a

miraculous healing. The pastor responded that he had.

"I was born with all kinds of congenital defects," the pastor explained. "I could neither see nor hear. My parents took me to many doctors, and they said there was nothing that could be done for me. Then, one day my mom took me to a tent meeting being conducted by a healing evangelist. He laid hands on me and prayed for me to be healed, and while he was praying, I suddenly started hearing and seeing. It was a glorious moment."

"Can you prove you were healed?" the reporter asked.

"Yes," the pastor responded confidently. "I have extensive medical records that prove my healing."

"Are you going to claim the reward?"

The pastor smiled and shook his head no. "It would be a waste of time," he observed. "Those fellows who signed that ad would never believe my evidence. They are like the religious leaders in Jesus' day who said they would believe Jesus was the Messiah only if He raised someone from the dead. Well, He raised Lazarus from the dead, and the religious leaders responded by murdering Him."

❖ A Heritage of Unbelief ❖

The ad and the television program brought back a lot of memories to me because the ministers who signed that ad represented the sect I had grown up in. I very well knew and understood their viewpoint about healing. It was the view that had dominated my thinking about God's power for nearly 30 years.

One of our cornerstone beliefs could be summed up in the statement, "The age of miracles has ceased." We believed that all aspects of the supernatural — miracles, demons, angels, etc. — had ceased with the death of the last Apostle. Our God was the Grand Old Man in the Sky who had retired at the end of the first century. To us He was the great "I Was," not the great "I Am." We laughed and scoffed at the people who still believed in a miracle-working God. We wrote them off as "ignorant" and "superstitious."

I remember when the movie *The Ten Commandments* came out. I watched it in fascination, marveling over the mighty miracles God performed for the Children of Israel as they escaped Egypt and then wandered in the wilderness for 40 years. The movie made me yearn for such a God today — a powerful, active, caring God.

But I could not bring myself to believe that such a God existed anymore.

We had put God in a box, and we spent most of our time telling people what God could not do. We did not realize that in the process we had made ourselves god — a false god.

❖ The God of Deism ❖

In theological terms, we were Deists. A Deist is a person who believes in God, but he believes in an impersonal God. The God of the Deists is remote and aloof. After He finished creating the universe, He turned His back on His creation and left it to operate according to certain immutable laws of nature. He left us to cope with life with our brains and His book, the Bible. A Deist would laugh at the idea of a personal, caring God who is willing and anxious to respond to the needs of His creatures. The Deist would argue that such a God is an imaginary crutch conjured up by those who don't have the strength to persevere with their own God-given abilities.

I encountered a good example of this type of thinking in 1986 when I used my radio program to ask people to pray for the safety and good health of a group I was about to take to Israel. An attorney in Louisville, Kentucky, wrote, "Having been raised in the Church of Christ, you will understand that while I wish you well on your journey, and a safe return to your home, I cannot offer prayers to God for that purpose as we do not believe God intervenes in human affairs now." He concluded the letter with these words: "Man is man, and God is God, and the two hardly ever meet."[1]

Since leaving the Church of Christ, I have spent 30 years moving among a great variety of denominations, and I have discovered that the Churches of Christ do not have any exclusive franchise dealership on Deism. In fact, I would be so bold as to say that it has been my observation that the vast majority of professing Christians are Deists.

❖ Examples of Deism in Action ❖

Do you remember in the 1970s when James Robinson was the darling of Southern Baptists? He was billed as "the next Billy Graham." He spoke regularly at First Baptist in Dallas, the largest of the Southern Baptist churches at that time. Then, one day on his television program, James announced that he had received a miraculous healing, and so had his wife. He told how a humble carpet-layer had come to his hotel room during one of his crusades. The man announced that God had sent him to pray for James and his wife, and he shared information about their afflictions that could only have come from God. The man laid hands on them, prayed, and they were healed.[2]

This good news of a miraculous healing was not received as such by many Southern Baptists. James' schedule of meetings for the next ten years was canceled almost overnight. He was suddenly an outcast.

The same thing happened to Jack Deere, a professor at Dallas Theological Seminary. His son was miraculously healed at a Vineyard conference when he was prayed over by John Wimber. Deere shared the good news with his colleagues at the seminary. The seminary responded by making it clear that he should move on.[3]

In the early 1980s I conducted a series of prophetic conferences in South Africa. In one of the cities I visited I met a remarkable missionary sponsored by the Independent Christian Churches in the United States. As we were talking one evening, he asked me if I believed in demons. I told him I did. He then revealed that the exorcism of demons had become one of his major ministries.

"People here in Africa worship everything from rocks to snakes," he explained, "and this opens them up to demonic invasion. Thus, demon possession is very common over here."

He asked me if I would like to participate in an exorcism. I was reluctant, since that is not my calling. But I agreed when he explained that my role would be to pray for him and his associate as they confronted the demon. The session proved to be an exhausting one, but it was thrilling to watch this man boldly and confidently confront the powers of darkness in the power of the Holy Spirit and in the name of Jesus.

When he finished that evening, the missionary called me aside and said, "Please do not tell anyone in the States that I am involved in the ministry of exorcism because none of my supporting churches even believe in the reality of demons. They would cut off my support if they knew what I was doing."

❖ Deism's Impact on Bible Reading and Prayer ❖

I am convinced that deistic thinking is the reason that so few Christians read the Bible regularly. After all, the Bible is full of stories about people who get into desperate conditions and then call out to God to deliver them. If you do not believe that God responds anymore to such pleas as He once did, then the Bible is really irrelevant.

The same is true of prayer. Why bother to pray to a God who is aloof and uncaring — and who no longer has the power to do anything, even if He wanted to?

In this regard, I remember that in my boyhood church we would never pray for healing because we didn't believe in it. Instead, we would pray for God to help the doctors remember what they had learned in medical school! In fact, if someone in our church had simply prayed, "Lord we are concerned about our sister who is ill. Please heal her," we would probably have experienced two or three coronaries in our congregation — simply because the word "heal" had been spoken.

If ever Christians needed the power of God in their daily lives, it is in these end times in which we are now living. Professing Christians need to get serious about what the Bible teaches regarding both the supernatural and the miraculous.

❖ Getting Serious about the Supernatural ❖

Regarding the supernatural, Christians need to wake up to the fact that they have been brainwashed by Western scientific rationalism. This is the viewpoint that denies the reality of anything that cannot be quantified in some way. Thus, according to this attitude, if something cannot be seen, touched, weighed, measured, or quantified in some other way, then it does not exist.

But the Bible teaches that there is a whole realm of reality that cannot normally be perceived by the senses. It is called the supernatural. Because so many Christians have rejected the supernatural, much of the Bible is either incomprehensible to them or irrelevant.

❖ The Reality of Demons ❖

An example can be found in Mark 1:32–34. In these verses we are told that the people of Galilee brought "all who were ill and those who were demon-possessed" to Jesus to be healed. The passage says, "He healed many who were ill with various diseases, and cast out many demons." It also says He would not permit the demons to speak.

Now, how about it? Were some of the people demon-possessed or not? The preachers of my heritage divided over the issue. Some took the position that those who were "demon-possessed" were merely emotionally ill, and since people in the first century did not understand emotional illness, they ascribed it superstitiously to demons. Others of our preachers argued that the demons were real, but that they all retired at the end of the first century!

I actually attended a meeting of ministers one time where this issue was debated. They could not agree on the nature of demons in the first century, but at the end of the meeting, they voted on whether or not demons exist today. The vote was 25 to 0 that demons are currently non-existent! I shuddered at the time as I thought how Satan's hordes must have been laughing over that silly vote, and how they must have been licking their chops over the prospect of attacking the churches of those ministers.

❖ The Reality of Angels ❖

Another example of a scripture that most Christians cannot deal with is found in Hebrews 1:14: "Are they [angels] not all ministering spirits, sent out to render service for the sake of those who will inherit salvation?" This verse asserts that there is an active ministry of angels in the world today in the service of Christians.

I will never forget how excited I got when I discovered this verse. It was one of the first insights the Holy Spirit gave me after I decided to stop playing games with the Scriptures by spiritualizing them to death. When I accepted the plain-sense meaning of this verse, I began to understand other seemingly cryptic verses like the one in Hebrews 13:2 that warns us to be hospitable toward strangers because "some have entertained angels without knowing it."

I also began to experience new power and confidence in my Christian walk as I began to rely on the ministry of angels. For example, I never fly anywhere without asking God to surround the plane with His holy angels. In like manner, I always ask the

Lord to post an angel at my home to protect it and my loved ones.
Corrie ten Boom relates a great example of the ministry of
angels in her book *The Hiding Place*.[4] She tells about the Nazis
taking her and others to a concentration camp. Upon arrival, the
women were told to strip naked and walk through a building where
they would be deloused. She had a small Bible hidden under one
armpit and a vial of liquid vitamins under the other. She knew
that if she took off her clothing, both items would be found. So,
in child-like faith, she prayed, "Lord, surround me with your holy
angels, and make me invisible." She walked right past two guards
at the door and all the way through the building, and no one said
a word to her!

❖ The Reality of Spiritual Warfare ❖

Ephesians 6:10–18 is another passage that means little to
most professing Christians because it deals with spiritual war-
fare. This passage clearly states that the struggles we have in this
life are "not against flesh and blood." Rather, they are against
"the rulers, against the powers, against the world forces of this
darkness, against the spiritual forces of wickedness in the heavenly places." These words are meaningless to a person who does
not believe in the supernatural.

It is no wonder that so many Christians live defeated lives.
Take, for example, the Christian who is trying to deal with an abusive boss on the job. Instead of recognizing his struggle as a spiritual one and responding to it by praying for the boss, he spends
his time fuming over his ill treatment and dreaming of revenge.

❖ The Supernatural and Christianity ❖

As the pressure on Christians increases in these end times, it
is going to become increasingly important for all those who pro-
fess Christ to get serious about the supernatural. The bottom line
is that the supernatural is inextricably intertwined with Christianity. Think about it:

God created the universe supernaturally.

God sustains His creation supernaturally.

God destroyed the earth supernaturally.

God has intervened in history repeatedly in supernatural ways.

Most significantly, God became flesh supernaturally.

Jesus repeatedly performed supernatural acts. He was resurrected supernaturally. He ascended to heaven supernaturally. He appeared supernaturally to John on the island of Patmos.
We Christians have been born again supernaturally. The Holy Spirit resides in us supernaturally. We communicate with God supernaturally. Someday soon, Jesus will return to this earth supernaturally. The supernatural is for real, and we need to get serious about it. Without a belief in the supernatural, it is impossible to "put on the full armor of God" that we may "be able to stand firm against the schemes of the devil" (Eph. 6:11).

❖ Believing in Miracles ❖

When it comes to the miraculous, our basic problem is that we have defined miracles out of existence. Most people would define a miracle as some action that violates a law of nature. That definition is too narrow.

It is true that some biblical miracles violated laws of nature, as when Jesus walked on the water. But this type of miracle occurs rarely in the Scriptures. There are four clusters of these miracles, separated in time. The first cluster relates to the miracles of creation. The second cluster occurred in conjunction with the deliverance of the Jews from Egyptian captivity. The third cluster came during the ministries of Elijah and Elisha when God spoke through them to call the Jews out of idolatry. The fourth cluster consisted of the miracles manifested in the ministry of Jesus.

The point that is often overlooked is that most biblical miracles never violated any law of nature. They were considered miracles not because of their supernatural essence, but because of their timing.

❖ A Miraculous Weather Forecaster ❖

Consider the prophet Elijah. He was sent to confront the evil king Ahab. To prove that he was speaking for the one and only true God, Elijah told Ahab that the heavens were going to be closed and that it would not rain again until he said so (1 Kings

17:1). There followed an intense drought that lasted three and a half years. Finally, when Elijah felt he had made his point, he prayed for rain, and God sent a gully-washer! (1 Kings 18:41–46).

Now, in what way did this miracle violate a law of nature? There is no law of nature that says it must rain in Israel every year. This was a miracle of timing. It stopped raining when Elijah commanded it to do so, and it started raining again when he prayed for it to do so.

Modern man would call it a "coincidence." And I'm sure many people in Elijah's time considered it to be just that. But you see, with a sovereign God, there are no coincidences; there are only God-incidences.

Think for a moment about how people would react to such an event today. Let's say that God sends a prophet to confront the Russian leader, and let's assume the prophet announces that it will not rain in Moscow again until he says so. Three years pass and there is no rain. Then the prophet prays publicly in Red Square, calling for rain — and it starts pouring. Do you think most people would consider it a miracle? I doubt it. I think most people would say, "Wow! That guy is a great weather forecaster. I wish we could get him on our television station."

❖ A Miraculous Escape from Jail ❖

Paul and Silas are sitting in a jail in Philippi. They are praying and singing hymns to God when, suddenly, an earthquake occurs. To their astonishment, the door of their cell opens and they walk out (Acts 16:19–34). They are delivered by a miracle of God. But what law of nature was violated? The answer is none.

There is nothing miraculous about earthquakes in Israel. They happen all the time. What was miraculous about this one was its timing. It just "happened" to occur at the moment Paul and Silas were praying for release. And it just "happened" to be focused in their area so that "the foundations of the prison house were shaken" (Acts 16:26).

❖ A Miraculous Pregnancy ❖

Hannah, a Jewish woman afflicted with a barren womb, goes to the temple and prays earnestly for the Lord to bless her womb, making it possible for her to bear a child. The Lord hears her prayer and answers it, enabling her to conceive (1 Sam. 1:9–20). When the child is born, Hannah returns to the temple and gives God all the glory. She also dedicates her son to God. The boy grows up to become the great prophet Samuel (1 Sam. 2:1–10).

Now, what aspect of this story violates a law of nature? Hannah had a husband, and she had sexual relations with him after her prayer (1 Sam. 1:19). Every aspect of this story appears to be perfectly natural. Yet, it is treated by the Bible as a miracle of God, and Hannah also viewed it as such. Why?

Again, it was a miracle of timing. She had a barren womb. There seemed to be no hope. But she prayed, and God heard and answered. He touched her womb and made it possible for her to conceive naturally.

Let's suppose we had a Hannah incident in a typical modern-day church. Let's say there is a woman who has gone to doctor after doctor seeking a cure for her barren womb. Finally, in a last act of desperation, she lingers one evening after church, and when the sanctuary is almost empty, she goes to the front, kneels, and pours out her heart to God, pleading with Him to have mercy on her. A month later she is pregnant. She rushes to church filled with joy and thanksgiving and begins to share her miracle with everyone. What do you think would happen?

In many churches, there would be an emergency meeting of the governing board. The woman would be called in and chastised for disturbing the peace of the congregation. She would protest, trying to explain that she had prayed for a miracle and God had given her one. The members of the governing board would then explain to her that when she prayed she had a "psychological experience" that subsequently enabled her to relax during sexual intercourse and thus conceive. In other words, the leaders of the church would try to explain away a miracle of God.

❖ Blindness to Miracles ❖

The fact of the matter is that most people are blind to the miracles of God. They are constantly writing off to "coincidence" or "luck" the special blessings that God brings into their lives. I am convinced that most professing Christians are so spiritually insensitive that they would not recognize a miracle if God slapped them in the face with one!

I'm reminded of the story of the little boy playing on the roof of his house. He suddenly loses his balance, falls, and starts sliding down the roof. Seized with terror, he begins crying out, "Save me, Lord, please save me!" Just as he reaches the edge, his pants catch on a nail, and he is saved from falling. He looks up, shrugs his shoulders, and says, "Never mind, Lord."

A similar story concerns a man in a flood. The waters have come up fast, and he is hanging out his second story window, crying out to God to save him. Along comes a motor boat to his rescue. He refuses to get in. "I believe in miracles," he explains. "I'm waiting on God to save me."

The water continues to rise. He is forced to the roof. He continues to cry out to God. A helicopter arrives and drops a rope ladder. He waves it away. "I'm waiting for God to save me," he yells.

The man wakes up in a strange place. "Where am I?" he asks.

"You're in Heaven."

"Heaven? What happened?"

"You drowned."

"Drowned! But I reached out to God in faith and believed He would deliver me. Why didn't He respond?'

"Well, He sent you a motor boat and a helicopter. What else did you want?"

The point is that we are often so busy looking for the spectacular, that we overlook the supernatural. The supernatural is not always spectacular.

Let's say you are in a financial bind. The rent is due and you are $200 short. You don't know what to do except pray. So, you cry out to the Lord. Later in the day you are cleaning up your desk top when you discover a piece of mail that had been covered up several weeks before and forgotten about. You open it and to your amazement it turns out to be a birthday card from your parents with a $200 check enclosed.

Sound familiar? All of us have stories like that. If it happened to you, would you start praising your luck or start babbling about coincidence? Or, would you bow your head and give God all the praise and glory? A "coincidence" is when God performs a miracle and doesn't get the credit for it.

❖ A Paradox about God's Power ❖

This brings me to my central point. It has to do with a paradox about the power of God.

Here's the paradox — God's power is unlimited, but you and I, as weak and silly as we are, can limit God's power in our lives by our unbelief.

I remember well the first time I was ever confronted with this fundamental truth. I was eating lunch with a godly man who had a deep personal relationship with the Lord. He began to talk to me about healing. He told me how he had been miraculously healed of a tumor. He also told me about a miraculous healing that his wife had experienced. As he witnessed the work of God in his life, I said nothing, but I must have had unbelief written all over my face, because he suddenly said, "You don't believe me, do you?"

I didn't know what to say in response. I didn't want to call him a liar or imply that he was a fool. So I just sat there staring at my plate. But he was insistent. Again he asked, "Don't you believe me?"

When I still hesitated about answering, he asked a different question. "Have you ever experienced a miraculous healing in your life?"

"I don't think so," I responded.

"Has your wife or children?"

"Not that I know of."

"What about anyone in your church?"

"I don't think so."

"Well, let me ask you this. Do you believe God could heal you if He wanted to?"

I thought for a moment and then answered honestly, "No, I don't think so."

"Then," my friend responded, " don't ever expect Him to do so. You see, David, God is a gentleman. He's not going to force a blessing on you."

His response pierced my heart. It started me thinking deeply about the nature of God and His power. I was driven to the Scriptures in search of answers, and the very first verse the Holy Spirit brought to my attention proved to be life changing. It was Hebrews 13:8 — "Jesus Christ is the same yesterday and today, yes and forever."

That verse went off like a bomb in my spirit. I suddenly realized that God had not retired in the first century. I realized that the miracle-working God of the Bible is still the God of history. He is still on the throne, He still hears prayers, and He still performs miracles. He is the God who does not change (Mal. 3:6).

I think I shouted "Hallelujah!" for a week. I was jumping the pews and hanging from the chandeliers. My friends thought I had gone Pentecostal overnight! But no, I had just discovered that my God was alive and well and still in control.

I had let God out of my box. I had decided to stop saying, "God can't do that." I was walking in a renewed faith that affirmed, "Nothing will be impossible with God" (Luke 1:37).

As I continued to search the Scriptures, I found example after example of the paradox that we who are so weak can limit the all-powerful Creator by our unbelief.

❖ Examples of the Paradox in Scripture ❖

A classic example is found in the first chapter of Deuteronomy. As the Children of Israel prepared to enter the Promised Land, Moses gave a speech to encourage and exhort them to always be obedient to God. The introduction leading up to Moses' oration reads as follows:

> It is eleven days' journey from Horeb by the way of Mount Seir to Kadesh-barnea. And it came about in the fortieth year, on the first day of the eleventh month, that Moses spoke to the children of Israel (Deut. 1:2–3).

Did you read that quote carefully? It states that it took the Children of Israel 40 years to make an 11-day journey! Have you ever had such an experience? I certainly have.

Why did it take them so long? We don't have to guess. We are given the reason in Psalm 78. The psalm presents an historical summary of the deliverance of the Children of Israel from Egypt and their wanderings for 40 years in the Sinai wilderness. The theme of the psalm is that the Jews constantly "put God to the test" in their hearts because of their unbelief (Ps. 78:18). The psalmist Asaph reiterates the incredible miracles that God performed — the dividing of the sea, their guidance by a cloud in the day and a fire at night, the provision of water from the rocks, and their daily feeding with manna. Then he states that "in spite of all this, they still sinned, And did not believe in His wonderful works" (Ps. 78:32). He then summarizes their attitude by asserting, "Again and again they tempted God. . . . They did not remember His power" (Ps. 78:41–42).

The New Testament contains a similarly dramatic example of people limiting the power of God by their unbelief. It can be found in Mark 6:1–6. This passage tells us that Jesus was able to perform very few miracles in His hometown of Nazareth. Mark says, "He wondered at their unbelief" (Mark 6:6). Matthew states, "He did not do many miracles there because of their unbelief" (Matt. 13:58). Think of it, their unbelief limited the power of Jesus! It also motivated Him to leave the town and move His ministry headquarters to Capernaum.

❖ A Personal Experience of the Paradox ❖

I have frequently experienced this spiritual barrier of unbelief in my own ministry. I remember an incident at a church in Indiana where I was holding a meeting. It was a very traditional church. One evening, in response to the invitation I offered at the end of my sermon, a lady came forward and asked that we pray for her to be healed of cancer. When I made that announcement, I immediately sensed a strong feeling of unbelief in the congregation.

I shared my discernment, and then I stated that I was concerned that the spirit of unbelief could limit my prayer for the lady's healing. So, I asked all those who believed in healing to come forward. There was a long pause. Finally, one person came to the front, and then another. We ended up with about 8 people out of 300! I then asked those 8 to join hands in a circle around the lady to form a spiritual shield of their faith to protect her from the congregation's unbelief. It was only when the shield was in place that I proceeded to pray for her healing.

❖ The Lure of the God of Deism ❖

In these perilous end times, we desperately need the power of God. Yet many, if not most, Christians continue to cling tenaciously to the God of Deism — a God who is aloof and impotent.

Why? I think there are at least two major reasons. First, many fear a powerful God because they want a God they can control. They want a God in a box because they want to be the God of their lives.

Second, many fear a transcendent, personal, and caring God because they don't want intimacy. They don't want a God who is constantly sticking His nose into their affairs.

❖ Challenges Regarding God's Power ❖

Where are you in your concept of God? Do you have God in a box? Do you view Him as the Grand Old Man in the Sky who once had great power but who has now run out of gas?

I challenge you to open that box and allow God to operate in your life in the fullness of His power. I challenge you to believe in a God who is still on the throne, still hears prayers, and still answers prayers miraculously. I challenge you to believe in the God of the Bible who never changes and with whom nothing is impossible. I challenge you to believe the words of 1 Peter 5:6–7:

Humble yourselves, therefore, under the mighty hand of God, that He may exalt you at the proper time, casting all your anxiety upon Him, because He cares for you.

Notice carefully the important words this passage ends with: "*He cares for you.*" The true God of this universe is a personal, caring God of unlimited power. His "mighty hand" is ready to assist you, waiting for you to reach out in faith.

Our God is an Awesome God,
He reigns from Heaven above
With wisdom, power, and love.
Our God is an Awesome God.[5]

Endnotes

1 Letter to the author from an attorney in Louisville, Kentucky, dated July 28, 1986.
2 James Robinson, *Thank God I'm Free: The James Robinson Story* (Nashville, TN: Thomas Nelson Publishers, 1988).

3 Jack Deere, *Surprised by the Power of the Spirit* (Grand Rapids, MI: Zondervan Publishing House, 1993), p. 37–38.

4 Corrie ten Boom with John and Elizabeth Sherrill, *The Hiding Place* (New York: Bantam Books, 1984). Originally published in 1971.

5 "Awesome God," words and music by Rich Mullins, ©1988 Edward Grant (ASCAP).

Chapter 5

❖ ❖ ❖

Relying on the Holy Spirit

ou can buy the Holy Ghost for a dime!" I will never forget those blasphemous words. I still recoil in horror every time I think of them, even though it has been 40 years since I heard them.

Believe it or not, they were shouted by a visiting evangelist as he preached to my boyhood church. He was known far and wide as a preacher who could "put down the Holy Ghost." Churches would call him in to stifle any "Holy Ghost emotionalism" that might be getting started.

He would preach mightily about the dangers of emphasizing the Holy Ghost — how it would lead to unrestrained emotionalism and then to irrational behavior. The climax of his sermon always came when he would reach into his coat pocket, pull out a tiny paperback New Testament, wave it in the air, and shout, "You want the Holy Ghost? You can buy the Holy Ghost for a dime!" It was the most emotional sermon I ever heard against emotionalism!

The point he was making is one that I grew up with — namely, that the Holy Ghost is the Bible. Our position was that the more Scripture you memorized, the more Holy Ghost you would receive. We had no concept of the Holy Ghost being a personage of the One God. To us, the Holy Ghost was an inanimate object.

I was 20 years old at the time I heard this sermon. I had already figured out that our concept of the Holy Ghost was dead wrong, which is the reason the sermon grated on me so strongly. My revelation about the Holy Ghost had come about seven years earlier when I was 13.

❖ Grappling with the Holy Ghost ❖

Keep in mind that when I was a teenager the only version of the Bible we had was the King James. It referred to the Holy Spirit as the Holy Ghost, and the use of the term "ghost" presented a major problem to me.

Ghosts were supposed to be something evil and scary. I was a Boy Scout, and when we would go on camping trips, we would sit around the campfire and tell ghost stories, trying to scare each other. We usually succeeded, and we often spent the night all sleeping in the same tent together!

With this background, I kept asking myself how this Holy Ghost in the Bible could be good. When I read about Him, He certainly seemed to be good, yet He was called a ghost. It just didn't make sense to me.

Then one Saturday morning I got on a city bus and went to the downtown area of my hometown of Waco, Texas. I paid nine cents to go to the Strand Theatre to see a double feature of cowboy movies. It was a regular Saturday morning ritual for me. Between the features they always showed a serial that usually left a distressed damsel tied to the railroad tracks. They also showed an animated comedy.

This particular morning, the comedy was one that I had never seen before. It was called "Casper, the Friendly Ghost." As I sat there watching this cute little friendly ghost helping people in trouble, it suddenly occurred to me that the Holy Ghost in the Bible must be a person like that ghost on the screen. That settled my theological struggle — until three years later, when I went through a rite of passage at our church called, "Young Men's Training Class." This was a required course for all 16 year olds. In it, we were taught how to pray publicly, lead in singing, and serve communion. We were also taught the fundamental doctrines of our church.

I will never forget the night we got to the topic of the Holy Ghost. The teacher asked, "Who can define the Holy Ghost for me?"

My hand shot up. "The Holy Ghost is like Casper, the

Friendly Ghost, and. . . ." That's as far as I got. The teacher cut me off in mid-sentence. He let me know in no uncertain terms that relating Casper to the Holy Ghost was downright silly. He made it clear to all of us that the Holy Ghost was the Bible. But he didn't convince me. I remained a secret believer in Casper.

❖ A Long History of Confusion ❖

I was to discover over the years that the confusion of my church about the Holy Spirit was nothing unique to it. Nor is the confusion anything new. It has existed throughout Church history. In fact you can find it in the New Testament. In Acts 19 we are told that when Paul came to Ephesus on his third missionary journey, he found some disciples. He asked them, "Did you receive the Holy Spirit when you believed?" Their astonishing reply was, "No, we have not even heard whether there is a Holy Spirit" (Acts 19:2).

That was a tragic situation. But what is even more tragic is the fact that almost 2,000 years later the same ignorance of the Holy Spirit exists in the modern-day Church. This was clearly revealed in a poll taken in 1997 by the Barna Research Group of Oxnard, California. The poll showed that only 40 percent of Americans believe in the existence of the Holy Spirit. But what was even more stunning was the response of "born-again Christians." More than five out of ten born-again Christians (55 percent) agreed that the Holy Spirit is a *symbol* of God's presence or power, but not a living entity![1] It appears that Christians have been brainwashed into believing that the Holy Spirit is an impersonal power like "The Force" in *Star Wars.*

We need to get serious about the nature and purpose of the Holy Spirit if we are to have any hope of living triumphant lives in these end times. Satan knows Bible prophecy. He knows he is living on borrowed time. He is determined to take as many people to hell with him as he can. He is determined to wreak havoc in the lives of Christians and in their churches. Our only hope of standing against his steadily intensifying attacks is learning how to rely on the power of God's Holy Spirit.

❖ The Causes of Confusion ❖

Why is there so much confusion about the Spirit, and why has this always been true in the Church? I think it relates in part to the self-effacing role of the Spirit. As we will see, one of His primary roles is to point people to Jesus as Savior and Lord. He does not draw attention to himself. He works behind the scenes. Another factor relates to the many symbols that are used of the Spirit in Scripture — things like wind, rain, and fire. These symbols seem to connote an impersonal force.

Our Creator God has been revealed to us as Father. That is a concept we can grasp. Jesus took on a human body and lived among us. We have biographies of Him. But for most people, the Holy Spirit is a shadowy entity difficult to grasp. Trying to get hold of the concept for many is like trying to nail Jell-O to a wall.

❖   The Identity of the Spirit   ❖

So, let's look for a moment at the identity of the Holy Spirit. The first thing you need to keep in mind is that the Spirit is never referred to as an "it." The Spirit is not an inanimate object. Regarding the Bible, the Spirit is intimately related to God's Word because it was the Spirit who inspired the biblical writers (2 Tim. 3:16), but the Bible is the sword of the Spirit, not the Spirit himself (Eph. 6:17). The Spirit works through the Bible to draw people to Jesus, although the work of the Spirit is not confined to the testimony of the Scriptures. The Spirit can witness directly to our spirits (Rom. 8:16).

The Holy Spirit is a person. The Spirit is always referred to directly in the Scriptures as "He." Referring to the Spirit, Jesus told His disciples that when He left, He would send a "helper" (*paracletos* in Greek, meaning a helper or intercessor). Jesus added, "And He, when He comes, will convict the world concerning sin, and righteousness, and judgment" (John 16:8). To Jesus, the Holy Spirit was "He" not "It."

The Bible says the Holy Spirit can be lied to (Acts 5:3–4). It also says the Holy Spirit can be quenched (1 Thess. 5:19) and grieved (Eph. 4:30). These are characteristics of a personality. You cannot lie to a chair, or quench a wall, or grieve a light fixture.

The Holy Spirit is the supernatural presence of God in the world today. Paul put it this way: "The Lord is the Spirit" (2 Cor. 3:17). Luke stated that the Holy Spirit is "the Spirit of Jesus" (Acts 16:7). Peter equated the Holy Spirit with God the Father when he told Ananias and Sapphira that they had lied to the Holy

Spirit (Acts 5:3) and then added, "You have not lied to men, but to God" (Acts 5:4). Remember that old axiom in geometry: "Things equal to the same thing are equal to each other."

The Holy Spirit is one of the three persons who constitute the One God. That's the reason we are told to be baptized "in the name of the Father and the Son and the Holy Spirit" (Matt. 28:19). As such, He is co-equal to Jesus and the Father, but He plays a different role.

❖ The Work of the Spirit ❖

This brings us to the work of the Spirit. The Holy Spirit has two roles — one toward the unbeliever and another within the believer. With regard to the unbeliever, the Holy Spirit is the Father's evangelist. With regard to the believer, He is the Father's potter. Let's consider these two roles in detail.

Jesus summarized the work of the Spirit regarding unbelievers. He said that the Holy Spirit would "convict the world concerning sin, and righteousness, and judgment" (John 16:8). Specifically, the Spirit convicts unbelievers of their sinfulness, impresses upon them the righteousness of Jesus, and points them to the judgment of Satan (John 16:9–11). The Bible makes it clear that no person can come to Jesus apart from the testimony of the Holy Spirit. Jesus put it this way: "No one can come to Me, unless the Father who sent Me draws him" (John 6:44). And how does the Father draw unbelievers to Jesus? He does is through the Holy Spirit who bears witness of Jesus as the Father's only begotten Son (John 15:26 and 1 John 5:7).

When a person responds to the witness of the Spirit by accepting Jesus as Lord and Savior, he is "born again" (John 3:3), and the Father gives that person a very special birthday present — the Holy Spirit (1 Cor. 12:13). That's right, the Holy Spirit ceases to be on the outside drawing the person to Jesus. Instead, He moves inside the person and takes up residence within him (Rom. 8:9). When He does so, His role changes.

❖ The Spirit in the Believer ❖

Within the believer, the Holy Spirit is the Father's potter. His role is to shape each believer into the image of Jesus (Rom. 8: 29 and Gal. 4:19), a process which the Bible refers to as sanctification

(Rom. 6:22 and 2 Thess. 2:13). The Spirit does this by first of all gifting us. Each person, when he or she is born again, is given at least one gift of the Spirit, and sometimes more than one (1 Cor. 12:4–11). If we are good stewards of our gifts, using them to advance the Lord's kingdom, we may be given additional gifts during our spiritual walk with the Lord.

The Spirit also accomplishes His work of sanctification by guiding us (Rom. 8:14), comforting us (Acts 9:31), strengthening us (Phil. 4:13 and 1 John 4:4), praying for us (Rom. 8:26–27), encouraging us (Rom. 15:5), defending us (Luke 12:11–12), and illuminating us as we study the Word (1 John 2:27).

The work of sanctification is a lifelong process. It continues until we die or we are raptured to meet the Lord in the sky. It is an inward work that applies to the soul.

To clarify this, let me explain that salvation is a process. We don't often think of it in this way. When asked if we are saved, we usually respond by saying, "Yes, I was saved in May of 1951." We normally give the date when we received Jesus as our Lord and Savior. That's okay, except for the fact that it leaves the impression that our salvation began and ended that day.

The fact of the matter is that the day you accepted Jesus, the only part of you that was born again was your spirit. Your spirit was brought to life by the regenerating power of the Holy Spirit, and you were justified before God. Justification is the first step in the salvation process. It refers to your legal standing before God. Because of your faith in Jesus, God forgives and forgets your sins, and you stand before the Father justified in the righteousness of Jesus (Rom. 5:18).

At that point, the second step in the process begins. It is called sanctification. The Holy Spirit moves in and begins the work of shaping your carnal soul into the image of Jesus. Your soul is your personality, your will, and your emotions.

When sanctification begins, you become involved in a spiritual struggle. Each time you start to make a decision, your regenerated spirit will pull you in the direction of God whereas your carnal soul will draw you to the world. That's the struggle Paul describes in his life in Romans 7 when he speaks of wanting to do what is right, but often ending up doing what is wrong (Rom. 7:7–25).

The final step in the process of salvation does not occur until the Resurrection or rapture. At that point, the bodies of believers will be glorified, which means they will be perfected and be made immortal (1 Cor. 15:51–55).

And so we have it — the three stages in the salvation process: justification (the spirit), sanctification (the soul), and glorification (the body).

❖ A Slow and Painful Process ❖

The work of sanctification is a slow and painful process. It is slow because the Spirit is a gentleman, and He does not force us to change all at one time. It is painful because we have a natural tendency to resist the work that the Spirit wants to do within us.

You see, the Spirit wants to take over the direction of our life. But we usually want Him to be a resident and not president. We want Him to reside within us but not preside. So we end up stifling the work of the Spirit, which is why we are commanded, "Do not quench the Spirit" (1 Thess. 5:19).

Most of us come to the Lord out of a very specific need. We want Him to straighten out a specific problem that is wrecking our life. Then, soon after we have accepted Him and received the gift of His Spirit, we discover that He is concerned about every aspect of our life, not just the problem that was bugging us. The Spirit begins to convict us of sins that never really bothered us all that much and which we would really prefer for Him to overlook. We welcomed the Spirit as a helper, but he begins to act like a meddler.

❖ The Transformation of a Drunk ❖

The drunk who comes to Jesus to get sober begins to feel bad about smoking. The person obsessed with sex wants to be delivered from lust and becomes convicted of using filthy language. The man who wants Jesus to deliver him from driving ambition starts feeling remorse for his neglect of his family. The woman who wants Jesus to liberate her from materialism and her reckless use of credit cards begins to feel uneasy about gossiping.

I'm reminded of the fellow whose life was being ruined by alcoholism. One night as he was thinking of killing himself, he decided instead to reach out to God. The gospel had been shared with him many times. He knew what to do, but He had never before been willing to repent and reach out to Jesus in faith.

He got on his knees, confessed his sins, and cried out to the Lord to save him. Instantaneously, he experienced a miracle of healing. He was delivered from any desire whatsoever for alcohol. He was overwhelmed by the Lord's response, and he decided to witness what had happened to him.

He sought out a pastor he knew who had been praying for him. He shared the good news of his salvation and his deliverance from alcohol. The pastor encouraged him to witness his faith in baptism and to get involved in the life of the church so that he could begin to grow spiritually. He did so, continuing to marvel over the miracle God had performed in his life. Then, one day on his construction job, he was telling a dirty joke at lunchtime, when he suddenly felt convicted that he shouldn't finish the story. He resisted the conviction and delivered the punch line. All his fellow workers got a big laugh, but he did not feel the usual satisfaction he had always experienced before when he told one of his smutty jokes.

The next time he told one of his stories, the words started sticking in his throat. He couldn't even finish the joke because he came under such strong conviction. He finally just broke off the story, claiming he could not remember the punch line. The Holy Spirit had delivered him from one of his worst habits.

A few weeks later, he was lighting up a cigarette when he felt a nudge from the Spirit. It was as if the Spirit was saying, "Hey, fellow, I'm living inside of you now, and I don't want it to be smoky in here." He decided to cut back to two packs a day. But he was still miserable. So, he decided to make a deal with God. He agreed to give up smoking if the Lord would just let him chew tobacco. But chewing didn't seem to placate the Spirit either. After months of struggle, he finally threw out all his tobacco products.

He was beginning to feel like a spiritual giant. God had delivered him from drinking, smoking, cussing, and telling dirty jokes. As he was sitting in his den on a weekend contemplating his spiritual growth, the Holy Spirit suddenly began to speak to him about his addiction to television sports. He began to feel very uneasy because this was his greatest source of pleasure. The Spirit seemed to be saying, "This is your fourth football game in one day. What about your football widow in the kitchen? Are you going to show any interest in her this weekend? And what about your football orphan — your ten-year-old son? Why don't you go outside and spend some time throwing a football to him?"

The Holy Spirit was really meddling now. *Football is sacred! Surely I can have one area of pleasure all to myself*, he thought. He brushed the Spirit aside. It was the fourth quarter, there were only 30 seconds left in the game. His favorite team was behind 2 points, but they were on their opponent's 20-yard line with one down left to go. What would they do? Kick a field goal or go for a touchdown?

As he leaned forward to watch the ending, he suddenly felt all the excitement drain from his body. He knew the time had come for him to drastically curtail his TV sports and spend more time with his family.

He also felt like it was time for him to give a testimony at church about the great work the Lord had been doing in his life. His pastor agreed.

"You will not believe what the Lord has been doing in my life," he began. "He delivered me from alcohol, cleaned up my language, stopped me from telling dirty jokes, released me from my bondage to tobacco, and — believe it or not — He even liberated me from my obsession with TV sports. It is amazing the spiritual progress I have made in such a short time." And just at that moment, the Holy Spirit began to convict him of his pride!

❖ The Goal of Perfection ❖

The Holy Spirit wants to fine-tune each of us into the image of Jesus because the Father is interested in nothing less than perfection in our lives (James 1:4 and 1 Pet. 1:13–16). Yes, He is a God of grace who will accept us in all our imperfections, but He desires that we be perfected (Matt. 5:48). Think of it this way. When a child takes its first step, his father rejoices. But no father is going to be satisfied with that one step. He will not be satisfied until the child can walk and then run without falling.

For this reason, Christians are commanded to "be filled with the Spirit" (Eph. 5:18). Jesus said He wanted us so full of the Spirit that the Spirit would flow out of us like "rivers of living waters" (John 7:38). But most of us are like 500-gallon drums with six inches of water sloshing around in the bottom.

So, what's the key? How can we become Spirit-filled and

stay that way? How can we walk triumphantly in the power of the Spirit, living as overcomers in these difficult end times?

❖ Receiving the Spirit ❖

The first step is to receive the Spirit. You cannot be filled with the Spirit if you don't even have the Spirit. There are many professing Christians who need to take this first step because they have never been born again.

You do not receive the Holy Spirit by being born into a Christian family. Nor do you receive the Spirit by attending church or submitting yourself to Christian rites like water baptism.

The first step is to develop a personal relationship with Jesus by sincerely accepting Him as your Lord and Savior and then manifesting that relationship of trust in Christian baptism — not as some formal rite for church membership but out of love for the Lord. The apostle Peter put it this way at the end of the first Gospel sermon that was ever preached: "Repent and let each of you be baptized in the name of Jesus Christ for the forgiveness of your sins; and you shall receive the gift of the Holy Spirit" (Acts 2:38).

The gift of the Spirit is once and for all, for "the gifts and the calling of God are irrevocable" (Rom. 11:29). You don't get a little of the Holy Spirit when you are born again. You receive all the Spirit that you will ever receive. Many teach otherwise. They teach that you must continue to seek a baptism of the Spirit that will secure more of the Spirit for your life.

That teaching is misleading. The Christian walk of sanctification is not a process of getting more and more of the Holy Spirit. No, it is a process of allowing the Spirit to get control of more and more of you!

❖ Releasing the Spirit ❖

That brings us to the second step in becoming a Spirit-filled person. First, we must receive the Spirit. Second, we must release the Spirit. This can occur at the time the Spirit is received if the person truly turns over every aspect of his life to the Spirit. But that rarely occurs. Usually it is a gradual process, as we wrestle with the Spirit over every aspect of our life that He desires to control.

The ultimate release often occurs after years of stifling the Spirit, when we encounter a crisis that overwhelms us, and we are driven to our knees in total desperation and complete humility. This experience happened to my wife and me 30 years into our Christian walk when our 16-year-old daughter ran away from home and disappeared without a trace for three months.

The experience brought us to the end of ourselves. We were totally desperate and completely helpless in our own power. The police showed no interest. We turned to the Lord, as we had never done before. We cried out to Him to protect our daughter and to bring her back home. In the process we experienced a release of the Spirit in our lives, and we were drawn into a deeper relationship with the Lord than we ever dreamed possible.

Ultimately, we found our daughter unharmed in Indiana. But we were never the same people again. Our relationship had been transformed with the Lord, each other, and our daughter.

❖ Evidence of Being Spirit-Filled ❖

There is no special sign of this release of the Spirit. It can be evidenced in a myriad of ways. For one person it may be the receipt of a new spiritual gift. For another, it may be an insatiable appetite for the Word of God.

Some people insist that the sign of a Spirit-filled person is the gift of tongues. Often, those who believe this make the terrible mistake of putting down Christians who do not have that gift, implying that they are second-class citizens in God's kingdom. Don't ever allow anyone to judge you by your gifts. The gifts of the Spirit are just that — gifts. They are not prizes that are earned by achieving certain levels of spirituality.

The gift of tongues alone cannot be the one and only true sign of a Spirit-filled person, because there are people with the gift of tongues who are meaner than a junkyard dog. They are not filled with the Spirit. Actually, the greatest evidence of a Spirit-filled life is not found in gifts but in fruit. Paul wrote: "The fruit of the Spirit is love, joy, peace, patience, kindness, goodness, faithfulness, gentleness, self-control . . ." (Gal. 5:22–23). You show me a person who can control his tongue, and I will show you a Spirit-filled person.

I think it should also be kept in mind that history is full of great Christian leaders who were filled to overflowing with God's Spirit, but who never spoke in tongues — men like Martin Luther, John Wesley, D.L. Moody, C.S. Lewis, and Billy Graham, to name only a few.

One other thing — the release of the Spirit is not a one-time phenomenon. It is something that can occur several times in one's life. The reason is that we are leaky vessels. We can get filled with the Spirit and then get our eyes off the Lord and start getting caught up on sin again. The only way to remain filled with the Spirit is to stay near the fountain — namely, Jesus. We must keep our eyes focused on Him (Heb. 12:2). And that is a daily struggle.

❖ Relying on the Spirit ❖

Which brings me to the third key to living a Spirit-filled life. First, we must receive the Spirit. Second, we must release the Spirit. Third, we must rely on the Spirit. This begins with a realization that the only way we can effectively serve the Lord is by relying on His power. The Holy Spirit is the one who anoints us with that power. Without it, we serve the Lord in our flesh, and both we and the Lord will be disappointed in the results.

We need to remember this important truth. It is so easy to forget it when we are dealing with "minor things" or when we are operating in an area where we are naturally talented.

When the Apostles needed men to wait tables in the Early Church, serving food to widows, what did they look for? Not what we would be inclined to look for. For such minor service, we would tend to look for anyone interested in the job, although we would prefer people who had the strength to carry heavy trays. But the Apostles put something else first. They sought out men who were filled with the Holy Spirit (Acts 6:1–6).

Our churches are going to come alive when we start following this example. The first qualification for any servant in the church should be whether or not the person is Spirit-filled. This should apply to elders, deacons, teachers, and choir members. Too often, church leaders are selected merely on the basis of political considerations — things like the prestige of the person's position in the community or their family connections within the congregation. The result is that we end up with contentious, domineering carnal leaders who know nothing about Spirit-filled, servant leadership.

Then there is the problem of relying on our natural-born talents. The talented singer or speaker often feels no need to pray for a special anointing of the Spirit. They forget that there is a big difference in a natural talent and a supernatural gift.

The naturally talented singer can sing "The Lord's Prayer" perfectly and produce a standing ovation. The Spirit-gifted singer may sing the same song and receive no applause at all because people have dropped to their knees with tears in their eyes to repent before the Lord. The most talented of people still need to humbly seek the Lord's anointing on their talent if they are to use it effectively to serve God.

Receive. Release. Rely. Let me conclude with two examples, one taken from the Bible, the other from history.

❖ A Biblical Example ❖

I am convinced that when Paul came to the Lord, he did so with a heart filled with pride. That is understandable when you consider that he was an intellectual trained in the law by one of the greatest rabbis, Gamaliel. He was also a talented writer, speaker, and debater. I think Paul felt that the Lord was really fortunate to have him on His side. After all, he could easily convert tens of thousands of his Jewish brethren. I realize this is a startling appraisal of Paul at the time of his conversion, but I think I can prove it from the Scriptures.

In Acts 8 we are told that after his baptism, Paul *immediately* began to preach Jesus in the Jewish synagogues (Acts 9:20). That is not the action of a typical, humble, new babe in Christ. A new Christian might begin to share his faith immediately with friends, family, and fellow workers, but he does not declare himself ready to start preaching. Time must be spent in the Word, getting intimately acquainted with the Lord.

Not only did Paul start preaching immediately, he did so with a cocky attitude, attempting to prove that the Jews were wrong (Acts 9:22). He had a debater's carnal spirit, determined to prove to all his Jewish brethren that they were wrong and he was right. How many people have you ever won to the Lord with such an approach? That's the same number Paul convinced — none! He didn't draw anyone to the Lord. Rather, he incited the Jews to murder, and they plotted to kill him (Acts 9:23). When the plot became known to Paul, he arranged for some fellow Christians to lower him over the wall of Damascus at night in a large basket (Acts 9:25).

Years later, while reviewing his life as a missionary, Paul wrote that the most embarrassing moment of his life was the night he was "let down in a basket through a window in the wall" (2 Cor. 11:30–33). In other words, it was the night he became a basket case!

Paul escaped to Jerusalem where he proceeded to do the very same thing again. He had obviously not learned from his mistake. Once again he entered the synagogues and spoke out boldly in the name of the Lord and tried to argue his opponents into submission (Acts 9:28–29). And once again, their response was to try to put him to death (Acts 9:29).

Finally, the brethren in Jerusalem decided to get Paul out of town. They did so by buying him a one-way ticket to his hometown of Tarsus. They even took him to Caesarea to make sure he got on the boat! (Acts 9:30)

What is said next in the Scriptures is really funny. You can almost hear the Holy Spirit sigh with relief: "So the church throughout all Judea and Galilee and Samaria enjoyed peace, being built up; and going on in the fear of the Lord and in the comfort of the Holy Spirit, it continued to increase" (Acts 9:31). Paraphrase: "Praise God, Paul is finally gone. Now the church can experience some peace and growth in the power of the Holy Spirit!"

Paul spent the next 14 to 16 years in Tarsus. What did he do? We are not told. I would assume that he spent that time studying the Word, learning new insights in light of his discovery of Jesus. I assume too that he learned by practice how to teach and preach in the power of the Spirit as opposed to the power of his flesh.

The next time we run across Paul, he is at a prayer meeting in Antioch (Acts 13:1). Suddenly, the Holy Spirit speaks: "Set apart for Me Barnabas and Saul [Paul] for the work to which I have called them" (Acts 13:2). The group fasted and prayed, laying their hands on the men, and then sent them on their way. "So, being sent out by the Holy Spirit" (Acts 13:4), Paul went forth to become the greatest missionary in the history of Christianity — "filled with the Holy Spirit" (Acts 13:9).

Paul received the Spirit when he received Jesus as his Messiah, but he quenched the Spirit as he attempted to minister in the flesh, relying on his natural talents. He had to be humiliated before he was willing to release the Spirit, and then he had to wait patiently for a special anointing of the Spirit before he could begin the ministry that God had in mind for him.

❖ An Historical Example ❖

The historical example of what it means to release the Spirit is found in the story of the European in the 1890s who saved his money for years to buy a cruise ship ticket to America. Finally, at the turn of the 20th century, he had enough money.

On the day of his departure, the man filled a large sack full of cheese and crackers because he had no money left to buy meals on the ship. He ate this paltry meal throughout the cruise, day and night. When the other passengers would go to their sumptuous meals, he would often peer through the dining room windows and wish that he could enjoy their fine food. But he always ended up in his room alone eating his cheese and crackers.

Finally, the last day of the voyage arrived. He was so glad because he was tired of his cheese and crackers, and furthermore, they were almost gone. This day he decided to sit on a deck chair and eat.

As he was eating, a passenger noticed him and asked, "Why are you sitting out here eating cheese and crackers?"

Embarrassed, he replied haltingly, "Well . . . you see . . . I'm a poor man. I was only able to raise enough money for my ticket. I couldn't afford to buy any meals, so I brought a large bag of cheese and crackers."

The passenger responded in amazement, "My dear man, didn't you know that all the meals were included in the price of your ticket? All the time you have been eating cheese and crackers, a great banquet has been waiting on you!"[2]

For 30 years, like that poor ignorant European immigrant, I was on the good ship Zion, and the captain was Jesus Christ. I was on my way to heaven, but I did not know what all was included in the ticket.

Release the Spirit, and come to the banquet!

Endnotes

1 Billy Bruce, "Americans: Is the Holy Spirit Real?" *Ministries Today,* p. 13. The Barna Research organization has a website that contains the results of many of their religious polls. It can be found at http://www.barna.org.

2 This story is adapted from a pamphlet by John Osteen, who at the time was pastor of Lakewood Church in Houston. The author has only pages torn from the pamphlet, so the title and date of the pamphlet are unknown.

Chapter 6

❖ ❖ ❖

Practicing Tough Faith

allup Says America Has a Shallow Faith." Those were
the headlines of a newspaper article that contained the
results of Gallup's latest polls on faith in America.
"We've become a more churched nation but not necessarily a more
Christian one," reported Gallup. He added that in America today
"God is important but not primary in people's lives." Despite
religion's continuing and widespread appeal, Gallup reported that
Americans are ignorant about doctrine, inconsistent in their beliefs, superficially faithful, and lacking trust in God. "So many
Americans say they believe in God," said Gallup, "but far fewer
are willing to trust Him, to be obedient and to follow His will."[1]

❖ A Biblical Contrast ❖

In contrast to the shallow faith of Americans at the beginning of the 21st century, let's take a look at the faith of the apostle
Paul in the first century as depicted in the following paraphrase:

I've worked much harder, been jailed more often, beaten
up more times than I can count, and at death's door
time after time. I've been flogged five times with the
Jew's thirty-nine lashes, beaten by Roman rods three
times, pummeled with rocks once. I've been ship-
wrecked three times, and immersed in the open sea for
a night and a day. In hard traveling year in and year
out, I've had to ford rivers, fend off robbers, struggle
with friends, struggle with foes. I've been at risk in the

city, at risk in the country, endangered by desert sun
and sea storm, and betrayed by those I thought were
my brothers. I've known drudgery and hard labor, many
a long and lonely night without sleep, many a missed
meal, blasted by the cold, naked to the weather.

And that's not the half of it, when you throw in the
daily pressures and anxieties of all the churches. When
someone gets to the end of his rope, I feel the desperation in my bones. When someone is duped into sin, an
angry fire burns in my gut (2 Cor. 11:23–28).[2]

These remarkable words of the apostle Paul need to be
brought to the attention of all Christians in these end times, particularly American Christians who have a shallow faith and have
never really experienced severe persecution for their faith. Paul
did not expect God to protect him from suffering simply because
he had put his faith in Jesus. He suffered mightily because of his
commitment to the Lord. But his suffering never prompted him
to throw up his hands in disgust and curse God.

Even when he was in prison facing a death sentence, he wrote:
"Rejoice in the Lord always; again I will say, rejoice!" (Philippians
4:4). He added, "Be anxious for nothing, but in everything by
prayer and supplication with thanksgiving let your requests be
made known to God" (Phil. 4:6).

❖ The Need for Tough Faith ❖

Paul knew how to practice tough faith. Unlike most of us,
the quality of his faith did not depend upon circumstances. It is so
easy to walk in faith when the circumstances of life are all very
positive. It is when the circumstances go sour that our faith is tested.

It happens when the doctor looks you in the eye and says,
"I'm sorry, but it's cancer." Or when the police call to tell you that
your son or daughter has been arrested and is high on drugs. Or
maybe it's a note from a spouse that says, "I no longer love you. I
have decided to leave." Perhaps it will be the loss of a job or the
death of a family member.

In these end times, a new factor is likely to be persecution
for your faith — the loss of a job or a promotion simply because

you are a Christian. Or perhaps ridicule and harassment at school or on the job because of your Christian convictions. Is your faith ready for the test?

❖ The Erosion of Tough Faith ❖

Many Christians today are sitting ducks waiting to be picked off by Satan when the economy goes belly-up. That's because they have been deceived by the popular "prosperity gospel." This is the false gospel that teaches that God wants all His children to walk in perfect health and financial prosperity. It appeals to the greed in people's hearts. The advocates of this gospel strut about in conspicuous wealth, living in mansions and driving luxury cars. They unashamedly point to their wealth as "proof" that God's hand is upon their ministry. Their disciples follow their lead by lusting after what they have, giving $100 so that they can get back $1,000, as if God were running some sort of money scheme.

When the good health and prosperity do not materialize for the faithful, then they are told it is because they don't have enough faith. They are condemned for their poverty or ill health. Spiritual suffering is added to their physical and mental anguish. It is a deceitful "doctrine of demons" (1 Tim. 4:1).

❖ The Fellowship of Suffering ❖

God has not promised His children a rose garden, at least not in this life. Jesus said His followers would be hated by the world (John 15:18–19). Paul wrote that those who are "fellow heirs with Christ" will suffer with Him, just as they will one day be glorified with Him (Rom. 8:17). Paul called on Timothy to join him in "suffering for the gospel" (2 Tim. 1:8). When the Sanhedrin council of the Jews flogged the Apostles for preaching the Gospel, Luke says that they went on their way "rejoicing that they had been considered worthy to suffer shame for His name" (Acts 5:41).

The Apostles' attitude was in accordance with the teaching of their Lord. In His Sermon on the Mount, Jesus had told them, "Blessed are those who have been persecuted for the sake of righteousness, for theirs is the kingdom of heaven" (Matt. 5:10). Getting more specific, He added, "Blessed are you when men cast insults at you, and persecute you, and say all kinds of evil against you falsely, on account of Me. Rejoice and be glad, for your reward in heaven is great, for so they persecuted the prophets who were before you" (Matthew 5:11–12).

Paul, of course, was not the only one in the Early Church who suffered persecution for the Lord. All of the Apostles, except John, were martyred for their faith.[3] A young deacon in the early church, Stephen, was stoned to death (Acts 7:59). *Foxe's Book of Martyrs* is filled with stories of Christians who were murdered for their faith during the early history of the Church.[4] Nor is Christian martyrdom a thing of the past. In 1998 more than 300,000 Christians died for their faith worldwide.[5] In fact, more Christians were martyred for their faith in the 20th century alone than in the previous 19 centuries combined.[6] In the Sudan during 1999, Christians by the thousands were crucified and thousands of others were sold into slavery.[7]

Those who teach the shallow and deceptive prosperity doctrine love to talk about the great heroes of the faith — people like Gideon, Barak, Samson, Jephthah, David, Samuel, and the prophets. They love to read aloud that section of Hebrews 11 that says these saints "conquered kingdoms, performed acts of righteousness, obtained promises, shut the mouths of lions, quenched the power of fire, escaped the edge of the sword, from weakness were made strong, became mighty in war, put foreign armies to flight" (Heb. 11:33–34).

But they always stop reading there because they detest the verses that follow: "Others were tortured . . . and others experienced mockings and scourgings, yes, also chains and imprisonment. They were stoned, they were sawn in two, they were tempted, they were put to death with the sword; they went about in sheepskins, in goatskins, being destitute, afflicted, ill-treated . . . wandering in deserts and mountains and caves and holes in the ground" (Heb. 11:35–38).

❖ The Seduction of Prosperity ❖

The United States of America is probably the only nation in the world where the prosperity doctrine could be preached without the preacher being laughed out of the pulpit. We are a people who have been seduced by "pillow prophets" who speak soft, sugar-coated lies. We chase after them, fulfilling the prophecy that "the time will come when they [Christians] will not endure sound doctrine; but wanting to have their ears tickled, they will accumulate for themselves teachers in accordance to their own desires; and will turn away their ears from the truth, and will turn aside to myths" (2 Tim. 4:3–4).

It's no wonder that American Christians flock to the Church of Prosperity. They want blessings without sacrifice. They have no interest in the Church of Commitment or the Church of Suffering. Most could not identify in any way with Paul's statement, "I count all things to be loss in view of the surpassing value of knowing Christ Jesus my Lord, for whom I have suffered the loss of all things, and count them but rubbish in order that I may gain Christ" (Phil. 3:8). Paul went even further. He said that in coming to know Jesus better, he wanted to experience "the fellowship of His sufferings, being conformed to His death" (Phil. 3:10). Those words sound insane to the modern-day, glitzy Christian caught up in the prosperity gospel or in the "seeker-sensitive" type of Christianity that soft-pedals the need for repentance and sacrifice.

But a day is coming soon when this will no longer be the case. America's days are numbered, and when the hammer of God's judgment falls, the righteous are going to suffer along with the unrighteous. In many cases the righteous will suffer even more because they will be subjected to persecution for their faith.

❖ An Example of Tough Faith ❖

That's why we need to be thinking about tough faith as never before. What does it mean, and how do we walk in it? Let's take a look at a classic example from the Scriptures. It is found in the life of the prophet, Habakkuk.

Habakkuk was a prophet whom God raised up to speak to Judah during the final years preceding that nation's destruction in 586 B.C. He was a contemporary of Jeremiah's.

Like the rest of God's prophets, his call for repentance and his threat of impending doom were messages the Jewish people did not want to hear. They mocked him and scoffed at him and claimed he was full of wind.

Finally, in a moment of self-pity, Habakkuk cried out to God, asking the Lord to vindicate him. "Lord, You have given me sensitive eyes to see violence, immorality and lawlessness, and I have preached my heart out against these things. But the wicked have overwhelmed the righteous, and no one pays any attention to me. When are You going to back up my message with some action? When are You going to validate me as a prophet by sending some judgment?" (Hab. 1:1-4). (Author's paraphrase throughout.)

The Lord's answer was not what Habakkuk wanted to hear. (How many times has that happened to you?) The Lord told him that He was going to do something so astonishing that no one would believe it if they were told in advance (Habakkuk 1:5–11). "You see, I am raising up the most savage warriors on planet earth — the Chaldeans. They are going to sweep through your nation like a wind and destroy your people and your temple. I am going to use the Chaldeans as a sword of my judgment" (Hab. 1:5–11).

Habakkuk was astounded by the Lord's answer. He had wanted some judgment for his people in order to get their attention. But he certainly did not want to see them destroyed. And at the hands of the Chaldeans? How could this be? They were the most evil and violent people in the world.

❖ Tough Questions ❖

Habakkuk cried out to the Lord again with a sense of desperation: "Surely, O Lord, You do not intend our destruction! Surely You want to just provide us with some correction. After all, aren't You the Holy One? If so, then I ask You, how can a Holy God work through those who are unholy? Let me put it to You another way, Lord — how can You punish those who are evil with those who are more evil?" (Hab. 1:12–17).

They were profound questions. But they were met with stony silence, which is always the case when Man questions God. For, as God told Job, "Who are you to question your Creator?" (Job 38–41).

God's silence made Habakkuk angry. So, he got his stubborn up. He climbed to the top of a tower and announced he was going to sit there and pout until the Lord answered his question (Hab. 2:1).

❖ A Tough Answer ❖

Finally, in the Lord's timing, the answer came. The Lord said, "The answer I'm going to give you is so important that I want you to write it in big letters on a tablet so that a person running by can read it at a glance" (Hab. 2:2–5). The Lord then gave him His answer.

Keep in mind the question: "How can You punish those who are evil with those who are more evil?" The Lord's answer: "The righteous shall live by faith" (Hab. 2:4).

It was a tough answer to a tough question. It was an answer that was difficult for Habakkuk to swallow. "The righteous shall live by faith." What did that mean?

❖ A Tough Command ❖

As Habakkuk contemplated God's response, the Lord in His mercy began to assist the prophet in understanding and accepting His answer. He proceeded to point out to Habakkuk that He was fully aware of the greed, treachery, cruelty, immorality and idolatry of the Chaldeans (Hab. 2:6–20). There was nothing Habakkuk could tell God about the Chaldeans that He didn't already know. The Lord promised a series of woes upon the Chaldeans, indicating clearly that their day of reckoning for their sins would come in due time (Hab. 2:6–20). The Lord concluded this speech with the words, "The Lord is in His holy temple. Let all the earth keep silence before Him" (Hab. 2:20).

Those are words that Christians sing all the time without knowing their context. Out of context, they sound so beautiful. In context, they are very pointed. For you see, what God was really saying to Habakkuk was, "I am on My throne, and I am in control. I am sovereign. You have no right to question Me as to My motives and My actions. Your responsibility is not to question Me but to trust Me. So, shut up and start trusting!"

❖ Role Playing ❖

It was a tough command that called for tough faith. To show you how tough it was, let's put ourselves in the position of Habakkuk for a moment. Assume that you are a modern-day prophet crying out to God concerning the United States.

"O God, You have given me a sensitive heart to see iniquity and injustice. Everywhere I look today in America I see both of these evils multiplying. Why do You allow the sins of our nation to go unpunished? We are rotten to the core, claiming to be a Christian nation while delighting in the sins of alcoholism, drug addiction, abortion, lawlessness, and every other abomination known to man. Even worse, we are intent on exporting our sinfulness to other nations through our immoral and violent movies and television programs.

"How long, O Lord, are You going to close Your eyes to the violence of the Mafia in New York and New Jersey? How long are You going to tolerate the swinging lifestyle of California and the crass materialism of Texas? When are You going to do something about the gambling in Nevada, the tobacco and whiskey in Kentucky, and the New Age voodooism in the state of Washington?

"When, O Lord, are You going to pour out judgment on our nation for our insufferable pride and our imperialistic desire to run the affairs of other nations?

"And when, Lord, are You going to avenge the blood of the more than 40 million babies we have slaughtered in the wombs of their mothers since 1972?

"Are you there, Lord? Are you paying any attention? Do You know what is going on? Do You care?"

And the Lord answers: "Calm down. Relax. I've got it all under control. You see, the Russians are coming. I have roused them up to invade Israel, and as they do so, they are going to launch an all-out nuclear attack against your country that will leave you devastated."

Stunned, you respond, "But Lord, how could You do such a thing? Those Russians are worse than we are! They are nothing but a bunch of barbaric God-haters. We're bad, but we aren't nearly as evil as they are. How can you punish an evil nation with one that is more evil?"

And the Lord simply says, "The righteous shall live by faith."

❖ Responding to the Challenge ❖

You see how tough the Lord's answer is? How would you respond? Would you shuck your faith? Wallow in despair? Retreat into self-pity? Let's look at how Habakkuk responded.

The very first thing Habakkuk did is what any person of faith does in a crisis. He went to his knees in prayer, and in that prayer, he cried out, "O Lord, in Your wrath remember mercy!" (Hab. 3:1–2).

It was a very human prayer, and thus a very pitiful one. Can you imagine the prophet's audacity in reminding God to show mercy? After all, he was speaking to the One who is the source of all grace and mercy — the God of lovingkindness (Ps. 86:15). God never has to be reminded to show mercy. That is His heart and His character. Even when He pours out His wrath, His fundamental purpose is to bring people to repentance so that they might be saved (Isa. 26:9 and 2 Pet. 3:9).

❖ A Vision of Hope ❖

Even as Habakkuk was begging for mercy for his nation, God showed him personal mercy. As Habakkuk wrestled for words, the Lord suddenly interrupted his prayer with a glorious vision that was designed to give him hope. It was a vision of the second coming of the Messiah when He will come to earth to reign over all the nations.

The vision is vivid, almost terrifying. Habakkuk sees the Messiah coming in glory with "rays flashing from His hands" representing His great power. He comes in wrath, with pestilence going before Him and plague following behind Him. He marches across the earth in indignation, trampling the nations in anger (Hab. 3:3–15).

In this vision, the Lord is saying to Habakkuk, "A day of reckoning is coming when I will deal with all the nations of the world in holy judgment" (Acts 17:31). Each one will receive what it deserves. You may never see justice and righteousness in your lifetime, but be assured that they are coming, for "the earth will be filled with the knowledge of the glory of the Lord, as the waters cover the sea" (Hab. 2:14).

By giving him a vision of the climax of history, God is calling Habakkuk to live with an eternal perspective. He is calling him to believe that "all things work together for good for those who love God" (Rom. 8:28).

❖ A Song of Tough Faith ❖

With his eternal perspective restored, Habakkuk meditates for a moment on the vision, trembling over the realization that God is serious about pouring out His wrath on Judah (Hab. 3:16). Then, suddenly, Habakkuk breaks forth with a song that surely must go down in history as one of the greatest expressions of tough faith that a poet has ever penned (Hab. 3:17–18):

Though the fig tree should not blossom
And there be no fruit on the vines,
Though the yield of the olive should fail
And the fields produce no food,
Though the flock should be cut off from the fold
And there be no cattle in the stalls,
Yet I will exult in the Lord,
I will rejoice in the God of my salvation.

Pause for a moment and consider what the prophet is saying here. He proclaims that even if all the crops and animals of Judah are destroyed, leaving the nation devastated, he will still praise God's Holy name!

❖ Trusting God ❖

Why? Because he has decided to submit himself and his nation to God's will, believing that God will do what is best for them although it means their immediate destruction. In short, he has decided to stop whining and start trusting. It has taken a lot of encouragement from the Lord and a major leap of faith on the part of the prophet. Habakkuk is now practicing tough faith.

And look what happened. The Chaldeans came. The city of Jerusalem and its temple were destroyed. The land was devastated, and the surviving Jews were taken into captivity. But 2,600 years later, where are the Chaldeans? In the dustbin of history. Where are the Jews? Regathered to their land, awaiting the appearance of their Messiah.

Only God has the long-term perspective. Only He knows how He will orchestrate history to the triumph of all His purposes. As we await the working out of His will, He calls us to walk in tough faith, with our eyes on Him rather than our fickle circumstances.

❖ Jeremiah's Tough Faith ❖

That's exactly what the prophet Jeremiah did after the Chaldeans had destroyed his nation, his hometown of Jerusalem, and his sacred temple. He wrote a funeral lament that appears in the Bible as the Book of Lamentations. It is the saddest book in the Bible. The first two and a half chapters are devoted to a eulogy for Jerusalem. Jeremiah pictures the city as an unfaithful wife who has experienced the rod of her husband's wrath (Lam. 1:1–2). He talks about how her majesty has departed because she did not consider her future (Lam. 1:6, 9).

As the prophet surveys the horrible destruction that he himself had so accurately prophesied, he personifies the city as a woman crying out to God, "Zion stretches out her hands; There is no one to comfort her" (Lam. 1:17). He weeps as he sees the evidence of cannibalism due to the long siege that the city experienced before its destruction. He cries out, "Should women eat their offspring, The little ones who were born healthy?" (Lam. 2:20).

He observes that the Lord "has poured out His wrath like fire" (Lam. 2:4). "He has swallowed up Israel . . . and He has violently treated His tabernacle [the temple] like a garden booth" (Lam. 2:5–6). The scene overwhelms Jeremiah. His heart is broken for his people and his nation. He totters on the brink of despair as he cries out, "My soul has been rejected from peace; I have forgotten happiness. So, I say, 'My strength has perished, And so has my hope from the Lord'" (Lam. 3:17–18).

❖ Remembering God's Faithfulness ❖

But at that precise moment, by a monumental act of will, Jeremiah decides he will not give in to his emotions. Rather than curse God, he decides to praise God in a magnificent statement of tough faith (Lam. 3:21–24):[8]

> But this I call to mind, and therefore I have hope:
> The steadfast love of the Lord never ceases,
> His mercies never come to an end;
> They are new every morning;
> Great is Thy faithfulness.
> "The Lord is my portion," says my soul,
> "Therefore, I will hope in Him."

The clouds of despair dissipate as Jeremiah reminds himself of God's lovingkindness in the past. The sunshine of God's grace breaks through to his heart. His hope is restored.

He knows his nation has gotten what it deserved. But he also knows he is dealing with a God who never changes. Just as He has been merciful in the past, Jeremiah is confident that the

Lord will show mercy in the future. So, he proclaims, "The Lord is good to those who wait for Him, To the person who seeks Him. . . . The Lord will not reject forever, For if He causes grief, Then He will have compassion According to His abundant lovingkindness" (Lam. 3:25–32).

❖ The Meaning of Tough Faith ❖

The lives of Habakkuk, Jeremiah, and Paul reveal to us the meaning of true faith. It is the kind of faith that continues to believe and trust even when everything seems to be going wrong. It is a faith that is not dependent upon external circumstances. Nor is it dependent upon feelings.

What is the key to developing this kind of faith that is so desperately needed in these end times? Paul gives us the answer. In his prison letter to the church at Philippi, he wrote:

> I have learned to be content in whatever circumstances I am. I know how to get along with humble means, and I also know how to live in prosperity; in any and every circumstance I have learned the secret of being filled and going hungry, both of having abundance and suffering need (Phil. 4:11–12).

What was the secret Paul had discovered? He reveals it in his next sentence: "I can do all things through Him who strengthens me" (Phil. 4:13). The secret is to trust God, remain focused on Jesus, and rely on the power of the Holy Spirit. Paul says if we will do that, then "God shall supply all your needs according to His riches in glory in Christ Jesus" (Phil. 4:19).

❖ Suffering in Hope ❖

Notice that the promise is to meet our needs, not to provide every materialistic delight that may enter our imagination. In that regard, we in America are soon going to learn the difference in needs and luxuries. When God judges our economy, we will learn that we can live without a lot of the electronic toys that we consider to be so essential today.

Christians will suffer along with the rest of society. But for those who know how to walk in tough faith, there will be a difference. They will suffer in confident hope. God never promises that His people will be immune to His judgments. He only promises that they will never taste the wrath He will pour out in the great Tribulation (1 Thess. 1:10). But with regard to His judgments, God does make a significant promise. He says in His Word that He will walk through those judgments with His children, constantly encouraging them, giving them hope, and providing their basic needs. Inscribe these words from Isaiah upon your heart:

> Do not fear, for I have redeemed you; I have called you by name; you are Mine! When you pass through the waters, I will be with you; And through the rivers, they will not overflow you. When you walk through the fire, you will not be scorched, Nor will the flame burn you. For I am the Lord your God, The Holy One of Israel, your Savior (Isa. 43:1–3).

Affirming the Lord's protection, King David wrote, "I have been young, and now I am old; yet I have not seen the righteous forsaken, Or his descendants begging bread" (Ps. 37:25). King Solomon put it this way: "The Lord will not allow the righteous to hunger" (Prov. 10:3).

❖ Going Against the Wind ❖

Many years ago a lady named Ella Wheeler Wilcox wrote a poem after her husband observed from the deck of their cruise ship that one sailing ship could travel west and another east in the same wind. She wrote:

> One ship drives east and another west
> With the selfsame winds that blow.
> 'Tis the set of the sails and not the gales
> Which tells us the way to go.
> Like the winds of the sea are the ways of fate,
> As we voyage along through life:
> 'Tis the set of a soul
> That decides its goal,
> And not the calm or the strife.[9]

Most people seem to have decided that the only way they can go in life is the way the wind is blowing. In our nation today, that wind is blowing toward immorality and violence, toward a disrespect for the sanctity of life. It is propelling people to call evil good and good evil. Unfortunately, there are many Christians, even Christian leaders, who have decided to set their sails to go with the wind and not against it.

Observing this phenomenon, Don Wildmon, the founder of the American Family Association has written:

> Jesus went against the wind, and it meant that He ended up on a cross. I think that is what we are afraid of — a cross. No one likes to be crucified. So we set our sails the easy way. . . .
>
> Many people have decided that they want Christ but not the cross. It is a contradiction. It can never be. The cross is at the very heart of Christianity. Remove it and there is no Christianity.[10]

Tough faith calls us to set our sails against the wind. We do that by setting our souls on Jesus.

Endnotes

1 Diane Winston, "Gallup Says America Has a Shallow Faith," *Dallas Morning News,* December 11, 1999, p. 1G and 4G. The results of Gallup's latest religious polls have been published in a book entitled *Surveying the Religious Landscape: Trends in U.S. Beliefs* (Harrisburg, PA: Morehouse Publishing Co., 1999). The book is co-authored by D. Michael Lindsay.

2 Eugene H. Peterson, *The Message: New Testament with Psalms and Proverbs* (Colorado Springs, CO: Navpress, 1995), p. 455–456.

3 Summaries of the deaths experienced by the Apostles can be found on the Internet at the following address: http://www.geocities.com/Athens/Ithaca/7730/Christians_martyrs/Christian.htm.

4 *Foxe's Book of Martyrs* by John Foxe was first published in 1563. It is available in many modern editions, some of which bring the accounts of martyrdom up through the 19th century. The entire book, as edited by William Byron Forbush, can be found on the

Internet at the following address: http://ccel.wheaton.edu/foxe/martyrs.

5 Two good sites on the Internet provide detailed information about worldwide Christian persecution and martyrdom. They are: Voice of the Martyrs at http://www.persecution.com and International Christian Concern at http://www.persecution.org.

6 Nina Shea, *Mindszenty Report,* Cardinal Mindszenty Foundation, April 1997.

7 "The Voice of the Martyrs Presents Sudan," an Internet report at http://www.persecution.com/country/country.asp?f_Country=7.

8 *The Holy Bible,* Revised Standard Version (Grand Rapids, MI: Zondervan Bible Publishers, 1962).

9 Donald E. Wildmon, "Against the Wind," *AFA Journal,* May 1998, p. 2.

10 Ibid.

Chapter 7

❖   ❖   ❖

Ordering Your Priorities

Every time I go to Israel I am reminded of priorities. The reminder is what the Jews call a "mezuzah." You will find one on every doorpost in Israel, including the ancient gates to the Old City.

They come in all sizes, and they are made of a variety of materials — stone, plastic, wood, glass, etc. They vary greatly in design, from the very colorful to the starkly somber.

The mezuzah is affixed to the doorpost on the right-hand side. Every time an Orthodox Jew walks through a door, he pauses and performs a ritual that is associated with the mezuzah. He puts the fingers of his right hand to his lips, then touches the mezuzah with those same fingers. In other words, he bestows a kiss upon the mezuzah.

Why? Because of what the mezuzah contains. You see, every mezuzah has a hollowed out section under its surface, and in that hollowed out place is a tiny scroll containing what the Jews call the "Shema." *Shema* is the Hebrew word for "hear." The Shema is a section of Scripture taken from Deuteronomy. It begins with the words: "Hear, O Israel!" It continues with a profound proclamation: "The Lord is our God, the Lord is one! And you shall love the Lord your God with all your heart and with all your soul and with all your might" (Deut. 6:4–5).

These verses are about priorities. They are a call to put God first in our lives. The mezuzah is a constant reminder of that call.

The importance of these verses cannot be over-emphasized. They are the cornerstone of the Hebrew Scriptures. Jesus attested to this when a lawyer asked Him, "Teacher, which is the great commandment in the Law?" (Matt. 22:36).

Jesus responded by quoting the Shema: "You shall love the Lord your God with all your heart, and with all your soul, and with all your mind. This is the great and foremost commandment" (Matt. 22:37–38). Then He added, "The second is like it, 'You shall love your neighbor as yourself' " (Matt. 22:39, quoting Lev. 19:18). Jesus concluded His response by observing, "On these two commandments depend the whole Law and the Prophets" (Matt. 22:40).

We as Christians would do well to have a mezuzah on each of our doorposts because we constantly need to be reminded of priorities. That is particularly true in these end times when we are bombarded by the world's priorities in advertising, movies, books, and television programs. It is so easy to get caught up in the fast lane and to get focused on the world's priorities of money, fame, and power.

❖ Questioning My Priorities ❖

The Lord used a novel approach to get my attention a number of years ago when I was allowing my ministry to take priority over Him. I was baby-sitting our oldest grandchild who was six years old at the time. Her first name is Reagan.

Before I tell you what happened, you need to know that Reagan was from birth what Texans often refer to as a "pistol" — meaning that she was feisty and always cocksure of herself. She was the type, at age six, who could listen to an explanation of Einstein's theory of relativity and say, "I knew that!"

Well, my wife and I were keeping her over a weekend. I was sitting in the den reading when she walked up and tugged on my arm.

"You know what, Paw-paw?" she asked. "I've got it all figured out!"

That, of course, was no surprise to me, but I wanted to get the specifics, so I asked, "Okay, what have you figured out?"

"God is boss of everything!" she proclaimed triumphantly. "He is boss of my daddy. Daddy is boss of my mother. Mama is boss of me. I am boss of my dog. My dog is boss of my cat. And my cat is boss of no one!"

I smiled and thought to myself, *She really does have her priorities in order.*

At that moment, the Lord spoke to my heart and said, "Yes, David, she does, but do you?"

What about you, dear reader? Are your priorities in order? Is God first in your life? Or, has God been replaced as the number one priority in your life by your family, your career, or your pursuit of money, power or fame?

❖ Testing Your Priorities ❖

I have a test for you that will help you determine your priorities. At first you may think it is a silly test, but please bear with me, because I think I can show you that it is not — that it is a test that should be taken seriously.

Let's assume that tonight, in the early hours of the morning, an angel appears to you and says, "Fear not! I have good news for you. God has sent me to tell you that you can have one request — anything you desire." What would you ask for? Your response will reveal your priorities.

Now take this seriously. Stop for a moment and think about it. Write your request at the top of this page or on a piece of paper. Have you paused to give your response serious consideration? Do you have an intense personal need? Finances? Healing? Maybe you desire to be selfless and altruistic, wishing for world peace or a cure for AIDS. Or perhaps you desire housing for the homeless or food for the hungry. What would you ask for?

Now, you may be thinking, "This is silly. No angel is ever going to appear to me and ask me such a thing." Well, don't be too sure about that because God has done it in the past, and the Bible says God never changes (Mal. 3:6 and Heb. 13:8). What He has done in the past, He may do again in the future.

❖ King Solomon's Priorities ❖

Can you think of an example in the past? Anyone who is familiar with the Old Testament will think immediately of King Solomon. Do you remember the story?

Solomon had succeeded the greatest king in Jewish history, his father, King David. He had big shoes to fill, and he was frightened. As he put it, "Give me now wisdom and knowledge, that I may go out and come in before this people" (2 Chron. 1:10). That's a Hebrew colloquialism for "Help! I'm in over my head!"

So, Solomon did the only thing he could think of — something he had witnessed his father doing on several occasions. He went to his knees in prayer. He cried out to God, "You have dealt with my father David with great lovingkindness, and have made me king in his place. Now, O Lord God. . . . Give me now wisdom and knowledge . . . for who can rule this great people of Yours?" (2 Chron. 1:8–10). The Lord was exceptionally pleased with this humble prayer. He responded to Solomon with these words:

> Because you had this in mind, and did not ask for riches, wealth or honor, or the life of those who hate you, nor have you even asked for long life, but you have asked for yourself wisdom and knowledge, that you may rule My people over whom I have made you king, wisdom and knowledge have been granted to you. And I will give you riches and wealth and honor, such as none of the kings who were before you has possessed, nor those who will come after you (2 Chron. 1:11–12).

Jesus was to echo these words a thousand years later in His Sermon on the Mount when, speaking of priorities, He said, "Seek first His kingdom and His righteousness, and all these things [the necessities of life] will be added to you" (Matt. 6:33).

The Lord kept His promise and richly endowed Solomon with great wisdom. He was a wise ruler who became a legend in His own time. He wrote inspired psalms and proverbs and the great "Song of Solomon." The Queen of Sheba journeyed to Jerusalem to test him with difficult questions, and he answered them all, prompting her to exclaim, "Blessed be the Lord your God who delighted in you, setting you on His throne as king for the Lord your God" (2 Chron. 9:8).

❖ Solomon's Apostasy ❖

It would be wonderful if we could conclude the story of Solomon at that point. For despite all his wisdom, he was soon to fall into apostasy. He was to turn his back on God and wallow in sin until his dying days.

The turning point occurred shortly after the visit of the Queen of Sheba. The Word says that King Solomon received 666 talents of gold, and from that moment on, his heart was given to money, women, and military power (2 Chron. 9:13). Solomon let his priorities get scrambled.

According to his own testimony, recorded in the Book of Ecclesiastes, Solomon decided to search for fulfillment in the things of the world. In the process, he descended into depravity. As he put it, "I did not withhold my heart from any pleasure" (Eccles. 2:10).

His wisdom ultimately prevailed. He repented of his sins and wrote off his search for pleasure as "vanity of vanities!" (Eccles. 1:2). On his deathbed he summed up his experience with these insightful words: "The conclusion, when all has been heard, is: fear God and keep His commandments, because this applies to every person. For God will bring every act to judgment, everything which is hidden, whether it is good or evil" (Eccles. 12:13–14).

❖ An Evaluation of Solomon ❖

In 1 Kings 11 the Holy Spirit presents a summary of Solomon's kingship. It is not a pretty picture. Solomon is portrayed as a man who chased after "foreign women" despite the fact that God had specifically commanded the Children of Israel not to marry foreigners lest they become corrupted by their idols (1 Kings 11:1–2). Solomon violated this injunction in a mighty way, taking 700 wives and 300 concubines, many from foreign, pagan nations.

And just as the Lord had warned, the foreign wives turned Solomon's heart toward pagan gods (1 Kings 11:3–4). He worshiped Ashtoreth, the goddess of the Sidonians, and he bowed to Milcom, the detestable idol of the Amonites (1 Kings 11:5). He even built altars for Chemosh, the despicable idol of Moab, and for Molech, the pagan god of Ammon (1 Kings 11:7).

The Holy Spirit sums it up in a remarkable sentence: "His heart [Solomon's] was not wholly devoted to the Lord his God, as the heart of David his father had been" (1 Kings 11:4).

Whoa! What did the Holy Spirit say? Read that sentence again. The Spirit compares Solomon with his father, David, and He says, "Solomon was nothing compared to David. David is your model because his heart was totally dedicated to Me."

David? Is the Spirit talking about the King David who was a liar, adulterer, and murderer? As if to emphasize that there has been no slip of the tongue, the Spirit repeats the statement two verses later: "And Solomon did what was evil in the sight of the Lord, and did not follow the Lord fully, as David his father had done" (1 Kings 11:6).

What's going on here? Aren't we dealing here with two sinners of equal magnitude? How can David be elevated in God's sight over Solomon?

❖ David's Sins ❖

My study has convinced me that there are at least four reasons. First, David never indulged himself in sin as Solomon did. David sinned mightily, but his sins were committed in moments of desperation or passion. He never willfully decided to give his life to sin as Solomon did.

Second, David was sensitive to sin. When he strayed from the Lord, he always came running back in repentance. Psalm 51, which contains his confession and repentance following his adultery with Bathsheba, is a classic example of his sensitivity to sin. It also illustrates the depth of his remarkable relationship with God.

He makes no excuses for his sin and acknowledges that he has sinned not just against man but against God himself (Ps. 51:1–4). He cries out for God to cleanse him of his iniquity and to give him a clean heart and a steadfast spirit (Ps. 51:2–10). He pleads for the Lord not to remove his anointing by the Holy Spirit (as he had seen the Lord do to his predecessor, King Saul). He concludes by asking the Lord to restore "the joy of Your salvation" (Ps. 51:10–12).

Then he makes a remarkable statement that reveals how well he knew the Lord. He says, "Lord, if I thought You would be pleased by my making a bunch of sacrifices, I would offer them to You all day. But I know You, Lord. I know that what You want is not a lot of empty religious ritual. Rather, what You desire is a broken and contrite heart. So, dear Lord, here is my heart. Take it and make it new!" (Ps. 51:16–17, paraphrased).

Do you see how different his repentance was to the way we

so often repent today? Our tendency is to bargain with God, using religious ritual: "Lord, if you will forgive me, I promise I won't skip Sunday morning worship again. Why, I will even volunteer to work in the children's ministry!"

❖ **Degrees of Sin** ❖

The third difference between David and Solomon is that David never committed the ultimate sin. Before I develop this point, I need to address a myth that exists in Christianity. It is the myth that "all sins are equal."

This statement is only partially true. All sins are equal in only one sense: any sin, no matter how big or small, will separate you from God and will require of you a Savior to reconcile you to God (Rom. 6:23). It doesn't matter whether the infraction is a white lie or murder, it condemns us before God, for He is perfectly holy, and He cannot countenance sin (Rom. 3:21–24).

Beyond that, all sins are not equal. The Bible says so. For example, Proverbs 6:16–19 says there are seven sins that the Lord particularly hates more than others, one of which is "hands that shed innocent blood." Jesus often emphasized the degrees of sin in His teachings. To the religious leaders of Israel He said, "Woe to you scribes and Pharisees, hypocrites, because you devour widow's houses . . . therefore you shall receive greater condemnation" (Matt. 23:14). When He left the Galilee for the last time, Jesus pronounced a curse on the three cities where He had focused His ministry, saying, "It shall be more tolerable for the land of Sodom in the day of judgment than for you" (Matt. 11:24). And when standing before Pilate, Jesus announced that the sin of the High Priest Caiaphas in turning Him over to the Romans was greater than Pilate's sin in condemning Him to death (John 19:11).

Because there are degrees of sin, there are going to be degrees of punishment in hell. Jesus taught this important truth in His parable of the faithful and unfaithful servants (Luke 12:35–48). Speaking of the punishment people will receive, Jesus says, "And that servant who knew his master's will, and did not prepare himself or do according to his will, shall be beaten with many stripes. But he who did not know, yet committed things deserving of stripes, shall be beaten with few" (Luke 12:47–48).[1]

❖ The Ultimate Sin ❖

Now, with these principles in mind, let's proceed to consider what I meant when I said, "David never committed the ultimate sin." I believe the Bible clearly indicates that in God's eyes the ultimate sin is idolatry. This is the plain inference of the "Shema" (Deut. 6:4–5). It is the reason that the first of the Ten Commandments is "You shall have no other gods before Me" (Exod. 20:3). It was the reason for the ministries of Elijah and Elisha. They were anointed to call the people of Israel out of idolatry, and when the people refused to repent, it is the sin that led to God's judgments upon both Israel and Judah. It is the sin that the apostle John singled out for special warning when he wrote, "Little children, guard yourselves against idols" (1 John 5:21).

Solomon literally wallowed in idolatry. He worshiped Ashtoreth, Milcom, Chemosh, and Molech (1 Kings 11:1–8). David never once bowed his knee to any pagan god.

In review, David never indulged himself in sin; David was sensitive to sin; and David never committed the ultimate sin.

❖ The Great Passion ❖

I think there is a fourth reason that David is elevated over Solomon, and it may well be the most important reason. David had an incredible passion for God, and it was this passion, more than anything else, that caused him to be remembered as "a man after God's own heart" (1 Sam. 13:14 and Acts 13:22).

This brings me to the point that I want to hammer home. David's great passion for God was rooted in his priorities. He revealed his priorities when God gave him the same opportunity as Solomon — namely, to ask for one thing. It's interesting how all students of the Bible know what Solomon asked for but seem unaware of what David requested.

Yet, what David requested was a thousand times more profound than what his son, Solomon, later asked for. What David requested proved to be the secret of his greatness.

Solomon asked for wisdom and knowledge. What did you ask for when I gave you the angel test at the beginning of this chapter? Compare now the requests of Solomon and yours to that of David's.

David's request is revealed in Psalm 27: "One thing I have

asked from the Lord, that I shall seek: That I may dwell in the house of the Lord all the days of my life, To behold the beauty of the Lord and to meditate in His temple" (Ps. 27:4). David asked for the most significant thing that could be requested — he asked for intimate fellowship with the Lord! "All I want is You, Lord! I just want to be in Your presence to behold Your beauty."

❖ Passionate Poetry ❖

It is a theme that runs throughout David's majestic poetry. In Psalm 26:8 he says, "O Lord, I love the habitation of Your house and the place where Your glory dwells." Can you say that? Do you find yourself yearning during the week to be in the Lord's house on Sunday? Do you hunger to be in His presence in worship? Or do you attend church out of a sense of duty? And while you are there, are you a clock-watcher? Is your only concern to get home before the kickoff? In Psalm 69:9 David says, "Zeal for Your house has consumed me." David's top priority was God.

In Psalm 63 David speaks of his passion for God in words that people cannot fully appreciate unless they know something about Israel's weather and topography. Israel is an arid land where water is one of the most precious commodities. During the land's two brief rainy seasons, every effort is made to collect and preserve every drop of water in preparation for the long dry season that usually stretches for seven months, from April through October.

In Israel, water is ever on one's mind. This was particularly true in the life of David because he spent many of his early years hiding out from Saul, and his favorite hiding place was in the Dead Sea area — a place renowned for its scarcity of potable water.

So, in Psalm 63:1, to emphasize his passion for God, David writes, "O God, my God! How I search for You! How I thirst for you in this parched and weary land where there is no water. How I long to find You!"[2] David is saying that his passion for God is as great as a man yearning for water in the middle of a desert.

❖ Infectious Passion ❖

When you have a spiritual leader who is truly in love with God, his attitude will be infectious. That was the case with David. His passion infected those around him. Take, for example, his worship leader, Asaph. In Psalm 73 Asaph expresses the same passion as his mentor: "Whom have I in heaven but You? And besides You, I desire nothing on earth . . . as for me the nearness of God is my good" (Ps. 73:25–28).

Just as David infected Asaph, so did Asaph have the same influence on the singers and musicians that he worked with. Psalm 42 was written by the sons of Korah, one of Asaph's choral groups. It is proof positive that something inspired really can be produced by a committee! The psalm begins with these words: "As the deer pants for the water brooks, so my soul pants for You, O God, for the living God" (Ps. 42:1–2).

❖ Imagining the Scene ❖

Every time I read those words, a vivid picture forms in my mind. I can remember walking in a dense forest many years ago in the foothills of the Alps in Austria. The forest was so dense that it was almost dark at mid-day. There was little vegetation on the ground because of the lack of light. There was mainly just a thick cover of pine needles. It was quiet, deathly quiet.

I sat down under a tree and started praying, when suddenly I heard a slight noise. I looked over my shoulder and saw a deer walking through the forest. It seemed not to have a care in the world.

As I watched the deer, my imagination came alive. I began to imagine what would happen if the silence of the forest were suddenly to be violated by a loud explosion — a gunshot. I could imagine the deer being wounded and then taking off, running for its life. I could imagine the deer running until it is covered with lather, until it is gasping for breath with every stride. I could imagine it continuing to run until it is overcome by a passion greater even than the fear of death — the passion for water. "As the deer pants for the water brooks, so my soul pants for You, O God." That was the intensity of David's passion for God.

❖ Passionate Humility ❖

Psalm 84 is another of the compositions of the sons of Korah in which they proclaim the passion of their spiritual leaders, Asaph and David. The psalm begins with them expressing, like David, their love of God's dwelling place and their yearning to be in the Lord's presence (Ps. 84:1–2). They then sum up their feelings in a remarkable statement: "A single day in Your courts is better than a thousand anywhere else! I would rather be a gatekeeper in the house of my God than live the good life in the homes of the wicked" (Ps. 84:10).[3] They are saying that they would rather serve as humble doorkeepers in God's house than to live in splendor in the mansions of the wicked. Here's how Eugene Peterson puts it in his paraphrase *The Message:* "One day spent in Your house, this beautiful place of worship, beats thousands spent on Greek island beaches. I'd rather scrub floors in the house of my God than be honored as a guest in the palace of sin."[4]

❖ Living with Passion ❖

An important thing to keep in mind about David is that he not only expressed a passion for God in his poems and songs, he also lived it. Yes, there were times when he took his eyes off the Lord and his priorities got mixed up, but he was always quick to restore them. Further, his spontaneous actions seemed always to express the priority of God in his heart.

A good example is to be found in the priorities he established when he became king of all of the Jews, both Israel and Judah. He did not do what most kings would have done. His first priority was not a census or a taxation or a military campaign. No, his first priority was a spiritual one. His overwhelming desire was to restore God as the focal point of his nation. His first priority was spiritual revival.

His predecessor, King Saul, had been an apostate king, trafficking in the occult. He had completely ignored the fate of Israel's most holy object, the ark of the covenant. The ark had been captured by the Philistines at the battle of Ebenezer (1 Sam. 4:1–11). When the ark was finally returned to Israel, it ended up in a farmhouse at a village called Kiriath-jearim, located about five miles northwest of Jerusalem. This site was only two miles from Gibeon where the tabernacle of Moses had been rebuilt following its destruction at Shiloh by the Philistines after they won the battle of Ebenezer (2 Chron. 1:13 and Ps. 78:60).

Yet, despite the fact that the ark was only a stone's throw from its proper resting place in the Holy of Holies, no one in Israel cared enough to put it in its proper place. The ark sat forgotten in the farmhouse for 67 years! (The 67 years were the last 20 years of Samuel's judgeship, the 40 years of Saul's kingship, and the first 7 years of David's reign in Hebron before he became king of all Israel and moved his throne to Jerusalem.)

But David had not forgotten the ark. When he was crowned king of all Israel, he announced that the first priority of his administration would be to provide the ark of God with a proper resting place. He was anxious to bring the symbol of the presence of God back into the central life of the nation.

Not only did he announce that he would bring the ark to the new capital city of Jerusalem, he also made a vow that must have astounded his people. Once again, it was a vow that demonstrated his passion for God. He vowed that he would not sleep in a building or in a bed until the ark had been provided a proper resting place! (Ps. 132:1–5). Think about that — a king announcing that he was going to sleep outside on the ground until the whole nation got its priorities in order!

❖ Spontaneous Passion ❖

Now, it is one thing to express a passion for God in poetry and song, and even to express it in one's official duties; it is something else to live it in private. Remember, anyone can have their priorities in order when they are in the spotlight. The real test comes in the unguarded moments. This point was summed up beautifully in a statement I saw on a sign at a high school in Los Lunas, New Mexico: "True character is revealed in the dark."

The Scriptures reveal that David lived with a passion in his heart for God even in his most unguarded moments. There are many examples of this in his life, but the one that has always impacted me the most is one that is not well known although it is recorded twice in the Scriptures (2 Sam. 23:13–17 and 1 Chron. 11:15–19).

The timing of the story in David's life is not entirely clear. In 2 Samuel the story is told following the recording of David's last words on his deathbed. The story seems to be inserted at this point as a fond remembrance of a great king. In 1 Chronicles the story is inserted immediately after David was crowned the king of all the Jews. But it appears to be a flashback to an earlier time, demonstrating both the loyalty of David's "mighty men" and David's passion for God.

The most likely setting is shortly after David was crowned the king of Judah and began his reign in Hebron, seven years before he became king of all Israel. It seems that before he could build up his army and consolidate his power, the Philistines attacked and conquered his hometown of Bethlehem. David and his "mighty men" apparently fled to his old stronghold at the Dead Sea where he had often hid from King Saul.

❖ A Passion for Water ❖

One night as they were sitting around a campfire, David began to think about water, which is a natural obsession for anyone in that terrible wilderness. Suddenly, he grew nostalgic. "You know what I would like right now more than anything I can think of?" he asked. "A drink of the water from the well of my hometown of Bethlehem." He then stretched and yawned, bid his warriors goodnight, and crawled back into his cave to go to sleep.

His soldiers looked at each other, and all had the same thought at the same time: "If David wants a drink of the water of Bethlehem, then he will have it!" You see, David was a symbolic type of the Messiah, and those men loved him with the same passion that we are to love our Savior.

They talked it over, and three of them decided to go to Bethlehem and fetch a pail of water for David. Those three brave men spent the next few hours of the night walking across the desert to Bethlehem. Then, at the risk of their lives, they sneaked through the Philistine guards posted around the town and drew a bucket of water from the well. Then, once again, they sneaked through the enemy lines and walked back across the desert to David's stronghold. It was not only a dangerous mission, it was an exhausting one — as anyone knows who has ever tried to lug five gallons of gasoline very far.

I can imagine them arriving in the early morning hours, tired but full of glee. They had a very special present for their beloved leader, and they could hardly wait for him to see it.

They placed the bucket right outside his cave and then sat down in a semi-circle to await his appearance. As the sun began to rise over the Dead Sea, they heard David stirring inside the cave. Their hearts began to pound in anticipation. Finally, David emerged, stretching and rubbing the sleep from his eyes.

David looked out across the Dead Sea, watching the first light of dawn break over the mountains on the other side. Then he looked down and saw the three men sitting before him with silly grins on their faces.

"What's with you guys?" he asked.

One of them spoke up and said, "Look at your feet, David."

David looked down and saw the bucket of water. "What's this?"

Almost in unison the three began to exclaim excitedly, "It's a bucket of water from the well in Bethlehem!"

David was incredulous. "How can that be?" he asked. "Bethlehem is occupied by the Philistines."

"We know," his men replied. "We went there last night and sneaked through their sentry lines."

"You mean you risked your lives for this water?" David asked in astonishment.

And then, David spontaneously did something that would impact the lives of those men for as long as they lived. He reached down, picked up the bucket of water, and said, "This water is too valuable to drink. There is only one thing that can be done with it." Then, to the utter astonishment of his men, David poured the water out on the ground as a drink offering to the Lord!

Is there any doubt that God was the first priority in David's heart? Is there any doubt that he lived moment to moment for God? The Word says, "The mouth speaks out of what fills the heart" (Matt. 12:34). David's heart was filled with God.

❖ Self-Examination ❖

What about you? Is God really first in your life — above all else? Do you have a passion for God? Do you yearn to fellowship with Him in His Word, in prayer, and in worship? Do you spend special time with Him daily? Does your heart cry out for His Son to return?

If not, then pray for God to give you the heart of David. Pray that He will lead you to have the same passion for fellowship with Him that David had. Ask Him to give you an insatiable appetite for His Word so that you might be drawn into a more intimate relationship with Him. Request that He will daily empower you through His Spirit to keep your priorities in proper order.

Because David had his priorities in order, he did not fear the two things that humanity fears the most — life and death. Since David was certain of his relationship with the Lord, he could speak of facing the challenges of life with confidence: "The Lord is my light and my salvation; whom shall I fear? The Lord is the defense of my life; whom shall I dread?" (Ps. 27:1).

Likewise, he could look death in the eye and not tremble. Speaking of the resurrection in one of the few Old Testament passages that refer to it, David wrote, "I would have despaired unless I had believed that I would see the goodness of the Lord in the land of the living. Wait for the Lord; be strong and let your heart take courage; yes, wait for the Lord" (Ps. 27:13–14).

I challenge you to get your priorities in order today, putting God first, family second, and career third. And I challenge you to rely daily on the Holy Spirit to help keep your priorities in that order.

Endnotes

1 *Holy Bible,* New King James Version (Nashville, TN: Thomas Nelson Publishers, 1990).
2 *The Living Bible Paraphrased* (Wheaton, IL: Tyndale House Publishers, 1971).
3 *Holy Bible,* New Living Translation (Wheaton, IL: Tyndale House Publishers, 1997).
4 Eugene H. Peterson, *The Message: New Testament with Psalms and Proverbs* (Colorado Springs, CO: Navpress, 1995), p. 774.

❖   ❖   ❖

Chapter 8

Keeping an Eternal Perspective

O ne of the greatest public servants in the history of England was William Gladstone (1809–1898) who served as prime minister four times during the latter half of the 19th century.

Gladstone was a committed Christian who always attended church. (By contrast, Prime Minister Tony Blair was the only British leader in the 20th century who regularly attended church services.) Gladstone also taught a Sunday school class throughout his adult life. In fact, his aim early in his life was to become an Anglican clergyman, but after his graduation from Oxford, his strong-willed father insisted that he enter politics.[1]

Shortly before he died, Gladstone gave a speech in which he told about being visited by an ambitious young man who sought his advice about life. The lad told the elder statesman that he admired him more than anyone living and wanted to seek his advice regarding his career.[2]

❖   A Remarkable Interview   ❖

"What do you hope to do when you graduate from college?" Gladstone asked.

The young man replied, "I hope to attend law school, sir, just as you did."

"That's a noble goal," said Gladstone, "Then what?"

"I hope to practice law and make a good name for myself defending the poor and the outcasts of society, just as you did."

"That's a noble purpose," replied Gladstone. "Then what?"

"Well, sir, I hope one day to stand for Parliament and become a servant of the people, even as you did."

"That too is a noble hope. What then?" asked Gladstone.

"I would hope to be able to serve in the Parliament with great distinction, evidencing integrity and a concern for justice — even as you did."

"What then?" asked Gladstone.

"I would hope to serve the government as prime minister with the same vigor, dedication, vision, and integrity as you did."

"And what then?" asked Gladstone.

"I would hope to retire with honors and write my memoirs — even as you are presently doing — so that others could learn from my mistakes and triumphs."

"All of that is very noble," said Gladstone, "and then what?"

The young man thought for a moment. "Well, sir, I suppose I will then die."

"That's correct," said Gladstone. "And then what?"

The young man looked puzzled. "Well, sir," he answered hesitantly, "I've never given that any thought."

"Young man," Gladstone responded, "the only advice I have for you is for you to go home, read your Bible, and *think about eternity.*"

❖ Good Advice ❖

Think about eternity! What good advice. Life goes by so quickly. It is like a vapor that is here one moment and evaporates the next. We are preparing for eternity. Are you ready?

Or, are you living like you expect to live forever? Are you focused on this life, determined to accumulate all the money, power, and fame you possibly can? Are you like the young man who visited Gladstone — are you a person who has never given eternity a thought? If so, the Word of God has a stern warning for you:

> And now I have a word for you who brashly announce, "Today — at the latest, tomorrow — we're off to such and such a city for the year. We're going to start a business and make a lot of money."

You don't know the first thing about tomorrow. You're nothing but a wisp of fog, catching a brief bit of sun before disappearing.

Instead, make it a habit to say, "If the Master wills it and we're still alive, we'll do this or that" (James 4:13–15, paraphrased).[3]

❖   The Fleeting Nature of Life   ❖

This passage always reminds me of an incident that occurred in my life several years ago. A dear friend of mine whom I had taught with in a Texas college called me one day and told me he had been diagnosed with prostate cancer.

"The doctor has given me only six months to live," he reported.

I told him I was very sorry to hear the news, and I promised to pray for him and his family. Then, I added, "But keep in mind, I may be dead before you."

"Oh? Do you have cancer, too?" he asked.

"No," I responded, "it's just that I do not have the promise of even one day of life, much less six months."

We all tend to live like we are going to live forever, when the fact is that we are all mortal and can die at any moment from a thousand different causes, natural or accidental. Ironically, the Bible tells us that we are to live like we are going to live forever — but not on this earth. We are to live in preparation for eternity, hopefully an eternity with God.

Most likely you are a born-again believer who has given serious thought to eternity, but who finds it difficult to maintain an eternal perspective. You repeatedly find yourself caught up with the problems of life, and the result is stress, anxiety, and even depression.

Living with an eternal perspective is one of the keys to living as an overcomer. It is a virtue that is going to become increasingly important as society continues to disintegrate and Christians come under increasing attack.

What is the secret to maintaining an eternal perspective? Much of the answer lies in your attitude about this world.

❖ Your Attitude toward the World ❖

Stop for a moment and think. What is your attitude about this world? Are you enthusiastic about it? Or do you feel uncomfortable with it? Do you love the world? Or do you often feel alienated from it? Are you at home in this world? Or do you feel like a stranger?

There's an old Negro spiritual song that always challenges me to examine my attitude toward the world. The first verse goes as follows:[4]

> This world is not my home,
> I'm just a passing through.
> My treasures are laid up
> Somewhere beyond the blue.
>
> The angels beckon me
> From heaven's open door,
> And I can't feel at home
> In this world anymore.

Do those words express your feeling about this world? What word would you use to summarize your feeling? Zealous? Anxious? Enamored? Estranged? Are you comfortable or do you feel ill-at-ease?

❖ My Attitude ❖

Let me ask your indulgence for a moment as I share my personal feeling about this world. The word I would use is "hate." Yes, I hate this world. I hate it with a passion so strong and so intense that I find it difficult to express in words.

Now, let me hasten to clarify my feeling by stating that I do not hate God's beautiful and marvelous creation. I have been privileged to marvel over the majesty of the Alps. I have been awed by the rugged beauty of Alaska. I never cease to be amazed by the creative wonders of God in the great American Southwest. I have been blessed to see the incredible beauty of Cape Town, South Africa. And I have been overwhelmed time and time again by the stark and almost mystical bareness of the Judean wilderness in Israel.

When I say that I "hate" this world, I'm not speaking of

God's creation. I'm speaking of the evil world system that we live in. Let me give you some examples of what I'm talking about:

• I hate a world where thousands of babies are murdered every day in their mother's wombs.

• I hate a world where young people in the prime of life have their lives destroyed by illicit drugs.

• I hate a world that coddles criminals and makes a mockery of justice.

• I hate a world that glorifies crime in its movies and television programs.

• I hate a world that applauds indecent and vulgar performers like Madonna.

• I hate a world where government tries to convert gambling from a vice to a virtue.

• I hate a world in which professional athletes are paid over a million dollars a year while hundreds of thousands sleep homeless in the streets every night.

• I hate a world where people judge and condemn one another on the basis of skin color.

• I hate a world that calls evil good by demanding that homosexuality be recognized as a legitimate, alternative lifestyle.

• I hate a world in which mothers are forced to work while their children grow up in impersonal day-care centers.

• I hate a world in which people die agonizing deaths from diseases like cancer and AIDS.

• I hate a world where families are torn apart by alcohol abuse.

• I hate a world where every night I see reports on the television news of child abuse, muggings, kidnappings, murders, terrorism, wars, and rumors of wars.

• I hate a world that uses the name of my God, Jesus, as a curse word.

I hope you understand now what I mean when I say, "I hate this world!"

❖ Jesus' Viewpoint ❖

But how I personally feel about this world is not important. The crucial point for you to consider is the biblical view. Let's look at it, and as we do so, compare the biblical view with your own.

Let's begin with the viewpoint that Jesus told us we should have. It is recorded in John 12:25 — "He who loves his life loses it; and he who hates his life in this world shall keep it to life eternal."

Those are strong words. They are the kind that cause us to wince and think, *Surely He didn't mean what He said.* But the context indicates that Jesus meant exactly what He said. So, what about it? Do you hate your life in this world or do you love it?

❖ The Viewpoint of the Apostles ❖

The apostle Paul gave a very strong warning about getting comfortable with the world. In Romans 12:2 he wrote: "Do not be conformed to this world, but be transformed by the renewing of your mind." How do you measure up to this exhortation?

Are you conformed to the world? Have you adopted the world's way of dress? What about the world's way of speech or the world's love of money? Are your goals the goals of the world — power, success, fame, and riches?

The brother of Jesus expressed the matter in very pointed language. He said, "Do you not know that friendship with the world is hostility toward God? Therefore whoever wishes to be a friend of the world makes himself an enemy of God" (James 4:4).

Are you a friend of the world? Are you comfortable with what the world has to offer in music, movies, television programs, and best-selling books? Friendship with the world is hostility toward God! In fact, James puts it even stronger than that, for at the beginning of the passage I previously quoted (James 4:4), he says that those who are friendly with the world are spiritual adulterers.

The apostle John makes the same point just as strongly in 1 John 2:15–16:

Do not love the world, nor the things in the world. If anyone loves the world, the love of the Father is not in him. For all that is in the world, the lust of the flesh and the lust of the eyes and the boastful pride of life, is not from the Father, but is from the world.

There is no way to escape the sobering reality of these words. Do you love the world? If so, the love of the Father is not in you!

❖ The Focus of Your Mind ❖

Paul tells us how to guard against becoming comfortable with the world. In Colossians 3:2 he says, "Set your mind on the things above, not on the things that are on earth." In Philippians 4:8 he expresses the same admonition in these words:

Finally, brethren, whatever is true, whatever is honorable, whatever is right, whatever is pure, whatever is lovely, whatever is of good repute, if there is any excellence and if anything worthy of praise, let your mind dwell on these things.

As these verses indicate, one of the keys to living a triumphant life in Christ — to living a joyous and victorious life in the midst of a world wallowing in despair — is to live with a conscious eternal perspective.

What does that mean? In the words of Peter, that means living as "aliens and strangers" in this world (1 Pet. 2:11). Similarly, in the words of the writer of Hebrews, it means living as "strangers and exiles" (Heb. 11:13). Paul said that we should not set our minds on earthly things "for our citizenship is in heaven" (Phil. 3:19–20).

The great Christian writer C.S. Lewis explained that to live with an eternal perspective means "living as commandos operating behind the enemy lines, preparing the way for the coming of the commander-in-chief."[5]

❖ A Biblical Example ❖

There is a powerful biblical example of what can happen when a believer gets his eyes off the Lord and starts focusing on transient things rather than eternal matters. It is found in Psalm 73.

All students of the Bible are familiar with Psalm 51 in which David confessed his sin of adultery with Bathsheba. But few seem to be aware of Psalm 73 which contains the confession of David's worship leader, Asaph.

In this remarkable psalm, Asaph confesses that he almost lost his faith when he lost his eternal perspective. It happened when he did something that all of us tend to do from time to time —namely, he took his eyes off the Lord and put them instead on the wicked. When he did so, he noticed the prosperity of the wicked and began to wonder if his devotion to God was really worth the effort (Ps. 73:1–3).

Has that ever happened to you? Surely it has. I think it has happened to all of us from time to time.

❖ Struggling with the Prosperity of the Wicked ❖

It's the end of the month, and the bills are due. You're sitting at your desk writing check after check. Suddenly, you reach that minimum balance you must maintain in order to pay the daily bills of the new month — food, gasoline, clothing, repairs, etc. But you still have a stack of bills to pay! You sigh in exasperation, wondering when you will ever be able to catch up with what you owe.

As you sit there staring dejectedly at your meager balance, you begin to think about a friend of yours at work. He is a vain and profane man, with a mouth like a sewer. He could not care less about God. He is unfaithful to his wife. He ignores his children. He is consumed with sports and gambles constantly. Yet, he never seems to have a worry. He lives in a beautiful house, drives a fancy car, and eats at the finest restaurants.

Your heart begins to fill with envy and anger. You feel like crying out, "Lord, I serve You faithfully, and all I ever seem to get in return is trouble. My colleague at work is a complete reprobate, and he doesn't seem to have a worry in the world! What's wrong? Am I spinning my wheels with You? Is my tithe a waste of my money? Is my faithfulness of no concern to You? The way things are going, I might as well serve the devil and get some enjoyment out of life!"

Sound familiar? Well, this is exactly what happened to Asaph.

He lost his eternal perspective, got his eyes on the wicked, and started wallowing in self-pity (Ps. 73:2–3).

❖ Asaph's Sin ❖

It's amazing how irrational we become when we allow self-pity to take over our thinking. When it happened to Asaph, he started fantasizing about the rich. He began to tell himself that they are "always at ease," always increasing in wealth, never facing the problems of other people (Ps. 73:4–5,12). All of which, of course, is utter nonsense. In fact, the opposite is true. The rich often tend to have far more problems than other people do. For one thing, they must constantly be concerned about their money — how to protect it and multiply it.

It was while Asaph was caught up in this fantasy world that he committed a grievous sin against God. He blasphemed the love and faithfulness of God by exclaiming: "Surely in vain I have kept my heart pure And washed my hands in innocence; For I have been stricken all day long And chastened every morning" (Ps. 73:13–14).

❖ Asaph's Turning Point ❖

Asaph was literally on the verge of losing his faith. His spirit was in turmoil. He was wrestling with monstrous doubt. The wrestling match continued until . . . "Until I came into the sanctuary of God; Then I perceived their end [the end of the wicked]" (Ps. 73:17).

Asaph is maddeningly vague at this point. He does not tell us what happened to him when he went to the Lord's house, except that his eternal perspective was restored. Was it a song that touched his heart? Could it have been a Scripture reading or a sermon? Perhaps it was a word of encouragement from a discerning friend. It might even have been a death in his family. We just don't know. All we know for sure is that something touched his heart and reminded him of the eternal destiny of the wicked.

He states that he was reminded that the wicked walk in "slippery places" and that God may cause them to be cast down at any moment, being swept away by "sudden terror" (Ps. 73:8–19). In other words, Asaph was reminded that life is very tentative — here one moment and gone the next.

❖ The Impact of Death ❖

I think this is the reason that the death of Princess Diana had such an enormous impact on the world. Here was a woman who had it all — everything the world dreams of having. She had beauty, charm, wealth, fame, and influence. She had the "good life." Yet, in one terrifying moment, it all disappeared. She was reduced to equality with all of us — a mortal person gone to meet her Creator.

It was a sobering event. It drove home the transitory nature of life. I'm sure it caused many people to pause and think about eternity for the first time in their lives.

The Bible says that most people live in lifelong fear of death. In fact, the Bible puts it even stronger than that. It says that most people live in "slavery" to the fear of death (Heb. 2:15). This is the reason that a death in the family, or the death of a friend or a celebrity, always has such an impact. It reminds us of our mortality, and it triggers our eternal perspective.

❖ A Personal Experience with Death ❖

I had an experience with death many years ago that I will never forget. It emphasized to me the fragility of life and the inevitability of eternity. It also impacted me with the importance of keeping my priorities in order at all times.

The setting was the Cajun country of southern Louisiana. I was holding a meeting at a fairly large church in Jennings, Louisiana. Following the Sunday evening service, I went to the door to greet people as they left. A young woman about 30 years old came up to me and enthusiastically thanked me for the message. She said she could hardly wait for the Monday evening service. I was speaking on the "Signs of the Times" that point to the soon return of Jesus. The Sunday message had caught her imagination, and she was excited.

"I have so many questions," she said, "but I'll have to hold them till later because I've got to rush to my job."

"Oh?" I responded. "What kind of job do you have on Sunday evening?"

"I run the skating rink," she answered, "and we've got a lot of church kids coming over to skate this evening. I've got to hurry and get the place opened."

I thanked her for her kind comments and urged her not to forget her questions. She left hurriedly.

❖ A Shocking Call ❖

About 10:30 that evening the phone rang at the house where I was staying. I heard my host, one of the congregation's elders, suddenly exclaim, "Oh, no! Oh, no!" He hung up the phone and yelled at me, "Get your coat. We've got to go to the hospital."

As we tore across town in his truck, he explained that the call had been about the young woman who managed the skating rink. She had been skating with the kids when she suddenly dropped to the floor. She had been rushed to the hospital. The situation looked critical.

The moment we walked into the hospital lobby, we knew she was dead. Groups of youngsters and friends from the church were gathered in small groups all over the lobby and down the main hallway. Some were praying. Some were singing softly. Some were just comforting one another with hugs of reassurance.

She had suffered a massive cerebral hemorrhage. She was only 32. Death had come instantaneously. The doctor said she was probably dead before she hit the floor.

❖ Reacting in the Lord ❖

Her older sister arrived and was given the terrible news. She was known as a woman of great faith. We tried to console her but she kept consoling us, reminding us that her sister was now with the Lord. She went from group to group encouraging them with the victory her sister now enjoyed.

Then her brother arrived. He was a man of the world. He had treated his sisters harshly because of their religious convictions.

When he learned of his sister's death, he was overcome with grief and guilt. He fell to the floor in a clump and began to weep and moan loudly.

His sister rushed to him, grabbed him by the shoulders and literally lifted him off the floor. She slammed him up against the wall and held him there with her forearm. Looking directly into his eyes, she said, "Don't weep for your sister. Weep for yourself. She's in heaven with the Lord. But if that were you in there on that table, you would be in hell!"

I was taken aback by what appeared to be a brutal approach to a grieving person. But it must have had the right impact because within a year that brother had accepted the Lord.

❖   Reacting Outside the Lord   ❖

I started moving up and down the hallway from group to group, praying with them and trying as best as I knew how to offer some consoling words. Suddenly, a side door flew open and in came two paramedics running and pushing a litter on wheels. On the stretcher was a man who looked to be 60. He was dressed in a tuxedo. They wheeled him into an emergency room.

A few minutes later a large entourage of "beautiful people" arrived, all dressed in tuxedos and evening gowns. They gathered outside the emergency room doors and waited for some word. I learned they had been partying at a nightclub and that the man had collapsed on the dance floor. They thought he had suffered a heart attack.

They were right. The doctor stepped into the hallway and delivered the grim news. The man was dead from a heart attack. They all stood there for a moment in a daze, and then they turned on each other like a pack of wild animals.

A daughter, dressed in a red evening dress, turned to an older woman and began to shout curses at her. The woman was her mother, the widow of the man who had just died. There was no consolation from daughter to mother. Only curses and accusations.

"It's all your fault," the daughter screamed. "You're the cause of his heart attack. You've never given him anything but grief."

"Look who's talking," the mother shouted back, "the biggest slut in southern Louisiana." It was a horrible scene — family members cursing and blaming each other.

❖   A Startling Contrast   ❖

I was standing at a corner of the hallway. Down one corridor I saw people cursing and clawing at each other. Down the other corridor I saw people consoling and loving one another. I saw death down one hallway. I saw life down the other. I saw the glory of dying in the Lord, and I saw the grim reality of dying with no hope.

Such an experience can jolt you out of your rut. It can grab you by the throat and turn you every way but loose. It certainly can force you to think about eternity.

I suspect that Asaph had some similar experience that propelled him to the Lord's house and compelled him to get his eyes back on the Lord. I think it is interesting to note that once his eternal perspective was restored, he looked back on his combat with doubt and marveled over how stupid he had been. He concluded that he was as "senseless and ignorant" as a beast (Ps. 73:21–22).

❖ Asaph's Faith Restored ❖

Asaph wrapped up his psalm by praising the Lord for His faithfulness in words reminiscent of Paul when he wrote, "If we are faithless, He remains faithful; for He cannot deny Himself" (2 Tim. 2:13).

Asaph expressed his restored priorities in memorable words:

Whom have I in heaven but You? And besides You, I desire nothing on earth. My flesh and my heart fail, But God is the strength of my heart and my portion forever. For, behold, those who are far from You will perish; You have destroyed all those who are unfaithful to You. But as me, the nearness of God is my good; I have made the Lord God my refuge, That I may tell of all Your works (Ps. 73:25–28).

The solution to Asaph's spiritual agony was the restoration of his eternal perspective. He was reminded that this life is fleeting, and a day of judgment is coming. He realized that he may never see justice in this life, but one day justice will prevail. He realized that he had been called to live by faith and not by sight.

❖ Another Test of Attitude ❖

Let me give you one last test for determining whether or not you are living with an eternal perspective: How do you feel about the Lord's return? This is an acid test that will determine whether you are in love with the world or the Lord. The attitude of the person who is in love with the world can best be expressed in these words: "I want the Lord to return, but. . . ." There is always a "but."

"I want the Lord to return, but I want Him to come after I have made a million dollars."

"I want the Lord to come, but I want Him to come after I've written a great novel."

"I want the Lord to come, but I want Him to come after I've made the cover of *Time.*"

"I want the Lord to come, but I want Him to come after I've built a great church."

"I want the Lord to come, but I want Him to come after I'm 85 years old and have experienced all that life has to offer."

What these people are really saying is, "I want Jesus to come, but I don't want Him messing up my life!" They are in love with the world.

You see, when you are in love with someone, you want to be with him or her. That's a fact of life. Watch people who have just fallen in love. They want to be with each other all the time. When they are apart, they are constantly on the phone talking about when they will be together again!

The same is true of the Lord. If you truly love Jesus, you will want to be with Him. You will talk with Him in prayer. You will fellowship with Him in His Word and in worship. But these forms of communication will never satisfy your longing to be in His presence, to have personal, intimate fellowship with Him, face to face.

❖ The Biblical Attitude ❖

You will be like Paul, willing to stay on in this world serving the Lord, but yearning for the day when you will be united with Him, either through death or His return (2 Cor. 5:8 and Phil. 1:23–24). A sense of yearning is characteristic of those who live with an eternal perspective. It can be found expressed throughout the Bible.

The patriarch Job stated that he looked forward to the day when his Redeemer would stand upon the earth because he knew that when that happened, he, Job, would receive a new body and would see the Lord. He added that the very thought was enough to cause him to faint! (Job 19:25–27)

Abraham "lived as an alien in the land of promise" because he yearned for "the city which has foundations, whose architect and builder is God" (Heb. 11:9–10).

Moses thought it was better to be ill-treated for the promised Messiah's sake than to own all the riches of Egypt because he was looking forward to his heavenly reward (Heb. 11:26).

David relished the promise of God that one day He will send His Son to terrify the nations with His wrath and reign as King on Mt. Zion (Ps. 2:5–6).

Isaiah's heart was so filled with desire to be with the Lord that he cried out, "Oh, that You would rend the heavens and come down . . . To make Your name known to Your adversaries, That the nations may tremble at Your presence!" (Isa. 64:1–2).

Jeremiah dreamed of when the Lord would "roar from on high, And utter His voice from His holy habitation" (Jer. 25:30).

Ezekiel spent nine chapters (40–48) describing in detail the glorious millennial temple of the Lord, obviously yearning for the day it would be built. He concluded the description with the reason for his yearning. He revealed that the city will have a new name: "Yahweh Shammah," which means, "The Lord is there" (Ezek. 48:35).

Daniel had visions about the Lord returning to reign over all the earth, together with His saints (Dan. 7:13–14,18, 27).

Micah cried out for the day when the Lord will dwell once again in Jerusalem and will "teach us about His ways" and "we will walk in His paths" (Mic. 4:2).

The Old Testament ends with Malachi looking forward to the day when the "sun of righteousness will rise with healing in its wings." He says his response will be to "go forth and skip about" like a calf released from a stall! (Mal. 4:2).

This yearning to be with the Lord continues throughout the New Testament. Peter exhorted us to live with our hope fixed confidently on the return of Jesus (1 Pet. 1:13–16).

Paul urged us to live with the love of the Lord's appearing in our hearts (2 Tim. 4:8). He also told the Church to pray, "Maranatha!" meaning, "Our Lord come!" (1 Cor. 16:22).

The New Testament ends with the words of John crying out, "Amen. Come, Lord Jesus!" (Rev. 22:20).

From beginning to end, we find people throughout the Scriptures who are in love with God and who are expressing that love by yearning to be with Him. In contrast, we find the Church of the 21st century yawning about the Lord's return. We are the church of Laodicea: penetrated by the world, rich and in need of nothing — not even the Lord who stands at the door knocking, asking to be let in (Rev. 3:14–17). Like that church, we are "neither cold nor hot." We are lukewarm. And the result is that we are apathetic and worldly. We desperately need to have our eternal perspective restored.

❖ A Practical Suggestion ❖

I suggest that the next time you let your eternal perspective slip, remember Psalm 73 and read it. When you finish, reverse the numbers and go to Psalm 37. There you will find a powerful summary of what Asaph learned. It is a psalm of Asaph's mentor, King David.

David says, "Do not fret because of evildoers. . . . For they will wither quickly like the grass And fade like the green herb" (verses 1–2). He tells us what to do instead: "Trust in the Lord, and do good. . . . Delight yourself in the Lord" (verses 3–4). Over and over again he warns us not to fret over evildoers, for he says the day will come when they will be "cut off" (verse 9). In contrast, "those who wait for the Lord" shall "inherit the earth" (verse 9).

❖ **What Is Your Attitude?** ❖

Are you focused on this world? Are you attached to it, or do you have a sense of the fact that you are only passing through, heading for an eternal home?

This life is transitory. This life is only a prelude to eternity. The songwriter Tillit S. Teddlie put it all in perspective when he wrote:

Heaven Holds All for Me

> Earth holds no treasures
> But perish with using,
> However precious they be;
> Yet there's a country
> To which I am going:
> Heaven holds all to me.
>
> Why should I long
> For the world with its sorrows,
> When in that home o'er the sea,
> Millions are singing
> The wonderful story?
> Heaven holds all to me.
>
> Heaven holds all to me,
> Brighter its glory will be;
> Joy without measure
> Will be my treasure:
> Heaven holds all to me.[6]

There is a more contemporary song that sums up the whole essence of what it means to live with an eternal perspective:

> Turn your eyes upon Jesus,
> Look full in His wonderful face,
> And the things of earth
> Will grow strangely dim
> In the light of His glory and grace.[7]

A number of years ago I was given the blessing of meeting a great man of God named Leonard Ravenhill, a prophetic preacher from England. After our meeting, we corresponded briefly. Right before he died, in the last letter he sent me, he enclosed a small card containing a brief, one sentence message. He urged me to memorize the message and live it daily.

That was July of 1988. I still have the card. It is worn and tattered because I have made it a point to keep it in my shirt pocket at all times. The message printed on it is simple but profound: "Lord, keep me eternity conscious."

Endnotes

1 Roy Jenkins, *Gladstone: A Biography* (New York: Random House, 1997).

2 There are many versions of this speech that circulate on the Internet, all making the same point. The version reproduced here is a composite prepared by the author.

3 Eugene H. Peterson, *The Message: New Testament with Psalms and Proverbs* (Colorado Springs, CO: Navpress, 1995), p. 572.

4 Albert Brumley, "This World Is Not My Home (I'm Just A Passing Thru)," a Negro spiritual of unknown origin arranged by Albert E. Brumley. Arrangement © by Albert E. Brumley.

5 The author was unable to locate the precise source of this quotation which is attributed to C.S. Lewis. Lewis refers several times to "living on enemy territory" in his classic, *Mere Christianity* (New York: MacMillan Publishing Co., 1960), p. 51.

6 Tillit S. Teddlie, "Heaven Holds All for Me," public domain.

7 Helen H. Lemmel, "Turn Your Eyes upon Jesus," © 1922, renewed 1950 by Singspiration, Inc.

Chapter 9

❖   ❖   ❖

Standing for Righteousness

saiah prophesied that a day would come when people would call "evil good, and good evil" (Isa. 5:20). That day has arrived. As evidence, just turn on any of the television talk shows which have been dubbed most appropriately as "Trash TV." I'm speaking of programs like those hosted by Jerry Springer, Geraldo Rivera, Montel Williams, and Jenny Jones. On these programs you will see a parade of moral perverts, like "mothers who sleep with their daughter's boy friends." And if anyone in the audience has the audacity to stand up and say, "I think what you are doing is wrong," the audience will turn on that person in mob fury, denouncing him or her as an "intolerant bigot."

❖   The Call to Virtue   ❖

Christians are admonished throughout the Scriptures to be virtuous. Peter writes, "Make every effort to supplement your faith with virtue, and virtue with knowledge, and knowledge with self-control, and self-control with steadfastness, and steadfastness with godliness, and godliness with brotherly affection, and brotherly affection with love" (2 Pet. 1:5–7;RSV). Paul cites a similar list of virtues in Galatians 5:22–23 and refers to them as "fruit of the Spirit."

Needless to say, virtues are supposed to be character traits that are good. The dictionary defines a virtue as "a characteristic of moral excellence or goodness." But the number one virtue being touted in America today is anything but good. It threatens to destroy both America and the Church.

❖ A Shift in Values ❖

Our number one national virtue used to be justice. That is the virtue that Martin Luther King Jr. used to convict our consciences and call us to repentance for racial injustice.

But justice is no longer the primary virtue in America. If you want to know what that virtue is, just ask your children, because it is being hammered into their heads on a daily basis in their public school classrooms. What is it? It is *tolerance!*

It sounds so good. It sounds so uplifting, so positive in nature. Your most likely response to your children is to say, "Oh, that's wonderful! Pay close attention to your teacher." But before you do that, let me warn you. The concept of tolerance being taught to our children today is anything but wonderful. It is downright dangerous.

❖ The New Tolerance ❖

How can something that seems so good be so terrible? After all, isn't tolerance a necessary virtue to prevent prejudice, bigotry, and hatred? The problem is rooted in the fact that the traditional concept of tolerance — the kind adults in America grew up with — has been redefined into a moral perversion.

The tolerance we grew up with was the kind that encouraged respect for differing viewpoints, religions, and lifestyles. It was the idea of treating with dignity and respect those who might disagree with us on fundamental concepts of life.

This traditional concept of tolerance is one of the foundation stones of American democracy. It produced the attitude of freedom of diversity — a freedom that has made it possible for Catholics, Protestants, and Jews to live together in peace.

But this traditional concept of tolerance has been replaced by the "new tolerance" that is being taught to our children today. The "new tolerance" demands not only respect, but also *endorsement and praise.* Thus, it is no longer sufficient for me to simply tolerate the homosexual lifestyle. To be truly tolerant, I must also *endorse* it and *praise* it. If I refuse to do so, I am a bigot!

❖ A Twisted "Virtue" ❖

The new form of tolerance is really no virtue at all because it is based on a lie. The lie that serves as its foundation is the belief that all values, beliefs, and lifestyles are equally valid. Thus, democracy is viewed as being no better than dictatorship. Capitalism is considered no better than socialism. Christianity is seen as being no better than Hinduism. To summarize it in modern jargon: "Different strokes for different folks," with all judgment put aside.

But there is an irony to this "new tolerance." The irony is that everything is tolerated except intolerance!

❖ The Root of the Problem ❖

This "new tolerance" is a product of modern society's rejection of God. You see, if there is no God, then there are no objective standards. Every person's opinion is as good and valid as any other person's is. No one has a right to judge or condemn anyone else — unless, of course, the person is exhibiting some form of intolerance!

That is the reason modern society hates the Ten Commandments so much. They are constantly ridiculed in the press. Ted Turner, the media mogul, has rewritten them, converting them into humanistic platitudes which he calls "The Ten Suggestions."[1]

In colleges and universities across America, the worst thing that can happen to a student is to be accused of intolerance. Merely the accusation will often result in the accused person being required to take a course in sensitivity training, and this course must be finished before any other credit course can be taken! And what happens in the course? The person is bombarded with propaganda in an attempt to brainwash him into believing that all lifestyles have equal merit.

❖ The Moral Consequences ❖

The "new tolerance" has created a moral vacuum that, in turn, has produced some very strange consequences.

A good example of what I am talking about can be found in the "Naked Guy" incident that occurred on the UCLA campus a couple of years ago. You probably remember seeing reports of it on television.

A student decided that he would start attending classes naked. For days he went from class to class stark naked, and no one was willing to stand up and say, "What you are doing is wrong. It is immoral. Put your clothes back on!" After all, to make such a statement would have been intolerant.

But when the incident got national attention through the media, the administration decided that something had to be done. So, the fellow was finally disciplined on the grounds of the politically correct charge of "sexual harassment."

Again, when God is removed from the picture, objective standards collapse, and all truth becomes relative.

This was illustrated vividly in a recent article in the *Journal of Higher Education.* Two college professors reported independently of each other that they had discovered their students were unwilling to make any moral judgments, even regarding the most obscene things. One reported that his students were unwilling to condemn the Holocaust; the other reported that his students could not bring themselves to condemn the Aztec practice of human sacrifice![2]

❖ **The New Academic Atmosphere** ❖

Josh McDowell has spent 30 years proclaiming Christ on college and university campuses all across America and around the world. He recently commented on the impact of the "new tolerance" by observing that students now respond to his message in a completely different way.

In the past when he would present the claim that Jesus is the only hope for the world, the response from students was, "Prove it!" Today the response is, "You have no right to say that! You're a bigot."

Josh summed up the new campus atmosphere by stating, "An imbecile's claim that Ronald McDonald is the only hope for mankind becomes equally valid with my claim that there is no hope apart from Jesus. I have no right to judge or condemn his claim, nor do I have the right to point out that he is an idiot."[3]

I used to teach comparative government and comparative political philosophy at the university level. In both courses, the purpose was to evaluate the competing truth claims. We would consider questions like these: Is democracy more valid than oligarchy? Is communism more valid than capitalism? Is existentialism more valid than rationalism?

Today such an approach would be considered hard-core bigotry! The purpose of comparative studies today is "to understand, appreciate, and *accept* competing systems."

Thus, a comparative religion course would no longer evaluate the truth claims of competing religions. Instead, it would strive to show you that Hinduism is as valid a religion as Christianity or any other religion in the world.

❖ The Plague of Multiculturalism ❖

This explains the danger of the current fad of multiculturalism — the hottest buzzword in American education.

Again, it sounds so good. But there are two serious problems with it. First, it is a thinly veiled attempt to dispense with the teaching of Western Civilization. The advocates of the "new tolerance" loathe the study of Western Civilization because it emphasizes the civilizing influence of Christianity, a religion which they despise because it is considered "intolerant."

The second problem with multiculturalism is that it teaches that one culture is just as good as another, and that is a lie! The Aztec culture that emphasized human sacrifices was not as good as a Christian culture that emphasizes the sanctity of life. The Indian culture that is based upon gross idolatry in the form of worshiping every aspect of creation is not as good as a Christian culture that focuses on the worship of the one true God.

Consider for a moment the different results of the culture of India, which is based on Hinduism, and the culture of America that has been based on Judeo-Christian principles. In India, hundreds of millions of people are starving to death as a result of their belief that all living animals are reincarnated human beings. Because of this belief, they will not kill the animals for food. People starve while animals of all kinds wander the streets. By contrast, the Judeo-Christian principles America was founded upon have produced the most abundant society the world has ever known.

These differences in India and America are obvious, but no judgments can be drawn according to the rules of the "new tolerance." That's because the "new tolerance" requires the abandonment of convictions. It demands indifference to evil. That's the reason that President Reagan was so roundly condemned by the press when he had the audacity to characterize the Soviet Union as "the Evil Empire."

❖ Implications for Christianity ❖

Christianity has been heavily impacted by the "new tolerance." For one thing, the "new tolerance" has been adopted by many mainline Christian denominations, and this has resulted in diluting their stand against the sins of society.

John 3:16 has been replaced as the central verse in these churches with Matthew 7:1 which says, "Do not judge so that you will not be judged." The result is that there are tens of thousands of silent pulpits in America today because pastors are unwilling to denounce gambling, abortion, homosexuality, euthanasia, pornography, or any other societal evil.

Someone needs to point out to these preachers that Matthew 7:1 applies to motives — not to words and actions. God alone knows motives, but we can certainly judge words and actions against the standards of God's Word. In fact, we are required to do so. The Bible tells Christians to test all things, ourselves included (2 Cor. 13:5 and 1 John 4:1). Jesus Himself *commanded* us "to judge with righteous judgment" (John 7:24).

❖ The Impact on Liberal Churches ❖

Another way the "new tolerance" has impacted Christianity is to be found among mainline, liberal denominations. What I'm referring to is their growing attitude of acceptance of pagan religions as legitimate avenues to God and salvation. As I have pointed out earlier, this attitude dominates both the National and World Councils of Churches.

The attitude is usually expressed in the following manner: "There are many roads to God because He has revealed himself in many different ways." Because of this apostasy, many Christian leaders are now taking the position that it is wrong to send out missionaries because they violate the cultural sensitivities of foreign peoples and because they communicate the idea that there is something superior about the Christian message.

All of which makes a liar of Jesus who said, "I am the way, and the truth, and the life; no one comes to the Father but through Me" (John 14:6). It also makes a liar of the apostle Peter who proclaimed in Acts 4:12 that "there is salvation in no one else [but Jesus]; for there is no other name under heaven that has been given among men, by which we must be saved."

❖ The Impact on Society ❖

A third impact on Christianity of the "new tolerance" is the fact that it is turning society against evangelical Christianity. In fact, I would put it even stronger than that. I would say it is fueling outright hatred and persecution of Evangelicals. The reason, of course, is simple. Evangelicals stand on the Word of God as their authority for all things, and because they do, they feel compelled to speak with moral indignation against the sins of society.

Society responds by shouting, "Bigots!" Evangelicals are written off and publicly denounced as "Bible-thumpers," "redneck zealots," and "self-righteous prudes."

Consider, for example, the response of the press and the general public to the 1997 decision by Southern Baptists to boycott the Disney Corporation. The Baptists were castigated in the harshest possible language for adopting the following resolutions:[4]

1. That there should be a right to display the Ten Commandments in all government offices, courthouses, and schools.

2. That Bible publishers should refrain from accommodating their translations to contemporary cultural pressures.

3. That Christians should boycott the Walt Disney Company for its flagrant promotion of homosexuality, adultery, infidelity, and violence.

4. That the United States government should take sanctions against foreign governments that promote religious persecution.

What is so terrible about these resolutions? Why did they result in a firestorm of criticism? The answer is simple. The resolutions make moral judgments.

❖ A Double Standard ❖

Do you see a double standard here? Think of it — It is okay to bash Christians, but it is morally wrong to criticize homosexuals. It is okay to put a crucifix in a jar of urine and call it art, but it would be totally unacceptable to put a rainbow pin in the same jar (because it symbolizes the New Age movement). It is okay to boycott an American corporation that pollutes the atmosphere or exploits foreign workers, but it is totally unacceptable to boycott a corporation that promotes gross immorality.

We are obviously living in a time when Christians need to take a stand for righteousness. It is also a time when Christians find it increasingly difficult to do so, due to the condemnation they will face.

Sometimes the consequences are worse than condemnation. They can mean the end of a career. I'm thinking of an incident I read about a number of years ago concerning a deputy sheriff in Nevada.[5] He was ordered to an abortion clinic, together with other deputies, and told to break up an anti-abortion protest. When he arrived, his heart was touched by the scene before him. He saw fellow Christians singing hymns while sitting in front of the clinic's entrance. Others were walking around reading Scripture aloud. Some were displaying posters with ghastly photos of aborted babies.

As the deputy surveyed the scene, he decided he was on the wrong side. He took off his gun and his badge, laid them on the ground, and then sat down with the demonstrators. He was arrested along with them, and he lost his job. But he had been true to himself and his Lord.

More professing Christians should (and must) follow this man's example, willing to lay their reputations and jobs on the line in behalf of righteousness. To do so is a Christian responsibility that is not stressed much in modern preaching.

❖ The Importance of Good Works ❖

Part of the problem is rooted in the Reformation. That transforming movement was fought over the issue of salvation. Is it by grace or works? Grace triumphed, as it should have, but in the process the Christian community seemed to forget about the importance of good works.

One of the cornerstone passages of the Reformation is found in Ephesians 2:8–9 where Paul wrote: "For by grace you have been saved through faith . . . not as a result of works, so that no one may boast." But the very next verse says that we are "created in Christ Jesus for good works, which God prepared beforehand so that we would walk in them" (Eph. 2:10). The point: We are not saved by works, but we are saved to do good works.

Paul repeated the point in Titus 2:14 where he stated that God has redeemed us and is purifying us as a people "zealous for good deeds." James, the brother of Jesus, summed up the issue well when he wrote, "For just as the body without the spirit is dead, so also faith without works is dead" (James 2:26).

❖ The Significance of Good Works ❖

Works are significant because they manifest our salvation. They are also significant because they manifest the love of God through us. They are important too because each of us will one day be judged of our works, not to determine our eternal destiny, but to determine our degrees of reward (2 Cor. 5:10).

The Bible reveals that there are a variety of good works we are called to do. We are admonished to show holiness in our personal lives (1 Pet. 1:13–16). We are called to show compassion for those less fortunate, like widows and orphans, the homeless, the hungry, and the oppressed (Ps. 41:1, Isa. 58:6–7, and James 1:27). In many other passages, both Old Testament and New, we are commanded to take a stand for righteousness.

❖ The Divine Concern for Justice ❖

The Creator of this universe is a God who is passionately concerned about justice. This concern is vividly expressed in Amos 5:21–24 where the prophet speaks against religious hypocrisy. He states that there is something more important to God than religious festivals, solemn assemblies, burnt offerings, and songs of praise. What is it? Amos thunders the answer: "Let justice roll down like waters And righteousness like an ever-flowing stream" (Amos 5:24).

This theme is found throughout the prophetic literature of the Hebrew prophets. Micah put it in the form of a rhetorical question: "What does the Lord require of you But to do justice, to love kindness, And to walk humbly with your God?" (Mic. 6:8). Speaking for the Lord, Isaiah declared, "Learn to do good; Seek justice, Reprove the ruthless, Defend the orphan, Plead for the widow" (Isa. 1:17).

❖ The Biblical Concern for Justice ❖

In like manner, the wisdom literature of the Bible is filled with admonitions to stand for righteousness and justice.

> Who will stand up for me against evildoers? Who will take his stand for me against those who do wickedness? (Ps. 94:16).

> Hate evil, you who love the Lord (Ps. 97:10).

> Burning indignation has seized me because of the wicked, Who forsake Your law (Ps. 119:53).

> Rescue those who are unjustly sentenced to death; don't stand back and let them die (Prov. 24:11).[6]

> Open your mouth for the mute, For the rights of all the unfortunate. Open your mouth, judge righteously, And defend the rights of the afflicted and needy (Prov. 31:8–9).

Another way the Lord lets us know about His passion for justice is through the descriptions He gives us of what life will be like during the millennial reign of His Son. In the classic passage in Isaiah 11:3–5, the emphasis is upon righteousness, fairness, and faithfulness. In Isaiah 9:7 we are told that the Lord's kingdom will encompass the whole earth and that it will be characterized by "justice and righteousness." Micah emphasizes that there will be no homeless or hungry people, and the earth will be blessed with peace (Mic. 4:1–4).

The teachings of Jesus are filled with calls to stand for righteousness. In His Sermon on the Mount, He called upon His followers to be the salt and light of the world (Matt. 5:13–14). He summed up his admonition by saying, "Let your light shine before men in such a way that they may see your good works, and glorify your Father who is in heaven" (Matt. 5:16). He also said that those who were "persecuted for the sake of righteousness" would be greatly blessed (Matt. 5:10).

❖ Our Faithless Response ❖

So often we respond to verses like these by saying, "Who am I? I'm nobody. No one will listen to me. The evil is so great, and I am so small. What good will it do for me to speak out?"

We tend to look on biblical characters as persons who had a special hot line to God. We put them on a pedestal and assume that the incredible things they did are impossible for us to do. Take Elijah, for example. He confronted an evil king and his depraved wife. He also stood toe to toe with the pagan priests of Baal. One man against the system. Yet, he prevailed.

We look at Elijah and shake our heads in wonder, never suspecting that we could do something equivalent. Yet the New Testament makes a startling statement: "Elijah was a man with a nature like ours, and he prayed earnestly that it would not rain, and it did not rain on the earth for three years and six months. And he prayed again, and the sky poured rain" (James 5:17–18). Look at it again: *"Elijah was a man with a nature like ours,"* but he was a man of faith, and that faith made all the difference. He was also a man of righteousness, and that was important, because the lead-in sentence of this passage is, "The effective prayer of a righteous man can accomplish much" (James 5:16). Those of us who are born again are righteous people, not because of our own righteousness, but because we have been clothed in the righteousness of Jesus (Rom. 4:1–10 and Gal. 3:27).

❖ The Power of One Person ❖

The Bible teaches that you should never underestimate the impact of one person called by God and empowered by His Holy Spirit. We are told that "God has chosen the foolish things of the world to shame the wise, and God has chosen the weak things of the world to shame the things which are strong" (1 Cor. 1:27).

One godly man in Ft. Worth, Texas, a dentist named Richard Neill, was able to get the "Phil Donahue Show" canceled from television. He did so first of all by standing up and speaking out against the filth that was being paraded on the program. When there was no positive response from the network, he launched a letter-writing campaign to the program's sponsors. He urged others to join him in writing them. The sponsors began to fall by the wayside until the program was canceled in 1996.[7]

One man against a network. He seemed to have no chance. But neither did David against Goliath. While the Philistines laughed, David marched forward fearlessly to face the giant. He cried out to Goliath, "You come to me with a sword, a spear, and a javelin, but I come to you in the name of the Lord of hosts" (1 Sam. 17:45). One small boy against an army, armed with the name of God!

❖ Biblical Examples ❖

The Bible is filled with examples of single individuals like David who stood up and made a difference. Throughout the Book of Judges are stories of individuals, both men and women, who stood against evil and brought renewal to their nation. The same is true during the period of the kings, such as when Nathan confronted David, Elijah faced down Ahab, and Josiah (age 16!) rallied his nation to God by purging his land of false priests and their idols.

As we move to the New Testament, we are confronted with the greatest example of all — Jesus of Nazareth. His impact on history has been summed up powerfully in an essay called, "One Solitary Life:"[8]

> He was born in an obscure village, the child of a peasant woman. He grew up in another obscure village, where He worked in a carpenter shop until He was 30. Then for three years He was an itinerant preacher.
>
> He never wrote a book. He never held an office. He never had a family or owned a home. He didn't go to college. He never visited a big city. He never traveled two hundred miles from the place where he was born. He did none of the things that usually accompany greatness. He had no credentials but himself.
>
> He was only 33 when the tide of public opinion turned against Him. His friends deserted Him. One betrayed Him; another denied Him. He was turned over to His enemies and went through the mockery of a trial. He was nailed to a cross between two thieves.
>
> While He was dying, His executioners gambled for His robe, the only property He had on earth. When He was dead, He was laid in a borrowed grave through the pity of a friend.

Twenty centuries have come and gone, and today He is the central figure of the human race.

All the armies that ever marched, all the navies that ever sailed, all the parliaments that ever sat, all the kings that ever reigned, put together, have not affected the life of man on this earth as much as that one solitary life.

You may be thinking, "Yes, but He was God in the flesh." Yes, he was. But remember, He emptied himself of His divine glory and powers when He became flesh, and He lived His life relying on the power of the Holy Spirit (Phil. 2:6–7 and John 5:19). That's why He spent so much of His time in prayer (Luke 11:1). When He left this earth, He gave us that same Spirit to empower and guide us (John 16:7,13–14).

It was the empowerment of the Holy Spirit that enabled one man, Paul, to evangelize the then-known world. The Holy Spirit called him while he was at a prayer meeting in Antioch (Acts 13:2). Luke says that when Paul began his first missionary journey, he was "sent out by the Holy Spirit" and was "filled with the Holy Spirit" (Acts 13:4, 9).

Outside the Bible, history is replete with examples of individual Christians who changed the world by taking a stand for righteousness.

❖ One Man against Slavery ❖

One of the classic examples is William Wilberforce who was born in England in 1759. He inherited great wealth and became a playboy. But in 1784, at the age of 25, he found Jesus and his life was transformed. He began to speak out against the slave trade and to expose its horrors in the House of Commons where he served as a representative.[9]

Wilberforce was mocked, ridiculed, castigated, and threatened with his life, but no one could silence him. At one point, when he became discouraged, John Wesley, who was on his deathbed, heard about it. Wesley asked for a pen and paper. He wrote Wilberforce the following note:[10]

Unless God has raised you up for this very thing, you will be worn out by the opposition of men and devils.

But if God be for you, who can be against you? Are all of them stronger than God? Oh, be not weary of well-doing! Go on, in the name of God and in the power of His might, until even American slavery shall vanish away.

Wesley died six days later (1791). Wilberforce took his words of encouragement to heart and persisted with his crusade. Sixteen years later, in 1807, he succeeded in getting the English slave trade abolished. It took another 26 years for him to achieve the abolition of slavery in England. The bill was passed in 1833, the year Wilberforce died at age 74.

❖   One Man against an Industry   ❖

A modern-day example of a Christian leader with a similar tenacious spirit is Don Wildmon, founder of the American Family Association. In the mid-1970s he was the pastor of a small Methodist church in Tupelo, Mississippi, when the Lord spoke to his heart, calling him to step out in faith and take a stand against the growing immorality, violence, and blasphemy in American movies and television programs.

The rest is history. Today his ministry spearheads the fight against the degradation that characterizes the entertainment industry. The very mention of his name causes the boardrooms of Hollywood and New York to tremble. His boycotts and letter-writing campaigns have brought one major corporation after another to their knees, begging for him to back off.

I remember well when he launched a campaign against the Holiday Inns. Here was a corporation that had built its empire as a family-oriented business, and then it began to feature X-rated movies in its rooms. I joined the protest and wrote a letter to the corporate headquarters stating my objections and making it clear I would boycott the use of their facilities.

Normally, such letters prompt a public relations response in the form of sugar-coated words which thank you for your input, but which rarely address the issue. But my letter must have hit a sore spot. One of the company's vice presidents sent me a handwritten diatribe in which he denounced me as a "fundamentalist fool" who was blindly following the leadership of a quack! He stated that they had thoroughly investigated Don Wildmon and had found him to be an "undistinguished person" with no particular academic credentials. He said they could find no reason for his influence and power.

❖ Using the Weak and Foolish ❖

The man's words reminded me of what Paul wrote in 1 Corinthians 1:27 — "God has chosen the foolish things of the world to shame the wise, and God has chosen the weak things of the world to shame the things which are strong." Paul added, "A natural man does not accept the things of the Spirit of God; for they are foolishness to him; and he cannot understand them, because they are spiritually appraised" (1 Cor. 2:14).

I've often wondered how many people God called before He got to Don Wildmon. I can imagine Him speaking to the heart of some big-city pastor of a mega-church, and the pastor responding, "Lord, who will listen to me? I only have a church of 5,000. I don't have a national mailing list or a television ministry." But Don Wildmon, who was totally unknown and had no resources whatsoever, not even a big church, said, "Here am I, Lord, use me," and God's anointing fell upon him. It happened because the Bible says, "The eyes of the Lord move to and fro throughout the earth that He may strongly support those whose heart is completely His" (2 Chron. 16:9).

❖ The Mocking Church ❖

In his ministry's publication, *The AFA Journal,* Don Wildmon often reports that his severest critics are clergymen who write him mocking letters, ridiculing his fight against filth in the entertainment industry. Wildmon uses these letters to point out that the biggest problem in America today is "300,000 silent pulpits." He argues they are silent on moral issues because too many pastors are afraid of stepping on sensitive toes. In response to their allegations that his efforts are "useless," he responds that God has not called us to win the battles, rather He has called us to take a stand. Victory will not come until Jesus returns. But in the meantime, we are not to sit idly by and allow evil to multiply.

Otherwise, we end up with tragedies like the Holocaust. People forget that Germany was full of churches, both Protestant and Catholic. But the prevailing attitude was one of "hear and see no evil." So, six million Jews went to the ovens while Christians looked the other way.

❖ A Call to Action ❖

How does all this apply to you and me? God is calling us to take a stand for righteousness in the midst of a society that has become so evil that it has forgotten how to blush. There are three things that each of us need to do in order to stand for righteousness.

First, you need to pray for God to lay an issue on your heart. You cannot actively oppose all the evil, for it is too great. You must focus your time and energy. Think of it this way: If you pour water on the ground, it runs every which way; but if you pour it into a channel that runs it over a water wheel, you can generate electricity.

So, pray for God to burden your heart with one particular issue. You may wake up in the night weeping for those in bondage to homosexuality. Or, while praying, you may begin to feel a great sense of compassion for women who are contemplating an abortion.

Once God gives you the burden, then change your prayer and start asking what He wants you to do about it. Remember, God does not call everyone to do the same thing. Take the issue of abortion, for example. He might call one person to be a frontline soldier who sits in the doorway of a clinic and risks arrest. He may call another to stand across the street and pray or serve as a sidewalk counselor. He might motivate another to write letters to newspapers and politicians. Others He might call to serve as financial contributors. He might even call you to adopt a baby that someone wants to abort.

Finally, after the Lord has identified your issue and told you what to do, then follow that popular slogan that says, "Do it!" He will give you the gifts you need to do the job, and He will give you the opportunities. Remember, He is actively searching the earth for people who have given their hearts to Him so that He might strongly support them (2 Chron. 16:9). Donald K. Campbell, author of *Judges: Leaders in Crisis Times*, wrote, "The requirement for usefulness is not ability, but availability and trust in God's enabling power."[11]

Here's how Paul put it: "I thank Jesus Christ our Lord, who has strengthened me, because He considered me faithful, putting me into service" (1 Tim. 1:12).

❖   A Monk Who Challenged an Empire   ❖

In the fourth century there was a monk by the name of Telemachus. He lived alone as a hermit in the desert seeking God. One day he became convinced that he was selfish rather than self-less, and he decided that he would spend the rest of his life serving people, enabling God to touch them through him.

He headed for Rome. He arrived when the Romans were celebrating a military victory over the Goths. Prisoners of war were being marched through the streets. He heard there was going to be a great victory celebration at the Coliseum, and he decided to go.

He was astonished to find 50,000 people cheering as the prisoners of war fought each other to the death in gladiator games. (Keep in mind that Rome had become officially Christian by this time.) Telemachus could not endure what he was witnessing. He was morally outraged, and he decided to take action.

He rushed down the steps, vaulted the retaining wall, and stepped between two gladiators, signaling for them to stop their combat. The crowd was enraged. They began to chant for the life of the monk. Finally, the commander of the games gave in to the blood lust of the crowd and gave the signal for Telemachus to be slaughtered. Suddenly, a hush fell over the crowd as people began to realize that they had encouraged the killing of a holy man — a minister of Christ. The games ended, and they were never resumed. Edward Gibbon wrote, "His death was more useful to mankind than his life."[12]

Never underestimate what one person can accomplish when that person is called and empowered by God.

Endnotes

1 Catholic League for Religious and Civil Rights, press release, "Ted Turner Embarrasses Himself in Public," February 17, 1999, p.1. Available on the Internet at http://www.freerepublic.com/forum/ a36cb624133b0.htm.

2 John Leo, "On Morality, Students Suffer 'Absolutophobia,' " *Birmingham News,* Birmingham, Alabama, July 15, 1997, page number unknown. Taken from his column, "On Society," which appears regularly in *U.S. News and World Report.*

3 Josh McDowell has spoken out extensively on the issue of values and the changing nature of tolerance. He has developed an outstanding seminar for teens entitled, "Right from Wrong." Details regarding this seminar and other resources on the topic of tolerance can be found at Josh McDowell's website: http://www.josh.org.

4 The Ethics and Religious Liberty Commission of the Southern Baptist Convention, "Resolutions of the Southern Baptist Convention," http://www.erlc.com/WhoSBC/Resolutions/Resolut.htm, "Resolutions for 1997."

5 According to information received from Troy Newman at Operation Rescue (oprescue@aol.com), this incident occurred in Las Vegas, Nevada.

6 *The Living Bible Paraphrased.* This passage has been the rallying call of the Pro-Life movement in the United States.

7 Personal interview of Dr. Richard Neill by the author on November 6, 1999.

8 There are many variations of this essay which most sources attribute to an "unknown author." However, the author is known. He was Dr. James Allan Francis. The original version can be found in his book *The Real Jesus and Other Sermons,* published in 1926 by the Judson Press of Philadelphia, PA. The essay appears in the last chapter, "Arise, Sir Knight!" on page 123. The version quoted here is a composite of several versions. The original version can be found on the Internet at http://www.sjvls.lib.ca.us/sjvls/francis.html.

9 Garth Lean, *God's Politician: William Wilberforce's Struggle,* (Colorado Springs, CO: Helmers & Howard Publishers, 1989).

10 Wayne Holcomb, editorial in the *Hill 'N Dale Herald* of the Hill 'N Dale Christian Church, Lexington, Kentucky, September 30, 1992, p. 2.

11 Donald K. Campbell, *Judges: Leaders in Crisis Times,* (Wheaton, IL: Victor Books, 1989), p. 46.

12 Edward Gibbon, *The Decline and Fall of the Roman Empire* (Chicago, IL: Encyclopedia Britannica, Inc., 1952), Vol. I, p. 484.

Chapter 10

❖　❖　❖

Persisting in Prayer

O ne of the greatest spiritual weapons we should be using in these end times is prayer, yet it is one that we seldom use. It's an old problem. In James 4:2 we find these words: "You do not have because you do not ask."

Let me ask you a question: If you were to stop praying, would it radically affect your life? Or is that question one that you can't answer because it's like that old trick question, "Have you stopped beating your wife?" In other words, is it possible that you are one of those Christians who couldn't stop praying because you have never really started?[1]

On the other hand, are you one of those Christians who pray regularly out of a sense of habit or a sense of duty — but who doubts seriously the power of prayer because you have never sensed its effect in your life?

Again, I ask: If you were to stop praying, would it radically affect your life?

Perhaps you are one of those Christians who would really like to pray, but you have fallen victim to the modern, "sophisticated" concept that prayer is merely a psychological exercise in self-help — and therefore you are turned off by the concept of participating in a sham — by, in effect, praying to yourself.

❖　**An Age of Unbelief**　❖

There is no doubt that we live in an age that does not believe in prayer. The world scoffs at the very idea of prayer. How many television programs or movies have you ever seen where, in the midst of some great crisis, the characters resort to prayer? No, the resort is normally to weapons.

The great tragedy is that Christians have become caught up in the philosophy of our age, a philosophy that has enthroned science as god. We are taught on every side that we live in an impersonal universe, a world that is a great, remorseless machine, obeying relentless laws. In the midst of it all, we tiny humans are nothing but transient pygmies.

The result is that we have a hollow god — a god who has no heart or compassion, for science cannot feel or laugh or show mercy. Science can only analyze, measure, dissect, weigh, and speculate. So, we feel a sense of meaninglessness, a loss of significance, an erosion of hope, and a lack of power.

❖ Meaningless Rituals ❖

Oh, many of us who call ourselves Christians go through the motions of prayer. But our prayers are often infrequent and vague and faithless. Most of us pray prayers that a stone god could answer:

> Father, we pray for all those who it is our duty to pray for.

> Father, forgive us of all our unforgiven sins.

Our prayers tend to be empty, meaningless rituals. We are like the king in Shakespeare's *Hamlet* who tried to pray for the forgiveness of his sin of murder in order to purge his feeling of guilt. His prayer was ineffective. As he put it, "It didn't even reach the ceiling."

When the king analyzed his problem, Shakespeare put words of wisdom in his mouth that are as profound as any that mere man has ever written about prayer: "My words fly up; my thoughts remain below. Words without thoughts never to Heaven go."[2]

Like this king, we are often guilty of praying without meaning. Consider, for example, the songs which we sing as prayers, but which we do not mean at all. In fact, we would be appalled if the Lord answered them. A good example is to be found in the popular prayer song, "Take My Life and Let It Be."[3]

> Take my silver and my gold,
> Not a mite will I withhold;
> Take my intellect and use
> Every power as Thou shalt choose.

Even when we occasionally pray honestly, earnestly, and specifically for something, most of us pray with little or no expectation of fulfillment. The proof of this is that when our prayers are answered, we either react with astonishment, or else we react with crass unbelief, attributing the answer to some natural cause or process — like luck.

❖ An Impotent God? ❖

There is a very special problem with prayer that exists throughout Christendom. Many Christians have been taught at one time or another that although God once worked wondrously, directly, and even miraculously in response to prayer to order the events of man, He no longer does so. God is different now, for at the end of the first century He placed the universe under the operation of certain immutable laws of nature, and therefore miracles are no longer possible. The age of the supernatural has passed forever. God is now limited in what He can do.

I know this attitude well because I grew up with it and because I still encounter it all the time. In my boyhood church, if the elders were asked to pray for a person who was ill, they always prayed, "Lord, please help the doctors to diagnose this problem correctly and, please help them to remember how to treat it properly." If they had prayed, "Lord, we are concerned about this person, please heal him," there would have been several coronaries in the congregation. We just didn't believe in supernatural healing.

What rank heresy all this is! I can think of few concepts more unbiblical. How can you believe in a God who retired in the first century when the Word says that He is "the same yesterday and today, yes and forever" (Heb. 13:8).

It is no wonder that the prayers of so many Christians lack power! Like the Deists of old, they have, in effect, denied that God still has any personal, intimate interest in His creation. They deny the supernatural and the miraculous — and many even deny the reality of the Holy Spirit as the supernatural presence of God in the world today.

In the process, they deny the power of prayer, for I ask you: Why pray if God is aloof, the supernatural is a sham, the age of miracles has ceased, and the Holy Spirit is nothing but a symbol of God?

❖ A God Who Never Changes! ❖

My friends, we need to wake up to the biblical fact that God is still the same today as in biblical times. He has not changed. In Malachi 3:6 He says, "I, the Lord, do not change."

We need to wake up to the fact that God's power is not limited. We need to believe the fact that God is still intensely interested in every minute detail of His creation. Also, we need to understand that God is still in control of history. In short, *God is still on the throne, He still hears prayers, and He still performs miracles.*

What nonsense it is when Christians deny the supernatural and the possibility of miracles and then bow their heads and pray! I say to you, if the age of miracles has ceased, then prayer is a farce. For how can God even hear us in prayer if something miraculous does not occur? After all, you and I are not radio transmitters!

The power of God is limitless, yet you and I, as weak and frail and silly as we are, have the power to limit the action of God in our own lives through our unbelief. We have not because we ask not, and when we ask, we do not ask in faith.

❖ The Example of Jesus ❖

In Luke 11:1 we are told that the disciples of Jesus asked Him to teach them how to pray. Have you ever stopped to think about the significance of that request?

We have no record of the disciples asking Jesus to teach them how to teach or preach or interpret the Scriptures. But they came to Him and said, "Lord, teach us how to pray." Why?

I believe it was because they had concluded in their observations of Jesus that His remarkable power was related to His prayer life. I think they saw that for Jesus, prayer was a *necessity.* It was more than an occasional practice on His part — it was a lifelong habit.

It was, in fact, an attitude of His mind and heart. It was an atmosphere in which He lived. He literally "prayed without ceasing" — as the apostle Paul urged us to do (1 Thess. 5:17).

Jesus prayed as He healed the sick. He prayed as He fed the hungry. He prayed as he raised the dead. He prayed for His disciples. He prayed for himself. And He prayed for us — for you and me — at the last supper when He prayed that all those who might believe on Him would be one (John 17).

The life of the greatest man who ever lived was a life of prayer. He prayed because He believed what He preached when He said, "The Son can do nothing of Himself" (John 5:19). He also said, "The Father abiding in Me does His works" (John 14:10). Jesus had a conscious and constant sense of *need,* and out of that sense there arose a continuing attitude of prayer.

❖ Our Self-Reliance ❖

How different are our attitudes in contrast! Our problem is that we have such an unexplainable attitude of self-sufficiency. Thus, we tend to think of prayer as an emergency measure, something to resort to when all our own efforts have failed.

But, you see, the secret of the life of Jesus is that He never once thought of managing things on His own. He never said to himself, *I'll just rely on my training, my experience, my knowledge, or the natural ability I was born with.* No — He said, "I can do nothing on My own initiative" (John 5:30).

That attitude should give us a clue as to why so many of us have a two-bit prayer life. Think back for a moment to the time you came to Christ. Think how you did it. If you did it with any sincerity and conviction at all, you had to do so with the attitude of a little child. It had to be a moment of humiliation in which you set all your pride aside — all your leverage, all your affluence, and all your influence. You could only come in the humility of a child.

That is the "stigma" of prayer. For you see, anytime you pray to God in honesty and sincerity, you are admitting your need of Him. You are admitting that you can't handle the situation. You are confessing that you do not have adequate leverage to cope with the problem. We don't like to do that because it hurts our foolish pride.

❖ Applying Prayer to Everything ❖

Another thing that we can learn from the prayer life of Jesus is that He considered *all* of life worth praying about. He didn't save prayer for just the "big" problems of life — for the emergencies. Like Jesus, you and I need to apply prayer to all aspects of our lives —

> To the phone call we're making
> To the letter we're writing
> To the vacation we're planning
> To the school report we're preparing
> To the game we're playing
> Yes, even to the room we are cleaning

Carl Sandburg summed it up beautifully in his poem, "Washerwoman:"[4]

> The washerwoman is a member of the Salvation
>   Army.
> And over the tub of suds rubbing underwear
>   clean
> She sings that Jesus will wash her sins away
> And the red wrongs she has done God and man
> Shall be white as driven snow.
> Rubbing underwear she sings of the Last Great
>   Washday.

The washerwoman in this poem is a good example of the biblical injunction that we are to "pray without ceasing" (1 Thess. 5:17). Living in the attitude of prayer is something that we need to learn how to practice moment by moment in these end times.

❖ Praying with Confidence ❖

Another thing that characterized the prayer life of Jesus is that He prayed with confidence. Consider, for example, His prayer at the tomb of Lazarus:

> Father, thank you for hearing me. (You always hear me, of course, but I said it because of all these people stand-

ing here, so that they will believe you sent me.) Then he shouted, "Lazarus, come out!" (John 11:41–42).[5]

What a marvelous prayer! Jesus thanked God in advance for hearing and answering His prayer. That is truly praying in confidence.

The tragedy is that although Jesus is supposed to be our perfect example in all things, we often respond to examples like this by shrugging our shoulders and saying, "Well, He had some sort of very special channel to God." We discount His humanity, and we overlook dozens of other biblical examples of confidence in prayer on the part of people other than our Lord.

Take Abraham, for example. He prayed for God to spare Sodom and Gomorrah if 50 righteous people could be found, and God agreed. When Abraham found the Lord so willing to relent, he decided to engage in some rather bold bargaining. "What about 45?" he asked. "Surely You won't destroy the cities over the lack of five people." Again, the Lord agreed. So, Abraham pressed the Lord's grace. He prayed again for 30, and then 20, and finally, 10. Each time, God, in His grace, agreed to Abraham's request (Gen. 18:20–33). It was a remarkable exercise in bold, if not audacious, prayer.

Or, consider King Hezekiah, the greatest king in the history of Judah. When he became critically ill, Isaiah came to him and told him to put his house in order for it was God's will for him to die. Hezekiah responded by boldly crying out to God in prayer, asking Him to change His mind. He reminded the Lord of his godly rule, and asked the Lord to heal him. God responded mercifully by granting him 15 more years of life (Isa. 38:1–5).

❖ The Relevance of Biblical Examples ❖

Again, we tend to respond to these examples as if they were irrelevant to us. "After all," we think, "Abraham and Hezekiah were saintly men who held special favor in the eyes of God. They had special 800 numbers direct to God's throne. Who am I, in contrast?"

The Bible answers that question if you are a Christian. It says that "the effective prayer of a righteous man can accomplish much" (James 5:16). You may be thinking, "But I'm not all that righteous," and you are right. But if you are a Christian, you have been clothed in the righteousness of Jesus (Rom. 5:17–19). Further, He serves as your high priest before the throne of God, interceding in your behalf (Heb. 8:1–2).

❖ The Prayers of the Unrighteous ❖

Sometimes God responds in remarkable ways even to the prayers of the unrighteous. He does not promise to hear their prayers, in the sense that He will answer them, but sometimes He does so in His grace and mercy.

A classic example can be found in the life of one of the most evil men ever to hold the throne of Israel — King Ahab. In 1 Kings 16:33 the writer says "Ahab did more to provoke the Lord God of Israel than all the kings of Israel who were before him." The prophet Elijah was sent by God to confront Ahab with a message of judgment. Elijah told him that he would lose his throne and his life and that the dogs would lick his blood from the streets (1 Kings 21:17–19). Amazingly, this evil man did not respond to Elijah's message by cursing God. Instead, he tore his clothes and put on sackcloth as a sign of repentance. He then fasted and humbled himself before God, praying for mercy (1 Kings 21:27).

The Lord was so moved by Ahab's actions that He sent Elijah back to him with a message of mercy. Elijah was instructed to tell Ahab that because he had humbled himself before the Lord, the evil which God had intended for his days would be delayed until the days of his sons (1 Kings 21:28–29).

Now, keep in mind that Ahab was not a man of God. His repentance did not last. He was a thoroughly wicked man whose remorse lasted only for a moment. But out of that moment came an earnest prayer which God in His loving kindness acknowledged.

❖ David's Boldness in Prayer ❖

In like manner, when King David was visited by the prophet Nathan and was informed that his child conceived with Bathsheba would die because of his sin against God, the Scriptures tell us that David went straight to his knees in prayer. So great was his remorse that he lay prostrate on the ground, fasted, wept, and cried out to the Lord to spare his child (2 Sam. 12:1–16).

When David was informed that his child had died, just as

Nathan had prophesied, his servants asked him why he had prayed to God to spare his child when he had been distinctly told by a prophet of God that the child would die. David's remarkable answer was, "While the child was still alive, I fasted and wept; for I said, 'Who knows, the Lord may be gracious to me, that the child may live' " (2 Sam. 12:21–22).

King David believed in prayer. He didn't have all the theological hang-ups we have today about the foreknowledge of God or the ordained will of God or the unchangeableness of God. What he did have was a beautiful personal relationship with God through communion in prayer.

❖ Prayer in Christian History ❖

Now, lest you conclude that confidence in prayer is something confined to the Old Testament kings and prophets, or the life of Jesus, or even New Testament times, let me hasten to point out that testimonies to the power of prayer ring out through all the long history of Christianity — from the struggling Christian in the pew to the triumphant martyr burning at the stake.

The greatest of the church fathers, Augustine, is a good example. This man, who lived about 350 years after Jesus, was, by his own admission, a sinner of enormous magnitude.[6] He was a womanizer who traveled from town to town engaging in all forms of sexual depravity. He finally decided to leave his home in North Africa to go to Rome, the center of debauchery.

The key to his life was his mother, Saint Monica, who was a devoted Christian. She had prayed for years for his salvation. When she heard of his plans to depart for Rome, she began to pray fervently around the clock, asking God to prevent him from going. He went anyway, and she continued to pray.

Her prayers were answered when Augustine met Bishop Ambrose in Milan and was led to a deep and abiding faith in Jesus. Augustine later wrote about his mother's prayers with these words: "What she asked for, that I remain in North Africa, was denied. What she hoped for, my conversion, was granted."[7] Augustine then described the nature of prayer in a parable. He wrote:

> A man in a boat who throws a rope at a rock; it's not with the idea of pulling the rock to the boat, but with

the idea of pulling the boat to the rock. Christ is the rock, and we throw the rope in prayer.[8]

❖ The Prayer of a Great Scientist ❖

I remember as a boy reading the inspiring autobiography of George Washington Carver, the eminent black scientist.[9] Carver was a dedicated Christian who had an active prayer life. Here's what he had to say about the relationship of prayer to his research:

> I went into my laboratory and I prayed, "Great Creator, tell me about the universe."
> The Lord replied, "You want to know too much."
> I asked, "Great Creator, tell me about the world."
> He replied, "George, pick something your own size."
> Finally, I said, "Great Creator, tell me about the peanut."
> The Lord replied, "Now, George, you've got something about your size. I'll tell you about that!"[10]

God proceeded to reveal to George Washington Carver more information about the peanut than any person had ever discovered.

❖ The Prayer Life of George Mueller ❖

The greatest example of the power of prayer in modern times that I know of is to be found in the life of George Mueller.[11] This remarkable man lived 93 years, from 1805 to 1898. For 60 years of that time, he operated an orphanage in Bristol, England, caring for a grand total of 10,000 orphans.

When Mueller established his orphanage, he decided he would run it entirely on faith and prayer. Not once during the next 60 years did he ask anyone except God for anything. He did no advertising. He sent out no fund-raising appeals. He simply relied on the grace and mercy of God.

God blessed his faith and faithfully answered his prayers. Mueller received a total of $7.2 million dollars (at a time when the dollar was worth a hundred times its value today). He built five large buildings capable of housing 2,000 orphans.

Remarkably, his orphans never missed a meal, although there

were some close calls. On one occasion, early in the history of the orphanage, all the children gathered for breakfast, and as hundreds of hungry kids sat expectantly, Mueller announced that there was no food. He then asked the children to join him in prayer. He prayed, "Father, we thank You for the food you are going to give us." (Does that prayer sound familiar? It should. It's the kind of confident prayer that Jesus prayed.)

They sat and waited. In a few minutes a knock came at the door. It was a baker: "I awoke early this morning with the idea of baking some bread for you."

A few minutes later there was another knock. It was a milkman who announced that his delivery wagon had broken down in front of the orphanage. He explained that he needed to get rid of his milk before it spoiled.

When Mueller prayed, he always satisfied himself first that what he was praying for was God's will. Then, resting on the promises of the Bible, he would go before the throne of God boldly in prayer like Abraham, pleading his case argumentatively, giving reasons why God should answer him. Once he was persuaded that a thing was right, he would continue praying for it until the answer came.

He kept a complete record of his prayers. It covered 3,000 pages and contained nearly a million words. It chronicles over 50,000 specific answers to prayers.

It also records prayers that seemed to go unanswered, which brings us to one of the greatest problems of prayers. Why is it that prayers often seem to go unanswered? It is a question all Christians struggle with from time to time, often challenging their faith in God.

❖ The Mystery of Unanswered Prayer ❖

King David enjoyed many remarkable answers to his prayers. But from time to time, God seemed distant to him. Psalm 6 presents him crying out to a distant God, pleading for healing. "I am worn out with pain; every night my pillow is wet with tears. My eyes are growing old and dim with grief because of all my enemies" (Ps. 6:6–7).[12] On another occasion he lamented, "Why do You stand afar off, O Lord? Why do You hide Yourself in times of trouble?" (Ps. 10:1). Similar words can be found in Psalm

13:1: "How long, O Lord? Will you forget me forever? How long will You hide Your face from me?"

Have you ever been in that position? Have you ever felt like there was no one at the other end of the line when you were praying? If you pray regularly, you have experienced the silence of God. It was a common experience in biblical times, and I believe it is even more common today for several reasons.

❖ Living in the Fast Lane ❖

One reason relates to the nature of the world we live in. Our spiritual sensitivity has been dulled by modern technology. Because of the rapid pace of life in modern industrialized society, it is often difficult to hear God when He answers. How can we hear Him when we are living in the fast lane, madly rushing from one appointment to another? How can we hear God when a radio or television or CD player is constantly blaring? How can we hear when we are always exhausted from stress? How can we hear when we simply refuse to take time to listen? The point is that God may be answering but we can't hear.

We have developed a fast food mentality about everything in life. We want fast transportation, fast communication, fast medicine, fast education — and yes, we want fast religion. We don't have the patience to wait on God. We want to press Him into our own timetable.

❖ Coping with Theology ❖

Modern theology is another problem. It has desensitized us to the voice of God by telling us that God no longer speaks to people as He did in Bible times. It's reflected in the feeling of unease that we experience when a person tells us that God has "spoken" to him or her. Such people are written off by the world as "religious fanatics," so believers tend to shy away from listening to the voice of God, whether audible or as expressed in dreams, visions, and other forms of revelation, even a special word from the Scriptures.

At the opposite end of the theological spectrum are those who believe that the God of the Bible still operates today, but they feel they can manipulate Him into doing whatever they please through the recitation of magic prayer phrases. They act as if they have God on a string, ordering Him to heal or provide finances. In the process, they make promises to their people that God never made — promises like, "It is always God's will to heal." Then, when God fails to honor those "promises," the people are dumped on spiritually by being told they are at fault. They are blamed for having a lack of faith, or they are told that they have sin in their lives.

What is the real reason that prayers sometimes go unanswered? The Bible teaches there are several reasons. Certainly unbelief and sin are two of the reasons, but they are not always the reason.

❖ The Barriers of Sin and Unbelief ❖

The importance of praying with faith is emphasized throughout the Bible. Jesus said, "Whatever you ask in prayer, you will receive, if you have faith" (Matt. 21:22;RSV).[13] James taught that when we pray we are to "ask in faith without any doubting, for the one who doubts is like the surf of the sea driven and tossed by the wind." He adds, "That man ought not to expect that he will receive anything from the Lord" (James 1:6–7). He calls such a person "double-minded" (James 1:8).

Sin is also portrayed throughout the Bible as a major hindrance to prayer. A powerful statement concerning this point can be found in Isaiah 59:1–2:

> Behold, the Lord's hand is not so short That it cannot save; nor is His ear so dull That it cannot hear. But your iniquities have made a separation between you and your God, And your sins have hidden His face from you so that He does not hear.

David emphasized this point in Psalm 66:18: "If I regard wickedness in my heart, the Lord will not hear." The writer of Proverbs put it another way: "The Lord is far from the wicked, But He hears the prayer of the righteous" (Prov. 15:29). In the New Testament a blind man healed by Jesus summed up this principle succinctly when he told the Pharisees, "We know that God does not hear sinners; but if anyone is God-fearing and does His will, He hears him" (John 9:31).

❖ The Barriers of Arrogance and Selfishness ❖

Arrogance and selfishness are also great barriers to effective prayer. Humility in approaching God is an absolute necessity. In the Old Testament the people of God were told to "humble themselves and pray" (2 Chron. 7:14). In the New Testament we are told, "Humble yourselves under the mighty hand of God, that He may exalt you at the proper time, casting all your anxiety upon Him, because He cares for you" (1 Pet. 5:6–7). Jesus illustrated the importance of humility in prayer in a vivid way in his parable of the Pharisee and the tax collector (Luke 18:9–14).

James pronounces condemnation on selfish, "gimme" prayers in James 4:3: "You ask and do not receive, because you ask with wrong motives, so that you may spend it on your pleasures." That statement always reminds me of the fellow who needed a car to get to work. He prayed, "Lord, You know I need a car. You know it is essential to my livelihood. So, Lord, please provide me with a brand new, red Corvette." God promises to supply our needs, not our wishful desires.

❖ The Barrier of God's Will ❖

The most difficult barrier to prayer for us to understand and accept is the will of God. God is sovereign. He cannot be manipulated or deceived. His wisdom is far above ours, and His ways are not our ways (Rom. 11:33).

We don't always know what is best for us. In fact, if the truth were known, we probably rarely know what is best for us. We must keep in mind that God's purpose is to shape us into the image of Jesus (2 Cor. 3:18). To do that, God must at times allow adversity to come into our lives, first to get our attention, and then to develop qualities like perseverance, patience, and compassion. How, for example, could you have true compassion for a sick person if you have never been ill?

The effectiveness of all prayer is conditioned by God's will. The apostle John wrote, "This is the confidence we have before Him, that, if we ask anything according to His will, He hears us" (1 John 5:14). We don't like this condition because most of us really don't want God's will; we want our own.

I often run into this problem when I am contacted by women with barren wombs who want me to pray for them to conceive a child. Sometimes they will make it clear to me that they are determined to have a child, even if they have to resort to artificial insemination. When this happens, I point out to them that they are trying to play God and that my prayers for them will avail nothing unless they are willing to say, "Lord, your will be done." That advice usually makes them angry because they are not willing to submit to God's will.

❖ Knowing God's Will ❖

The other troublesome type of person I often encounter is the one who thinks they know God's will, when they really don't. I remember well the first time I ever encountered one of these people. I was in a Sunday school class, and we were going around a circle praying for specific prayer requests. When it came my turn, I started praying for a critically ill person. I asked the Lord to heal the person, and then I added, "if it be Your will."

A woman in the circle exploded over those words. She rudely interrupted my prayer by sneering, "If it be God's will? What do you mean? Of course it's God's will. You are not praying in faith!"

Well, the fact of the matter was that no one in that prayer circle knew for sure what God's will was for that critically ill person. It may have been His will to call that person home to be with Him.

Sometimes I am confident of God's will. I love to pray for lost people because I know for certain it is God's will that they be saved (2 Pet. 3:9). I love to pray for backsliders because I know it is God's will for them to repent and move on with their sanctification (Rom. 6:19–23). I love to pray for troubled marriages because I know it is God's will to heal them since He hates divorce (Mal. 2:16). But often, I simply do not know God's will, and so I pray for His will to be done, knowing that He is anxious to cause all things to work together for good for those who love Him (Rom. 8:28).

❖ God's Permissive Will ❖

Demanding your own will in prayer can get you in big trouble because God may decide in His permissive will to let you have your own way. You see, God has a perfect will and a permissive will. For example, it is His perfect will that all people be saved. But in His permissive will, He allows unrepentant rebels to be lost.

As we saw earlier, Hezekiah was not willing to accept God's perfect will that he die. He whined and cried and begged for a longer life. God granted his wish, giving him 15 more years. But look what happened during those years. He sired Manasseh, who became the most evil king in the history of Judah (2 Kings 21:1–2), and in a moment of pride, he showed the riches of the temple to the representatives of the king of Babylon, whetting their appetite to conquer Jerusalem (Isa. 39:1–6).

❖ Discerning God's Will ❖

How can we know the will of God? One way to seek God's will is to search His Word, praying for Him to give you insight and discernment. The Word is "living and active and sharper than any two-edged sword . . . able to judge the thoughts and intentions of the heart (Heb. 4:12).

Another way is to get to know God. The better you know Him, the easier it will be for you to discern His will. And the only way you can get to know Him is to spend time with Him in His Word and in prayer. It's like getting to know anyone. You have to spend time with them. As you do so, you come to know their likes and dislikes.

God hears prayer, and He answers prayer. When He does not seem to answer, when He appears to be silent, we need to review the hindrances to prayer to see if any exist in our lives. If they do not, then we need to exercise faith that God has heard and will answer in His own time and in His own way.

❖ Various Answers to Prayer ❖

The answer may be "Yes" — as it often is. But the answer may be "No," as it was when Paul prayed for deliverance from his "thorn in the flesh" (2 Cor. 12:7). God refused to remove the problem, but He granted Paul the grace to cope with it (2 Cor. 12:9). The answer may also be "Wait!" In that case the Lord may be calling us to patience and perseverance, and even to suffering. Or, He may have something better in mind for us than what we think is best.

The answer might even be one that we do not understand, or one that on the surface appears to be unpleasant or foolish. This type of answer often requires the greatest faith, as when God

told Abraham to pull up stakes and go into the desert to an unknown destination so that he, who was too old to have children,
could become the father of a great nation. Or consider the foolishness of God when He told Moses at the Red Sea to lift his rod
when there was no means of escaping the Egyptian army. Or think
of Joshua who was told to conquer Jericho by marching and blowing horns.

❖ Your Will or God's? ❖

The bottom line is whether you always want what you ask for
or whether you want God's will to be done in your life. The will of
God is what is always best for you. Consider the following prayer:

> I asked for strength, that I might achieve.
> He made me weak, that I might obey.
>
> I asked for health, that I might do great things.
> I was given grace, that I might do better things.
>
> I asked for riches, that I might be happy.
> I was given poverty, that I might be wise.
>
> I asked for power, that I might have the praise of men.
> I was given weakness, that I might feel the need of God.
>
> I asked for all things, that I might enjoy life.
> I was given life, that I might enjoy all things.
>
> I received nothing that I asked for;
> All that I hoped for.
>
> My prayers were answered.[14]

An "unanswered prayer" resulted in the greatest blessing the
world has ever received. The prayer was prayed in anguish by a
desperate man in a lonely garden 2,000 years ago: "Father, if it is
possible, let this cup pass from Me" (Matt. 26:39). But this prayer
really was answered, because when Jesus prayed it, He added,
"Not as I will, but as You will" (Matt. 26:39).

Let us praise God for the answer He gave to that prayer. Let
us praise God for the answers He still gives to prayer.

❖ Praying in the End Times ❖

How then shall we pray in these end times? The answer is earnestly, persistently, specifically, and in faith. As to subject, there are two things in particular we need to pray for — one is national revival and the other is for those in positions of authority.

The Bible strongly urges us to pray for our public officials (1 Tim. 2:1–3), from the city council to the Congress, from mayors to the president, and from local courts to the Supreme Court. Prayer for public officials is especially important because Satan is the "ruler of this world" (John 12:31). Yes, he was defeated at the Cross, but all aspects of his defeat have not yet been actualized. That's why John wrote long after the Cross, "The whole world lies in the power of the evil one" (1 John 5:19).

God is the one who puts all governmental leaders in their positions of authority, and He is the one who removes them (Dan. 2:21). But the moment He entrusts governmental authority to any person, Satan moves that person up on his hit list and comes against them, seeking to compromise and control them. That's why there has always been widespread political corruption and always will be. That's why we are exhorted to pray for our governing authorities.

❖ Praying for Revival ❖

We also need to pray fervently for national revival. Our nation may have descended into paganism, but there is still opportunity for spiritual revival. The greatest national revival recorded in the Bible was one that occurred in Judah during the reign of Josiah. It occurred after the reign of Judah's most evil king, Manasseh, a man who reigned for 55 years, longer than any other of Judah's kings (2 Chron. 33:1–2).

When Josiah ascended to the throne at age 8, there appeared to be no hope for his country. But the Bible says that when he was 16, he "began to seek the God of his father David" (2 Chron. 34:3). He purged the land of idols and slaughtered the priests of the false religions. He repaired the temple, restored God's Word to his people, and publicly repented for his nation (2 Chron. 34:3–21). In response, God poured out His Spirit, just as He had promised He would do many years before when He told Solomon, "If

My people who are called by My name humble themselves and pray and seek My face and turn from their wicked ways, then I will hear from heaven, will forgive their sin and will heal their land" (2 Chron. 7:14).

❖ A Call to Prayer ❖

In these end times, let's pray as we have never prayed before, that God will raise up righteous governmental leaders who will govern according to His Word, and not according to public opinion polls. Let's pray with even greater zeal for the Lord to raise up godly spiritual leaders to call our nation to repentance and lead us into national revival.

That revival can begin with you, in your heart. What you must do is humble yourself, repent, and seek the Lord in prayer in behalf of yourself, your family, your church, your state, and your nation.

If God could launch a national revival through a 16-year-old boy, why couldn't He do the same through you? You may be thinking, *But Josiah was a king, and I am only a housewife or a simple day laborer.* But if you are born again, then you are a child of a King — the King of this universe. That makes you spiritual royalty, so don't underestimate what you can accomplish through the power of God's Spirit.

Throw aside the doubts and the excuses, and *pray!*

Endnotes
1 The first time I encountered the thought-provoking question, "If you stop praying, would it radically affect your life?" was in the devotional book on prayer entitled *Pray!* The book was written by Ben Haden (Nashville, TN: Thomas Nelson, Inc., 1974). On the general subject of prayer, I highly recommend the books of Charles L. Allen. They include *God's Psychiatry, Prayer Changes Things, All Things are Possible Through Prayer,* and *The Lord's Prayer.*
2 William Shakespeare, *Hamlet*, Act III, Scene 3. The text of this play is available on the Internet at http://www.gh.cs.usyd.edu.au/~matty/Shakespeare/texts/tragedies/hamlet_0.html.
3 Frances R. Havergal, "Take My Life and Let It Be," 1874, public domain.

4 Carl Sandburg, *Complete Poems* (New York: Harcourt Brace Jovanovich, 1950), p. 105.

5 *The Living Bible Paraphrased* (Wheaton, IL: Tyndale House Publishers, 1971).

6 Augustine, *The Confessions of Saint Augustine,* translated by Edward B. Pusey (New York: Modern Library, 1999). The text of Augustine's *Confessions* is available on the Internet from the Collier Books edition: http://ccel.wheaton.edu/augustine/confessions/confessions.htm.

7 Augustine, Book 5, Chapter VII, Section 15.

8 Haden, *Pray!* — no page numbers in the book.

9 George Washington Carver, *George Washington Carver: In His Own Words,* Gary R. Kremer, editor (Columbia, MO: University of Missouri Press, 1991, reprint edition). An excellent modern biography is *George Washington Carver: Scientist and Symbol* by Linda O. McMurray. (New York: Oxford University Press, 1981).

10 There are many variations of this prayer in the many biographies that have been written about Carver. One can be found in *George Washington Carver* by Rackham Holt (Farden City, NY: Doubleday Co., Inc., 1943), p. 239–240. The version I have quoted is a composite of the various versions.

11 Faith Cox Bailey, *George Mueller* (Chicago, IL: Moody Press, 1980).

12 *The Living Bible Paraphrased.*

13 *The Holy Bible*, Revised Standard Version (Grand Rapids, MI: Zondervan Bible Publishers, 1962).

14 Source unknown. This prayer has been published in many different versions and has been attributed to a great variety of sources. The version presented here is a composite prepared by the author.

Chapter 11

❖ ❖ ❖

Surrendering in Worship

A young boy was fascinated by the huge American flag that his pastor always had displayed on the wall behind the pulpit. One Sunday morning the boy went up to his pastor and asked, "Pastor, why do you always have that big American flag on the wall?"

The pastor leaned down, patted the boy on his head, and replied, "Son, that flag is to honor those who have died in the service."

To which the boy replied, "Which service? The morning or evening?"

❖ Death in Worship ❖

Have you ever "been there and done that"? It's certainly not a new problem in the Church.

Luke tells us that the Church of the first century suffered from the same problem. In Acts 20 he says that when he and Paul were in Troas, they experienced a casualty in worship. Paul got long-winded and preached to midnight, and a young man named Eutychus, who was sitting on a windowsill on the third floor, fell asleep and dropped to the floor. Luke says he was "picked up dead," but Paul brought him back to life (Acts 20:7–12).

❖ Life in Worship ❖

In contrast, the Bible also records some glorious worship experiences. One that comes to mind is what Isaiah experienced when, as a teenager, he went to the temple in Jerusalem to mourn the loss of the only king he had ever known — King Uzziah (Isa. 6:1–8).

As Isaiah lamented the loss of his king, he suddenly discovered the King of kings! John tells us that Isaiah was given the blessing of seeing Jesus in a pre-incarnate appearance (John 12:41).

As Isaiah put it, "I saw the Lord sitting on a throne, lofty and exalted, with the train of His robe filling the temple" (Isa. 6:1). Angelic beings called Seraphim were flying around the Lord's throne crying out, "Holy, Holy, Holy is the Lord of hosts, The whole earth is full of His glory" (Isa. 6:3).

Isaiah was instantly aware of his sinfulness as he stood in the presence of pure holiness. He covered his face with his hands and cried out, "Woe is me, for I am ruined! Because I am a man of unclean lips . . . For my eyes have seen the King, the Lord of hosts" (Isa. 6:5). But then, something transforming occurred.

One of the Seraphim took a burning coal from the temple's altar, touched it to Isaiah's mouth, and proclaimed, "Behold . . . your iniquity is taken away, and your sin is forgiven" (Isa. 6:7). Isaiah experienced the grace of God!

The Lord then asked, "Whom shall I send, and who will go for Us?"

At that moment, Isaiah surrendered to the Lord. Reaching out to God, he cried, "Here am I. Send me!" (Isa. 6:8).

❖ Created for Worship ❖

What a contrast we have in these two worship services. In one there was death; in the other, rebirth. Which characterizes your usual worship experience? How would you describe what you have experienced in worship recently? Simulating or deadening? Exciting or boring? Intimate or impersonal? Participatory or passive? Joyous or somber?

Worship is a serious matter, and the time is long overdue for the Church to get serious about it. We were created for the purpose of worship. To emphasize this point, Jesus said that God the Father actively seeks worshipers who will worship Him "in spirit and truth" (John 4:23–24). King David, who was one of the most passionate worshipers who ever lived, wrote in Psalm 22 that God inhabits the praises of His people (Ps. 22:3).

Worship is essential to our spiritual growth. Our spirits were designed to feed upon it, just as they feed upon the Word. This is one of the reasons that the author of Hebrews admonished us to never forsake the assembling of the saints (Heb. 10:25).

Despite the importance given to worship by the Scriptures, most worship services today seem to contribute more to apathy than anything else. In the words of Paul, they have "a form of godliness" but "they have denied its power" (2 Tim. 3:5). There is religion but no Spirit, and in the absence of the Spirit, there is deadness.

❖ Song Leading vs. Worship Leading ❖

When I conduct a meeting at a church, I always send the pastor a letter in which I explain that there are two keys to a successful meeting. One is prayer before I get there; the other is worship while I'm there. To implement the latter, I always tell the pastor to find a worship leader as opposed to a song leader.

The sad thing is that the pastor often calls me and asks the difference in a song leader and a worship leader! There is an enormous difference. A song leader leads people in singing, like the director of a choir. A worship leader guides people into the presence of God.

A good worship leader must first of all be a person filled with the Spirit. He must be humble, and he must have a passion for God. He must be willing to be transparent before the congregation, dropping all pretense as he gives himself in worship to the Lord.

One of the most effective worship leaders I ever encountered was a fellow who would lead the worshipers into a song and then would disappear into the congregation with his microphone, continuing to guide the service but determined that people would focus on the Lord and not on him. You could hear his voice, but you could not see him! It reminded me of the humble black man, William J. Seymour, who led the Azusa Street revival that gave birth to the Pentecostal movement in the early 1900s. He always preached from behind a sheet that hung from the ceiling because he wanted folks to concentrate on the Word of God and not him.[1]

❖ Problems with Worship Today ❖

What is wrong with the worship of the Church today? Why does it so often lack power? Why does it so seldom bring us into the presence of God?

Well, for one thing, it is usually stifled by tradition. Few things in life are as powerful as tradition. Jesus was crucified for violating the sacred traditions of the religious leaders of His day. They were outraged when He called them hypocrites for neglecting the commandments of God in order to hold on to the traditions of men (Mark 7:6–8).

All of us tend to be slaves of tradition to one degree or another. We get into a rut, and we get comfortable in it. Worship becomes a meaningless habit of empty ritual that has a numbing effect. We go through the motions, but there is no substance. We end up worshiping our traditions instead of God.

The seven deadliest words in the Church are, "We've never done it that way before." I saw a cartoon that reminded me of these words. It showed a fellow walking up the steps of a gallows. His hands were tied behind his back. The hangman was waiting at the top. The fellow had paused halfway up and was looking down at the crowd of spectators. Incredulously, he says, "All I did was suggest a change in worship!"

I'm also reminded of the story of the traveling salesman who stopped to attend a church he had never visited before. Halfway through the sermon, he yelled, "Praise the Lord!" A few moments later an usher tapped him on the shoulder and whispered in his ear, "We don't praise the Lord in this church."

Do you have some sacred traditions of worship that you are not willing to surrender? Does ritual mean more to you than relationship? Have your traditions become idols that stand between you and God?

❖ Hardened by Doctrine ❖

Another problem with worship today is that it has often become hardened by doctrine. The church I grew up in put its emphasis in worship on what was referred to as "the New Testament pattern." But that pattern was more imaginary than real.

The fact of the matter is that there is no prescribed ritual or pattern of worship in the New Testament. It is highly doubtful that the Jewish church in Jerusalem worshiped in the same manner as the Gentile church in Antioch. And what about the Ethiopian eunuch who returned to Africa with only the Hebrew Scriptures? I would imagine that the worship he established in the first

African church was heavily patterned after the ritualistic worship of the Jewish temple.

The closest thing to a pattern of worship that exists in the New Testament is found in 1 Corinthians 14:26. Yet it is one that my boyhood church would never have considered following since it mentions speaking in tongues: "When you assemble, each one has a psalm, has a teaching, has a revelation, has a tongue, has an interpretation. Let all things be done for edification" (1 Cor. 14:26).

❖ Freedom in Christ ❖

The fact of the matter is that we have the freedom in Christ to worship as the Holy Spirit leads (Rom. 14:1–15:7). If any group wants to give special spiritual significance to the Sabbath rather than Sunday, they have the right to do so. No one has a right to condemn them, and they have no right to condemn those who do not honor the same day. The same is true of the use of musical instruments. I grew up in a church that condemned the use of musical instruments in worship. That was wrong. We had the freedom in Christ to sing a cappella, but we did not have the freedom to condemn those who used musical instruments.

The same is true regarding many other aspects of worship such as the frequency of communion. Some churches observe the Lord's Supper yearly; others observe it quarterly; others, weekly; and some, daily. Jesus said, "As often as you eat this bread and drink the cup" we are to do it in remembrance of Him (1 Cor. 11:25–26). He didn't prescribe how often. His focus was on meaning rather than frequency.

❖ Legalistic Bickering ❖

When the focus shifts from meaning to method, we become modern-day Pharisees. The church I grew up in is a good example of this. We divided every way imaginable — and some unimaginable — over the method of communion. We had one-cup brethren who would not associate with those who used multiple cups. We had the wine-before-the-bread brethren who disassociated themselves from those who took the bread first. There were those who insisted that the symbol of the Lord's blood had to be wine, whereas most insisted on grape juice. Some demanded that communion come before the sermon, but others insisted it come last in the service to give it more importance.

Observing all this legalistic bickering, a friend of mine expressed the opinion that he was sure glad that foot washing had never become an ordinance in our church. "Just think," he said, "if we practiced foot washing, we would have undoubtedly divided over such things as whether or not the feet should be wiped dry with a towel or be blown dry with a hair dryer!"

❖ Suppressed by Prejudice and Fear ❖

Another major hindrance to worship in these end times is prejudice and fear. We often find ourselves shying away from perfectly legitimate biblical worship practices because some other group does them. In the church of my heritage, we could not have stained glass windows or choirs because "the denominations have them." (We considered ourselves to be "non-denominational.") We couldn't take up love offerings because that practice was considered to be "Baptist." Kneeling was thought of as "Episcopalian," and the mourner's bench was taboo because it was "Methodist."

All that sounds downright silly. But it is no sillier than mainline denominations today who refuse to clap their hands because it's "Pentecostal," or refrain from raising their hands because it's "Charismatic," or resist dancing because it's "Messianic."

The church I grew up in was never expressive in worship unless we had a certain famous black evangelist come to town who always brought his own song leader with him. Then, we would clap our hands tentatively as we sang, because "black people expect that." I'm glad God has a sense of humor, otherwise I don't know how He could put up with us when it comes to our prejudicial hang-ups about worship. We need to put the prejudice and the fear aside concerning the methods of worship and focus instead on the meaning.

That's what David did when he danced before the ark of the covenant as it was carried into Jerusalem. He threw tradition to the wind as he exhorted the people to shout, sing, blow trumpets, and clang cymbals while he twirled and leaped before the ark in a frenzy of celebration. His wife was embarrassed by this behavior and rebuked him for it. David's response, put in modern English, was, "Honey, you ain't seen nothing yet!" (2 Sam. 6:12–23 and 1 Chron. 15:25–29).

❖ Victimized by Time ❖

Our worship has been stifled by tradition, hardened by doctrine, and suppressed by prejudice and fear. It has also been victimized by time. We live in a hurry-up world of fast food and fast medicine. We also want fast worship, particularly if the kick-off time for the TV football game is 12 noon! When it comes to worship, the attitude of many Christians seems to be "the less, the better." It's so amazing when you stop to think about it. We seem to lack time-consciousness about all other activities. We rejoice when we attend a sports event and it goes into overtime. We feel like we are getting more for our money. But not so at church.

Most Christians seem to want the kind of church I saw in a cartoon. It had a signboard that read: "The Lite Church," and explained the meaning of the name by specifying that it was the church of "the 7.5% tithe, the 45-minute worship service, the 12-minute sermon, the 8 commandments, the 3 spiritual laws, and the 800 year millennium."

Are you a spiritual time watcher? If so, I have a question for you. If you are miserable one hour a week in the Lord's presence, why do you think you will enjoy being in His presence for eternity? I suspect that for those of you who are time conscious, you will never have to worry about that problem. The reason, of course, is that if you are uncomfortable one hour a week in the Lord's presence, it's because you have no personal relationship with Him — which means, in turn, that you are not born again, for the essence of salvation is knowing the Lord. That's not my opinion. It is from the Bible. Jesus said, "This is eternal life, that they may know You, the only true God, and Jesus Christ whom You have sent" (John 17:3).

❖ Distorted by Attitude ❖

Another problem with contemporary worship is that it has been distorted by attitude — by the attitude we bring to it. So many believe that the essence of worship is the long face, clothed in dignity, piety, and liturgy. The result is that our worship services often resemble a funeral service more than anything else, and that is a tragedy, for it communicates a lie. We do not worship a Lord who is hanging on a cross. Nor is He lying in a grave in Israel. Our Lord is alive! He is sitting at the right hand of His

Father in Heaven. We need to celebrate His victory over death.

Yes, there is a time in worship to move from celebration to adoration, from rejoicing to loving, from thanksgiving to surrender, from exclamation to introspection, and from handclapping to weeping. But worship should begin with celebration — celebration of who God is and what He has done for us. The Psalmist expressed this in Psalm 105:1-2 where he urged us to "give thanks to the Lord. . . . Sing to Him . . . Speak of all His wonders [what He has done]. Glory in His name [who He is]."

We are not the "Frozen Chosen." We are called to be a "Rejoicing Remnant": And the ransomed of the Lord will return And come with joyful shouting to Zion, With everlasting joy upon our heads. They will find gladness and joy, And sorrow and sighing will flee away (Isa. 35:10).

❖ A Negative Worship Experience ❖

In all my years of traveling among a great variety of churches, I have experienced some glorious worship services, but I have also had to sit through some that were horrendous. I remember a church in Kentucky where the song leader (who was anything but a worship leader!) got up on a Sunday morning and literally snarled at the congregation. I figured he must have had a fight with his wife on the way to church. Barking orders like a Marine drill sergeant, he snapped, "Everyone turn to number 254! That's 2-5-4!" Then, to my total amazement, he growled, "The name of this song is 'Stand Up, Stand Up, for Jesus,' but I don't want to inconvenience any of you, so we're going to sing it sitting down." It was anything but an inspirational moment.

By the time I got up to preach, it was like chipping away at ice. I decided I had to take drastic action. So, when I got back to my motel, I got down on my knees and prayed, "Lord, do something about the cranky song leader. Deliver us from him."

That night when I returned for the evening service, the elders of the church were huddled in the foyer having a meeting. I asked what was wrong. They explained that the song leader had been called by his boss and told that he must go to Tennessee immediately to take care of some business. I had prayed him right out of the state! I found it hard to conceal my joy. I then convinced the elders to let me get on the phone and find a true worship leader.

❖ Perverted by Concept ❖

Sometimes our worship is perverted by concept. Many Christians consider worship to be a spectator sport, so they come as an audience, expecting to be entertained. The concept is one of "I pay my money, and I expect the pros to deliver."

But true worship requires participation. To worship, one must get involved. If anyone is the audience, it is God, but in true worship, even God is not an audience. He gets involved. He enthrones himself upon our praises (Ps. 22:3). He ministers to our spirit. He encourages us and empowers us. I have even been in worship services where people were healed by the Lord without anyone ever touching them or praying for them.

God does not sit aloof on His throne analyzing our worship and then grading it by holding up a card with a number on it — like a judge at an ice skating competition. He is a personal God who desires intimacy with us. He is responsive.

Wouldn't it feel strange if you told the one you love how much you love him or her, and continued to do so for an hour — only to have that person sit stone-faced without giving any response? I think you would get turned off very quickly. That is what happens when people approach God in rigid, stylistic worship that is based on a conception that God is aloof, distant, intransigent, and unresponsive.

There is another concept we often bring to worship that has a stagnating effect. It is the self-centered concept that we are giving God an opportunity to minister to us. This concept results in the worshiper coming selfishly to receive rather than to give.

The paradox of worship is that God can minister to us only to the degree that we are willing and able to lose ourselves in praise and adoration of Him. We must humble ourselves and reach out to the Father as little children, crying "Abba! Father!" (Rom. 8:15).

❖ Remedies for the Problems ❖

Let's review. I have pointed out that the worship of the contemporary Church has been stifled by tradition, hardened by doctrine, suppressed by prejudice and fear, victimized by time, distorted by attitude, and perverted by concept. What can we do about these problems? How can we bring renewal to the worship of the 21st century Church?

The first thing we need to do is focus on developing a personal relationship with God. The reason this is so important is because true worship is based on intimacy. You cannot truly worship God until you know Him — not know *about* Him, but know Him.

❖ Knowing God ❖

I grew up in an atmosphere where I knew a lot about God, but I didn't really know Him. I had no personal relationship with Him. Let me give you an example of what I'm talking about. I am an admirer of Billy Graham. I have listened to many of his sermons. I have read all of his books, and I have read several of his biographies. I know a lot *about* Billy Graham, but I do not know him. I have never met him. I have never sat down one-on-one, looked him in the eye, and talked with him about personal matters. Likewise, it is possible to know a lot about God, but not really know God at all.

This is one of the main reasons that changes in worship can cause such major problems in a church. You see, it is one thing to sing songs *about* God. It is quite another to sing love songs *to* God. A person who only knows about God has no problem singing a song like "Faith of Our Fathers." But if you suddenly ask that person to sing a song like, "I Love You, Lord," the person will get very uncomfortable. Think how you would feel if someone were to ask you to sing a love song to someone you've never met!

The introduction of true worship into any church takes time. It must be preceded and accompanied by a lot of teaching and preaching about God and worship. Unfortunately, what usually happens is that a young pastor who is starved for intimacy in worship goes to a conference where he experiences two or three days of divinely inspired worship. He returns home anxious for his congregation to have the same experience. Then, without any preparatory teaching, he hides the songbooks, projects choruses on a screen, and demands that his congregation stand for 30 minutes while they sing. To the pastor's dismay, the congregation is not edified in the least. Rather, all hell breaks loose, and he finds himself looking for a new church.

The Church today is full of worldly, carnal Christians who do not desire intimacy with God. They prefer a ritual God at arm's length who is not concerned with their sins.

❖ Opening Ourselves to the Spirit ❖

Another important key to worship renewal is opening ourselves up to the outpouring of the Holy Spirit that characterizes these end times. Unless we do that, our attitudes will never change. The Holy Spirit is desirous of raising up a Church in these end times that has given its heart to worship. Jesus is about to return, and the Father desires that He return on a cloud of praise.

The Bible clearly prophesies that one of the characteristics or signs of the end times will be a revival of worship. Specifically, the Bible says there will be a revival of Davidic praise worship with its lifting of hands, clapping, shouting, waving of banners, and dancing. The prophecy is found in Amos 9:11–12:

> "In that day I will raise up the fallen tabernacle of David, And wall up its breaches; I will also raise up its ruins And rebuild it as in the days of old; That they may possess the remnant of Edom And all the nations who are called by My name," Declares the Lord who does this.

❖ Prophetic Fulfillment ❖

Most Christians are familiar with this prophecy because it is quoted in Acts 15. The occasion was a special conference of church leaders that was called in Jerusalem to consider the momentous implications of Gentiles being added to the Church. In the midst of the debate, James, the leader of the Jerusalem church, quoted this prophecy from Amos to prove that it was God's intention to someday include the Gentiles in His scheme of redemption.

This usage of the prophecy has historically led to the conclusion that the term, "the tabernacle of David," refers to the Church, and perhaps it does in a spiritual sense. But the context of the passage in the Book of Amos makes it clear that the prophecy will find its ultimate fulfillment in something other than the establishment of the Church.

Note that the prophecy begins with the words, "In that day." What day? A quick glance at the prophecy in its context shows that the "day" being referred to is the period of time when the Jews are re-gathered to the land of Israel (see Amos 9:14–15).

That began in the 20th century. There were 40,000 Jews in Israel in 1900. Today, there are nearly five million. They re-established their state on May 14, 1948, and they have re-gathered their people from the four corners of the earth.

Has anything happened since 1948 that could constitute a literal fulfillment of the restoration of the "tabernacle of David"? To answer this question we must first seek to understand the meaning of the term, "tabernacle of David." What did Amos have in mind when he used this term?

❖ The Tabernacle of Moses ❖

To fully understand the tabernacle of David, we must first begin with a consideration of the tabernacle of Moses. It was a nomadic temple that moved with the Children of Israel as they crossed the wilderness of Sinai in search of the Promised Land. Its Holy of Holies contained the ark of the covenant where the Shekinah glory of God resided.

When the Children of Israel entered the Promised Land, they settled the tabernacle of Moses at Shiloh in Samaria. There the sacrificial ceremonies were conducted for 400 years during the period of the judges. By the end of that chaotic period, the Children of Israel were engulfed in spiritual darkness, having fallen victim to idolatry and immorality.

One day during the judgeship of Samuel, as the Israelites were preparing to fight the Philistines, they decided to take the ark of the covenant into battle with them, as if it were some sort of good luck charm. They evidently reasoned that God would never allow the Philistines to capture the ark, and therefore they would win the battle. The Lord was not pleased by this action, so He allowed the Philistines to defeat the Israelites and capture the sacred ark (1 Sam. 4:1–11). They also proceeded to destroy the tabernacle of Moses at Shiloh (Jer. 7:12). Israel had become "Ichabod," (meaning, "no glory") for the glory of God had departed (1 Sam. 4:21).

❖ The Odyssey of the Ark ❖

Plagues afflicted the Philistines, so they sent the ark back to Israel on an ox cart. It finally came to rest eight miles west of Jerusalem in a town called Kiriath-jearim (called Abu Gosh today) where it stayed for approximately 70 years (20 years under Samuel's judgeship, 40 years under Saul's kingship, and almost 10 years into David's kingship). The tabernacle of Moses was moved to Nob for a while (1 Sam. 21:1) and then on to Gibeon (about ten miles northwest of Jerusalem) where it remained until the temple of Solomon was built (2 Chron. 1:3).

Now, note something very important. During this 70-year period of transition between the judges and the kings, there was no Shekinah glory in the tabernacle of Moses located at Gibeon. The Holy of Holies was empty. The priests continued to minister at the tabernacle, offering daily sacrifices, but it was all dead ritual, for the glory had departed.

The astounding thing is that the ark was located in a farmhouse situated only about five miles from Gibeon. It would have been very easy to restore the ark to the tabernacle of Moses, but no one cared enough to do so. The ark was ignored, and it became a symbol of Israel's apostasy.

❖ Saul vs. David ❖

Saul did not have a heart for the Lord, so he ignored the estrangement of the ark from its proper resting place. But when David became king, he was determined to correct this situation, for he was a man after God's own heart (1 Sam. 13:14). David had to wait seven and a half years until he became king of all Israel (he was king of only Judah during his first years in power — see 2 Sam. 5:5).

David was determined to bring God back into the heart of his nation, and he recognized the symbolic significance of the ark in accomplishing this purpose. He was so determined to provide a proper resting place for the ark that it became the top priority of his kingship. In this regard, we are told in Psalm 132 that when David became king of all of Israel, he "swore to the Lord" that he would not sleep in a bed until he could provide a proper "dwelling place for the Mighty One of Jacob" (Ps. 132:1–5).

❖ The Tabernacle of David ❖

The amazing thing is that David brought the ark to Jerusalem rather than returning it to the Holy of Holies in the tabernacle of Moses at Gibeon. David pitched a tent in Jerusalem (probably on a slope of Mount Moriah), placed the ark inside, and instituted a whole new concept of praise worship. Instruments of worship were introduced. Special psalms of praise were written and sung. Incredibly, special priests were appointed to minister music before the ark *continually* (1 Chron.16:6, 37) — whereas only the high priest had been allowed to minister before the ark once a year in the tabernacle of Moses.

In fact, the Scriptures indicate that there was such great intimacy with the Lord, that David would actually lounge before the ark (1 Chron. 17:16). It is probably during these times of intimacy that he wrote new songs to the Lord (Ps. 40:3).

David's revolution in worship was very radical. There was no singing or celebration at the tabernacle of Moses. The worship there was one of solemn ritual focused on sacrifices. The only joy that had ever been evidenced in the worship of the Israelites had occurred spontaneously, as when Miriam danced with a tambourine and rejoiced over the destruction of Pharaoh and his army (Exod. 15).

The Psalms make it clear that the praise worship inaugurated by David was a worship of great joy that was characterized by handclapping (Ps. 47:1), shouting (Ps. 47:1), singing (Ps. 47:6–7), dancing (Ps. 149:3), hand waving (Ps. 134:2), and the display of banners (Ps. 20:5). The worshipers were encouraged to praise God with every form of musical instrument, from the gentle lyre to the "loud crashing cymbals" (Ps. 150: 3, 5).

❖ The Davidic Revolution ❖

But why? Why did David so radically change the worship of Israel? We are told in 2 Chronicles 29:25 that he did so in response to commands of God given to him through the prophets Nathan and Gad. But why didn't the Lord simply tell David to put the ark back in the Holy of Holies in Gibeon? Why did God tell him to revolutionize the worship of Israel?

The Bible does not tell us why. We can only guess. My guess is that God wanted to give David a prophetic glimpse of the glorious Church Age to come when animal sacrifices would cease, worshipers would have direct access to God, and worshipers would come before the Lord in rejoicing with a sacrifice of praise. I think there was also another reason. I believe the Lord wanted to give the Church a model for Spirit-filled worship.

For one generation (about 30 years under David and 12 years into Solomon's reign), two tabernacles existed in Israel. In Gibeon there was the dead, liturgical worship that characterized the tabernacle of Moses. In Jerusalem, there was the lively, spontaneous worship that characterized the tabernacle of David. The worship in Gibeon was the performance of ritualistic symbolism. The worship in Zion was the experience of the presence of God. At Gibeon, the priests offered the sacrifice of animals. At Zion, the offering was the sacrifice of praise: "Come before Him with joyful singing. . . . Enter His gates with thanksgiving And His courts with praise" (Ps. 100:2–4). Study for a moment the listing of differences between the two forms of worship as outlined in Table 2.

Table 2
A Comparison of Worship at Gibeon and Zion

The Tabernacle of Moses in Gibeon	The Tabernacle of David in Jerusalem
1. Form	1. Substance
2. Type	2. Reality
3. Liturgy	3. Spontaneity
4. Ritual	4. Celebration
5. Sacrifice of Animals	5. Sacrifice of Praise
6. Tradition	6. Innovation
7. Deadness	7. Life
8. Heaviness	8. Joy
9. Religion	9. Relationship
10. Intercession	10. Intimacy
11. Symbols	11. God

❖ The Prophetic Significance ❖

The tabernacle of David served as a joyous bridge between the spiritual deadness that had come to characterize the tabernacle of Moses and the Spirit-filled glory that would characterize the temple of Solomon.

In like manner, since the re-establishment of the nation of Israel in 1948, God has been raising up the tabernacle of David again to serve as a joyous bridge of transition between the dead worship of mainline Christendom and the glorious worship that will characterize the millennial temple of Jesus Christ. As I said before, God wants His Son to return on a cloud of praise.

The literal tabernacle of David today consists of those churches that have rediscovered the true meaning of worship and have given their people the freedom in Christ to worship God with all their energy, resources, gifts, and talents.

❖   The Worldwide Spread   ❖

Appropriately, God began to focus His revival of the tabernacle of David in Jerusalem in the early 1980s. It occurred when the International Christian Embassy decided to host a celebration of the Feast of Tabernacles. Zechariah 14 says that during the millennial reign of Jesus the nations will send representatives to Jerusalem each year to celebrate this feast and that any nation that fails to do so will not receive rain. The embassy decided it would be appropriate for Gentiles to start rehearsing for the Millennium, so they sent out a call worldwide for Christians to come to Jerusalem to celebrate the feast and to show their support of Israel.[2]

The embassy also decided to give an emphasis to Davidic praise worship which was springing up all over the world at that time through a sovereign move of the Holy Spirit. They brought together Christendom's best practitioners of celebratory worship.[3]

The result was an explosion of Davidic worship all over the world as the thousands of Christians who came to Jerusalem took what they had experienced back home with them in their hearts and on videos. The embassy's celebration has continued to this day, with 4,000 to 6,000 Christians attending annually from every continent.

❖   A Move of the Spirit   ❖

The rediscovery of the true meaning of worship is the reason that renewal in worship is sweeping Christendom worldwide. It is a move of the Spirit. It is a fulfillment of prophecy. It is a mark of the end times. It is a sign of the soon return of Jesus. It is preparation for that day very soon when:

You will go out with joy And be led forth with peace; The mountains and the hills will break forth into shouts of joy before you, And all the trees of the field will clap their hands (Isa. 55:12).

That is the day when the tabernacle of David will be restored completely. As we pray for it, and prepare for it, let's cry out in our spirits, "Maranatha!" (1 Cor. 16:22).

Endnotes

1 Frank Bartleman, *Azusa Street* (South Plainfield, NJ: Bridge Publishing, 1980), originally published in 1925.

2 The International Christian Embassy in Jerusalem has a website at http://www.intournet.co.il/icej. Videos of the Embassy's annual celebration of the Feast of Tabernacles are available through this site or by writing to P.O. Box 1192, Jerusalem, Israel 91010.

3 One of the foremost practitioners and teachers of Davidic worship in the world today is Randall Bane who heads up a ministry called David's House. The ministry conducts conferences featuring Davidic praise worship and also distributes teaching programs on video tape. To contact the ministry, write to P.O. Box 411831, Kansas City, MO 64141. The ministry's website is located at http://www.davidshouse.org.

Chapter 12

❖ ❖ ❖

Clinging to Hope

H ope is essential to life. Without it, people descend into deep depression or commit suicide or simply lie down and die. During the Holocaust, Viktor Frankl, who later became a world-renowned psychiatrist, was a prisoner in one of the Nazi death camps. He observed that every year as Christmas approached, hope would sweep the camp that the prisoners would be released on Christmas Day. It was an irrational hope, but it was hope. Then, when Christmas would come and go without a release, hundreds of prisoners would just lie down and die. Without hope, they could not live.[1] Frankl concluded, "It is a peculiarity of man that he can only live by looking to the future."[2]

❖ A Desperate Need ❖

The world desperately needs hope in these end times. We live in a world of increasing fears — fear of nuclear holocaust, economic collapse, plagues like AIDS, terrorism, war, and — of course — fear of life and of death. Christians also need hope, particularly as they face increasing persecution.

Some might respond by saying, "Christians are the only ones who have any hope!" That is true, but the problem is that most professing Christians cannot articulate their hope beyond a vague statement like, "My hope is heaven."

❖ An Ignored Virtue ❖

I came to this realization one day when I was reading Paul's great love poem in 1 Corinthians 13. It ends with the famous phrase, "There are three things that remain [or abide] — faith, hope, and love — and the greatest of these is love" (1 Cor. 13:13).[3]

As I thought about those words, it suddenly occurred to me that I had heard hundreds of sermons on faith and hundreds on love, but I could not think of a single one about hope. At that moment the Lord impressed upon my heart that hope is the most ignored of the Christian virtues. I knew instantly why that is true. It's because hope is directly related to one's knowledge of Bible prophecy, and there is no topic in the modern Church that is more ignored than prophecy.

Stop and think about it for a moment. What is your hope? How would you explain it to an unbeliever? Could you get beyond the words, "My hope is heaven"?

❖ My Heritage ❖

During the first 30 years of my life I received almost no teaching about Bible prophecy, and I lived with little hope. If you had asked me to define my hope, I would have given you a pathetic answer based more on Greek philosophy than Hebrew theology.

I was taught that if I died before the Lord returned, I would experience "soul sleep." In other words, I would lapse into total unconsciousness and lie in my tomb until the Lord returned. At His return, I was taught that a "big bang" would occur that would vaporize the universe. My soul would be resurrected, and I would go off to an ethereal world called heaven where I would float around on a cloud and play a harp eternally.

For me, it was a grim picture. I didn't like the idea of lying comatose in a grave for eons of time. The "big bang" scared me to death. I was repulsed by the idea of becoming some sort of disembodied spirit without any individuality or personality. I certainly could not get excited about playing a harp forever. In fact, I found that idea downright hilarious.

You see, I grew up in a church that believed it is a terrible sin to play a musical instrument in a worship service. Yet, we were going to play harps in heaven eternally! It made no sense to me, so I wrote it off as a bunch of silly nonsense.

I had no one to blame but myself because I did not study God's Word, as I should have. When I finally started doing that, and the Holy Spirit began to lead me into a study of Bible prophecy, I started making discoveries about the future that ministered great hope to my spirit. In fact, I got so excited about my discoveries that I started jumping the pews and hanging from the chandeliers, shouting "Hallelujah!" and "Praise the Lord!" People thought I had gone Pentecostal overnight! No, I had just discovered God's marvelous promises for the future that are designed to give us hope in the present.

❖ The Fallacy of Soul Sleep ❖

The first discovery I made concerned "soul sleep." I found out it is an unbiblical concept. It is true that when we die, our bodies "sleep" metaphorically, but the spirits of the dead never lose their consciousness.

Jesus clearly taught this in His story about the rich man and Lazarus (Luke 16:19–31). When they died, their spirits went to hades. The rich man's spirit went to a compartment in hades called "torments." The spirit of Lazarus went to a compartment named "Abraham's bosom." On the cross, Jesus referred to Abraham's bosom as "paradise" (Luke 23:43). The two compartments were separated by a "great chasm" which could not be crossed.

In Jesus' story, both men are pictured as fully conscious. They even carry on a conversation with each other. Their souls are not asleep.

Further evidence of consciousness after death can be found in Revelation 7. John has been taken up to heaven and is being given a tour of the throne room of God. He sees "a great multitude . . . from every nation and all tribes and peoples and tongues," standing before the throne of God "clothed in white robes" and waving palm branches in worship (Rev. 7:9). They are fully conscious as they cry out, "Salvation to our God who sits on the throne and to the Lamb" (Rev. 7:10).

John wants to know the identity of these people. He is told that they are martyrs for Christ coming out of the "great tribulation" (Rev. 7:14).

Here are two scenes in Scripture of people after death who are fully conscious. But note that there is one very important difference in the two scenes. In Jesus' story, the saved are in hades in a compartment called "Abraham's bosom" or "paradise." In John's vision the saved are in heaven. Why the two different locations?

❖ Hades and Heaven ❖

The answer is that before the Cross, the souls of the saved did not go directly to heaven. They could not go there because their sins were not forgiven. Their sins were only covered by their faith, not forgiven. There can be no forgiveness of sins without the shedding of blood (Lev. 17:11 and Heb. 9:22). Forgiveness for those who died in faith before the Cross had to await the shedding of the blood of the Messiah.

That's the reason Jesus descended into hades after His death on the cross (1 Pet. 3:19–20). He went there to proclaim the shedding of His blood for the sins of mankind. There must have been great shouts of rejoicing by the Old Testament saints who had been waiting for this good news. Now their sins were not only covered by their faith, they were forgiven by the blood of Jesus. That made them candidates to be ushered into the presence of the Father in heaven. And that's exactly what happened when Jesus later ascended into heaven. He took with Him "a host of captives" (Eph. 4:8), referring to the saved who had been retained in hades, awaiting the shed blood of the Messiah.

❖ Hades and Hell ❖

A lot of misunderstanding about all this has existed throughout the history of Christianity because translators confused hades with hell.[4] The two are not the same. Hades (called sheol in the Old Testament) is a temporary holding place of the spirits of the dead. Hell is the ultimate destiny of the unsaved. No one is in hell today. The first to go to hell will be the Antichrist and his false prophet (Rev. 19:20). They will be joined by Satan at the end of the Millennium when he will be thrown into the lake of fire (Rev. 20:10).

The unsaved are currently in hades in the compartment called "torments." At the end of the Lord's millennial reign, they will be resurrected, judged, condemned, and consigned to the "lake of fire," which is hell (Rev. 20:11–15). Notice that in Revelation 20:14 the text specifically says that both "death and Hades" will be thrown into the lake of fire. This means both the body (death) and the soul (hades) will be assigned to hell.

❖ Paul's Affirmations ❖

Since the Cross, the spirits of the saved have been ushered immediately into the Lord's presence in heaven by His holy angels. Paul affirms that paradise was moved from hades to heaven. In 2 Corinthians 12:2–4 he states that he was taken up to the "third heaven," which he identifies as "paradise." The first heaven is the atmosphere of this planet. The second heaven is outer space. The third heaven is where God resides.

Paul also affirms consciousness after death. In 2 Corinthians 5:8 he wrote that he would prefer to be "absent from the body and to be at home with the Lord." He repeated this sentiment in his Philippian letter where he wrote, "to live is Christ and to die is gain" (Phil. 1:21). He elaborated on the meaning of this statement by adding that his desire was "to depart and be with Christ" (Phil. 1:23).

❖ The Intermediate State ❖

My second discovery was that we are not destined to an ethereal existence as disembodied spirits. Immediately after death both the saved and the lost receive a body that I am going to call an "intermediate spirit body." I have given it that name because it is a body that is intermediate between our current fleshly body and the ultimate, glorified body that saints will receive at the time of their resurrection.

The Bible does not tell us much about this body except that it is tangible and recognizable. An example of it is found in 1 Samuel 28 where we are told that King Saul, in his rebellion against God, sought the counsel of a witch. She, in turn, attempted to call up her familiar demon spirit. Instead, the Lord sent Samuel who had died some time before. The moment Samuel appeared, both the witch and Saul recognized him. Samuel proceeded to pronounce judgment upon Saul, telling him that his kingdom would be given to David and that the next day, "you and your sons will be with me" (1 Sam. 28:8–19). The next day Saul and his three sons, including Jonathan, were killed by the Philistines (1 Sam. 31:1–6).

Another example of the intermediate spirit body can be found in Matthew 17 where the story is told of Jesus' transfiguration.

This was when His disciples were given a glimpse of His coming glory. As they witnessed this marvelous event, suddenly two people appeared and began talking with them. The two were Moses and Elijah (Matt. 17:1–5). It is quite possible that these two appeared again at the ascension of Jesus. Luke tells us that as the disciples gazed intently at Jesus while He was ascending into heaven, two men in white suddenly appeared and told them, "This Jesus, who has been taken up from you into heaven, will come in just the same way as you have watched Him go into heaven" (Acts 1:11). The men are not identified. They could have been angels, but they might also have been Elijah and Moses.

An additional example of intermediate spirit bodies is one I have already mentioned. It is the scene John saw in heaven that is recorded in Revelation 7. He saw a great multitude, too many to be counted. They were standing before God's throne dressed in white robes and waving palm branches. John was told that these were martyrs coming out of the great Tribulation (Rev. 7:9–14).

❖ Glorification ❖

When Jesus returns, the Bible says He will bring with Him the spirits of the saved (1 Thess. 4:13–14). He will resurrect their bodies in a great miracle of re-creation (whether their bodies are preserved, rotted, cremated, or dissolved in the ocean). In the twinkling of an eye, He will reunite their spirits with their resurrected bodies and will then glorify their bodies (1 Thess. 4:15–16). Then, those saints who are alive will be caught up (raptured) to meet the Lord in the sky, and they will be transformed on the way up (1 Thess. 4:17).

All my life I have heard people say, "There are two things in life that no one can avoid: death and taxes." That statement is wrong. The only thing we cannot avoid is taxes and more taxes. A whole generation of believers will avoid death — the generation living when the Lord returns for His Church. It's no wonder that Paul concluded this great passage in 1 Thessalonians by saying, "Therefore, comfort one another with these words" (1 Thess. 4:18).

What is a glorified body? Paul wrote a whole chapter about the topic in 1 Corinthians 15, and he ends up raising about as many questions as he answers. According to Paul, our glorified bodies will be imperishable, gloriously pure, powerful, and spiritual (1 Cor. 15:42–44).

Paul further states that the glorified body will be immortal, and as such will no longer be subject to death (1 Cor. 15:53–55). This is an important point. Many in Christendom believe in the immortality of the soul. That is not a biblical concept. It comes from the writings of Plato, a Greek philosopher. The Bible says that God alone possesses immortality (1 Tim. 6:16). We do not receive immortality until we are given our glorified bodies. Immortality is a gift of grace to the redeemed.

❖ The Nature of the Glorified Body ❖

Paul made a statement in his letter to the Philippians that I think provides us with a framework for understanding what our glorified bodies will be like. He wrote that when Jesus returns, He "will transform the body of our humble state into conformity with the body of His glory, by the exertion of the power that He has even to subject all things to Himself" (Phil. 3:20–21). In other words, our glorified bodies are going to be like Jesus' resurrection body.

Now, think about that for a moment. After His resurrection, Jesus had a tangible body that could be touched and recognized (Luke 24:41–43 and John 20:27–28). People had difficulty recognizing Him at first, but that is understandable. If you buried your best friend one day, and he knocked on your door the next, would you recognize him? Wouldn't you assume he was someone who looked like your friend? Once the disciples realized that Jesus had truly been resurrected, they had no more difficulty recognizing Him, even at a distance (John 21:1–7).

So, Jesus had a body similar to the ones we have now. It was tangible and recognizable. It was also a body that ate food. Jesus is pictured eating with His disciples several times, including a meal of fish on the shore of the Sea of Galilee (Luke 24:30–31, 41–42 and John 21:10–13). I must admit that I get excited when I read these accounts of Jesus eating, and also when I read about our eating with Him in heaven at the "marriage supper of the Lamb" (Rev. 19:7–9). I have this fantasy that we will be able to eat all we want in our glorified bodies and not have to worry about gaining weight! (That should be sufficient to prompt many of you to shout, "Maranatha!")

❖ A Different Dimension ❖

The resurrected body of Jesus was similar to ours in many respects, but there were also some differences. Jesus' body seemed to have a different dimension to it, for He could pass through a wall into a locked room (John 20:26), and He could move from one place to another almost instantly (Luke 24:30–36). One moment He was on the road to Emmaus, the next He was in Jerusalem, and then He would appear in the Galilee area.

His disciples were so startled and frightened by His ability to vanish and reappear suddenly at another place that they thought they were seeing a spirit. But Jesus countered that idea immediately by telling them, "Touch Me and see, for a spirit does not have flesh and bones as you see that I have" (Luke 24:39). When the Word says that our glorified bodies will be "spiritual" in nature (1 Cor. 15:44), it does not mean we will be ethereal spirits. It says our natural body will be raised a spiritual *body*, not a spirit. We will still have a body, but it will no longer be controlled by the old sin nature, the flesh. Rather, it will be a body yielded completely to the control of the Holy Spirit.

There is one other thing the Bible reveals about the glorified body that should be a source of great comfort. The glorified body will be a perfected body. That means the blind will see, the deaf will hear, the lame will walk, and the mute will speak. Those who are mentally impaired will have their minds healed (Isa. 29:18–19, 32:3–4, and 35:5–6). There will no longer be any pain or death (Rev. 21:4). God will "wipe away every tear," and "there will no longer be any mourning, or crying, or pain" (Rev. 21:4).

❖ Meaningful Activities ❖

My first discovery was that there is no such thing as "soul sleep." We remain conscious after death. My second discovery was that we are not destined to be disembodied spirits. We continue to have a body — first, an intermediate spirit body, and then a glorified body. My third discovery was that we are not going to be bored stiff playing harps for eternity. We are going to be engaged in some meaningful activities.

If you are a believer and you die before the Lord returns, you will go to heaven where you will be involved in worship (Rev. 7:9–14) and service (Rev. 7:15). Admittedly, the Bible does not get specific about our worship and service, but we can be assured that we will find both to be fulfilling and edifying. It could also be that this will be a time of rest, preparing us for the time of vigorous service that will follow, when the Lord returns to earth.

❖ Judgment and Rewards ❖

At the time of the Rapture (most likely before the Tribulation), both the living and dead in Christ will receive their glorified bodies. We will be in heaven with the Lord during the Tribulation. This will be the time of our judgment, not to determine our eternal destiny, but to determine our degrees of reward. Each of us will stand before the judgment seat of Jesus and be judged as to how we used our spiritual gifts to advance His kingdom (2 Cor. 5:10). Our works will be judged as to quantity, quality, and motive (1 Cor. 3:13–15 and 4:5). Some will experience embarrassment as all their works are burned up as worthless (1 Cor. 3:13–15). Others will receive great rewards.

Some of the rewards will relate to the degree of ruling authority we will be granted during the Lord's millennial reign (Luke 19:11–27). Others will consist of crowns and special robes. There will be a "crown of righteousness" for those who lived yearning for the return of Jesus (2 Tim. 4:7–8). A "crown of life" will be given to those who persevere under trial (Rev. 2:10 and James 1:12). Faithful elders and pastors will receive a "crown of glory" (1 Pet. 5:4). Soul winners will be given a "crown of rejoicing" (Phil. 4:1 and 1 Thess. 2:19). An "imperishable wreath" will be given to those who exercise self-control (1 Cor. 9:25). Even the clothing we receive will indicate our degrees of reward. It will in some way reflect "the righteous acts of the saints" (Rev. 19:8).

At the end of this time of judgment, we, the bride of Christ, will sit down at a banquet table in heaven to celebrate our union with our bridegroom, Jesus. The Bible calls it the "marriage supper of the Lamb" (Rev. 19:9). It will be a time of unparalleled celebration. The heavens will ring with "Hallelujahs!" (Rev. 19:1–6).

❖ Witnesses of Glory ❖

When the meal is completed, we will return to earth with Jesus (Rev. 19:11–14). We will be there in our glorified bodies when His foot touches the Mount of Olives and that mountain is split in half (Zech. 14:1–9). We will be there to shout "Hosanna to the Son of David! Hosanna to the King of kings!" as He rides down the Kidron Valley on His white horse and approaches the Eastern Gate. We will be there to witness the supernatural opening of that gate as it welcomes Jesus to the holy city of Jerusalem:

> Lift up your heads, O gates, And be lifted up, O ancient doors, That the King of glory may come in! Who is the King of glory? The Lord strong and mighty, The Lord mighty in battle (Ps. 24:7–8).

We will be there to shout, "Hallelujah!" when Jesus is crowned King of kings and Lord of lords and begins His glorious millennial reign.

❖ The Millennial Reign ❖

During the Lord's reign, the redeemed are going to be doing anything but floating around on clouds playing harps. We are going to reign with Jesus over those who are allowed to enter the Millennium in the flesh (which will be those believers who are alive at the end of the Tribulation). Jesus will reign over all the earth from Jerusalem (Isa. 2:1–4) as King of kings and Lord of lords (Rev. 19:16). David, in his glorified body, will reign as king of Israel (Ezek. 37:24). Those of us who will be glorified saints will be scattered all over the earth to assist with Jesus' reign (2 Tim. 2:12).

Think of it — every person on earth who is in a position of governing authority will be a glorified saint. Some of us will be in administrative positions, sharing in Jesus' reign as presidents, governors, or mayors (Luke 19:11–27). Others will serve as judges (1 Cor. 6:3). Most of us will serve as "shepherds," or teachers, trying to bring those who are born during the Millennium to faith in Jesus (Isa. 66:18–21 and Jer. 3:15).

None of us will serve as legislators because the law will be given by Jesus himself, and it will be perfect (Isa. 2:1–4). There will be no abomination known as the Texas Legislature or the United States Congress. Nor will there be any lobbyists or political parties.

The Lord will rule with "a rod of iron" (Ps. 2:9 and Rev. 2:27).

The government of the world will be a theocracy, with Jesus serving as both the spiritual and political leader. "He will be a priest on His throne, and the counsel of peace will be between the two offices" (Zech. 6:13).

We will be given the blessing of seeing this old sin-sick world flooded with peace, righteousness, and justice, "as the waters cover the sea" (Isa. 11:9). There will be no homeless people or hungry people (Isa. 65:21–22 and Mic. 4:4). Peace will envelope the earth (Isa. 2:4). The Lord's reign will be characterized by righteousness, fairness, and faithfulness (Isa. 11:4–5). "The whole earth will acknowledge the Lord and return to Him. People from every nation will bow down before Him" (Ps. 22:27).[5]

❖ The Eternal State ❖

When the Millennium ends and we move into the eternal state, the Bible does not go into detail as to what our activities will be. It tells us only three things: we will see the face of God (Rev. 22:4); we will serve the Lord (Rev. 22:3); and we will reign with Him forever (Rev. 22:5).

Seeing the face of God is an exciting prospect, for the Bible says that no one has ever seen His face (Exod. 33:20 and 1 Tim. 6:16). I believe the promise of seeing God's face means we are going to enjoy intimacy with Him forever. Much of that, undoubtedly, will be in the form of worship. I think it also means we will grow in our knowledge of the Lord forever. He is infinite, and no matter how much we come to know Him, there will be just that much more for us to experience. I feel certain that one aspect of this will be the eternal study of His Word. I get excited over all this as I think of singing the Psalms with David and studying the Book of Romans with Paul.

As for service, I would imagine, for one thing, our gifts and talents will be magnified and that we will use them to glorify the Lord. Thus, a singer will be able to sing with a perfection and range never before achieved, and a painter will be able to paint with a glory never imagined.

Reigning with the Lord forever implies that we will be reigning over someone. Who that will be, I do not know. Perhaps it will be the mysterious "nations" referred to in Revelation that seem to inhabit the new earth (Rev. 21:24–27 and 22:2).

❖ Our Eternal Home ❖

This brings me to the final discovery I made when the Holy Spirit led me into an in-depth study of Bible prophecy. I discovered that the redeemed are not going to live eternally in an ethereal world called heaven. I learned, instead, that our eternal home is going to be on a new earth. Most Christians are amazed by this truth, which shows how little Bible prophecy is taught in the Church today.

Since the Bible teaches that the current earth is eternal (Ps. 78:69 and Ps. 148:6), I have concluded that the "new earth" will be the current earth renovated by fire. It is true that Peter said that the current earth will be "destroyed" by fire (2 Pet. 3:10,12), but in the context it is clear that he is referring to a radical transformation of the current earth. Earlier in the same passage he referred to the original earth as having been "destroyed" by water, speaking of the Noahic flood. The earth of Noah's day did not cease to exist, but the flood "destroyed" it in the sense that it radically changed the nature of the earth — tilting it on its axis, splitting the continents apart, laying down the fossil record, depositing the marine organisms that would become petroleum deposits, and creating the ocean depths and the mountain heights.

At the end of the Millennium, fire will be used by God to burn away the pollution of Satan's last revolt (2 Pet. 3:12). In the midst of that fiery inferno, God will reshape the earth like a hot ball of wax. He will refresh it and restore it to its original perfection (Acts 3:21). He will then lower the new Jerusalem down to the new earth, with the redeemed inside (Rev. 21:1–2). Then, He himself will come to earth to live in our presence eternally! "The tabernacle of God is among men, and He shall dwell among them, and they shall be His people, and God Himself shall be among them" (Rev. 21:3).

Heaven is where God resides. When the new earth is supplied, heaven will descend to earth as God takes up residence on this new earth. So, it is true that the redeemed will live eternally in heaven, but heaven will be on earth.

❖ The Redemption of All Creation ❖

God loves His creation, and He intends to redeem it — all of it — and not destroy it with some mystical "big bang." Jesus died on the cross not only to redeem mankind but also to redeem the creation. That's the reason the high priest in Old Testament times sprinkled the blood not only on the mercy seat of the ark, but also on the ground in front of the ark (Lev. 16:15).

The blood on the mercy seat of the ark was a symbolic prophecy pointing to the fact that the blood of the Messiah would cover the law of God (the tablets inside the ark) with the mercy and grace of God. The blood on the ground was a reminder that the sacrifice of the Messiah would make it possible for the curse to be lifted and for the animal and plant kingdoms to be returned to their original perfection (Isa. 11:6–9 and Rom. 8:18–23).

❖ An Unjustified Fear ❖

Many people are afraid of Bible prophecy. They say it is full of "doom and gloom." That is true for those who have rejected the Lord. But for those who know Him and love Him, there is only good news. The Old Testament ends with an example of what I'm talking about. It says, "For behold, the day is coming, burning like a furnace; and all the arrogant and every evildoer will be chaff; and the day that is coming will set them ablaze" (Mal. 4:1). That is bad news. But the very next verse contains incredibly good news for believers: "But for you who fear My name, the sun of righteousness will rise with healing in its wings; and you will go forth and skip about like calves released from the stall" (Mal. 4:2).

Bible prophecy is full of glorious promises that are designed to give God's people a strong sense of hope as they live as strangers and pilgrims in the midst of an increasingly evil, God-rejecting world. When you read these wonderful promises, you can understand why Paul wrote these words:

> No eye has seen, nor ear heard, nor the heart of man conceived, what God has prepared for those who love him (1 Cor. 2:9).[6]

❖ A God of Hope ❖

As this verse indicates, we cannot even begin to imagine the marvelous blessings God has in store for the redeemed. But the very next verse says that the Holy Spirit has revealed those blessings to us in God's Word (1 Cor. 2:10). The sad thing is that most Christians are ignorant of those promises and therefore have no idea what Paul meant when he wrote, "For I consider that the sufferings of this present time are not worthy to be compared with the glory that is to be revealed to us" (Rom. 8:18).

In Romans 15:13 Paul wrote, "Now may the God of hope fill you with all joy and peace in believing, so that you will abound in hope by the power of the Holy Spirit." Our God is a God of hope who desires to fill us with hope. If you know Jesus as your Savior, you are an heir to some incredible promises, and if you know those promises and believe in them, you can live in this evil world with hope, joy, and great expectations.

Endnotes

1 Viktor Frankl, *Man's Search for Meaning* (New York, NY: Washington Square Press, a division of Simon & Schuster, 1963, revised and updated edition in 1998).

2 Ibid., p. 115.

3 *The Living Bible Paraphrased* (Wheaton, IL: Tyndale House Publishers, 1971).

4 The confusion of hades with hell continues today, even in modern translations. For example, in Jesus's story of the rich man and Lazarus, recorded in Luke 16, the translators of the *New International Version* (Grand Rapids, MI: Zondervan Publishing House, 1965) refer to the men being in "hell," when the Greek text says hades (Luke 16:23). The *New American Standard Version* is consistent in its translation of hades as hades. The *King James Version* was very inconsistent in its translation of hades, sometimes using hades and sometimes hell. The *New King James Version* (Nashville, TN: Thomas Nelson Publishers, 1995) is more accurate, and in Luke 16:23, it translates hades as hades.

5 *Holy Bible*, New Living Translation (Wheaton, IL: Tyndale House Publishers, 1997).

6 *The Holy Bible*, Revised Standard Version (Grand Rapids, MI: Zondervan Bible Publishers, 1962).

Part Three

Victory over
Paganism

❖ ❖ ❖

Chapter 13

❖   ❖   ❖

Living on Borrowed Time

I s paganism going to triumph? The painful answer is yes — for a brief period of time. The Bible teaches that society will continue to disintegrate the closer we get to the time of the Lord's return (2 Tim. 3:1–5). The climax of degradation will occur when a person called the Antichrist (1 John 2:18) takes over the world (Rev. 13:7) and rules with an iron hand for seven years during a period called the Tribulation (Rev. 6–19). He will be the personification of paganism and all the evil it represents (Dan. 8:23–25). He will be possessed by Satan (Dan. 8:24), and he will attempt to murder all Christians and Jews (Rev. 12:13–17).

The Bible indicates that the Church will be taken out of the world before this madman takes power (1 Thess. 1:10), but millions will come to Christ during the Tribulation, only to be hunted down like wild animals and slaughtered (Rev. 7:9–14).

The triumph of paganism will be brief but terrible, so terrible, in fact, that the Bible indicates it would result in the destruction of all life if it were not ended supernaturally (Matt. 24:21–22). That end will come swiftly and decisively after seven years when the Lord Jesus Christ breaks from the heavens in His glorious second coming (Rev. 19:11–21).

Victory is coming. But there are some terrible years ahead for planet Earth before that victory will be realized.

❖   How Close?   ❖

How close are we to the end-time climax of history? I believe that the signs of the times indicate that we are living on the

231

threshold of the Tribulation. The term, "signs of the times," refers to Bible prophecies about the end times that are being fulfilled in our day and time.

One hundred years ago there were no definite signs indicating the end times. Today, those signs are everywhere. One would have to be spiritually blind not to discern that we are living on borrowed time.

A few years ago I spoke at a prophecy conference in Orlando, Florida. One of the other speakers was a great man of God from Abilene, Texas, named Elbert Peak. He was over 80 years old and had been preaching about Bible prophecy for 60 years. His topic was the "Signs of the Times." I'll never forget how he began his message:

> I have been speaking on the signs of the times for 60 years. When I began, the signs were few and far between. Today, they are everywhere. In fact, they are so abundant, I am no longer looking for signs; I am listening for sounds — the shout of an archangel and the blowing of a great trumpet.

❖ The Turning Point ❖

The turning point occurred in 1917. On November 2, 1917, the British government issued the Balfour Declaration.[1] That momentous document declared that the British would prepare Palestine to become a homeland for the Jewish people.

The leading evangelical spokesman in London at the time was F.B. Meyer. He immediately recognized the prophetic significance of the Balfour Declaration. He responded to it by sending out an invitation to evangelical leaders in England to meet with him on December 13 to discuss the document's spiritual implications.[2] On December 11, General Allenby liberated Jerusalem from 400 years of Turkish oppression. The road to Zion was being opened to the Jews.

When Meyer's meeting convened two days later, there was a great sense of God moving sovereignly in history to fulfill promises He had made thousands of years ago. One of the speakers that day was Dr. G. Campbell Morgan. He proclaimed, "We all feel today that never in the history of the Church have the signs seemed so definitely to point to the fulfilling of Gentile times as they do today. Our loins should be girt about and our lamps should be burning. We should be occupying until He comes."[3]

❖ Organizing for Action ❖

Those who assembled that day were the "who's who" of the evangelical movement in England. They decided to form an organization called the Advent Testimony Movement whose purpose would be to proclaim the Lord's soon return, urging Christians to evangelize the lost and commit themselves to holiness. The organization adopted a manifesto that contained seven points:[4]

1. The signs of the times point toward the close of the times of the Gentiles.

2. The return of our Lord may be expected at any moment when He will be manifested as evidently as to His disciples on the evening of His resurrection.

3. The completed Church will be translated to meet the Lord in the air, and to be forever with the Lord.

4. Israel will be restored to their own land in unbelief, and be afterwards converted by the manifestation of Christ as their Messiah.

5. All human schemes of world-reconstruction must be subsidiary to the Lord when all nations will be subject to His rule.

6. Under the reign of Christ there will be a further effusion of the Holy Spirit upon all flesh.

7. The truths embodied in this statement are of the utmost practical value in determining Christian character and action with reference to the pressing problems of the hour.

With this manifesto as a foundation, that organization went forth and began to proclaim the imminent return of the Lord in conferences held all over England, Europe, America, and the British Empire. The organization still exists today, known as the

Prophetic Witness Movement International. Its efforts have spawned hundreds of other ministries around the world that are today proclaiming the same message.

❖   Additional Signs   ❖

Since those exhilarating days in 1917, many other equally significant and exciting events have occurred that have increased the fever pitch of expectation of the Lord's return. The nation of Israel has been re-established (May 14, 1948). The city of Jerusalem has been reoccupied by the Jews (June 7, 1967). The Arab nations have come against Israel (the wars of 1948, 1967, 1973, 1981, and 1991), and all the nations of the world are now turning against Israel over the issue of Jerusalem. Europe is reuniting, and Russia is threatening the Middle East.

In short, all the pieces of the end-time prophetic puzzle are in place for the first time ever, and the message is clear: *Jesus is returning soon!* He is at the very gates of heaven awaiting His Father's command. We are living on borrowed time. We should be listening for sounds rather than looking for signs. And we should be facing the new millennium with expectant hope.

❖   Knowing the Season   ❖

Many people scoff at these events and refuse to give them any spiritual significance because they believe there is nothing that can be known about the timing of the Lord's return. They usually base this conclusion on the words of Jesus in Matthew 24:42–44 where He stated that He would return "like a thief in the night."

But Paul makes it clear in 1 Thessalonians 5:1–6 that Jesus' statement does not apply to believers: "But you, brethren, are not in darkness, that the day should overtake you like a thief. . . ." He then proceeds to explain why. "For you are all sons of light and sons of day. We are not of night nor of darkness; so then let us not sleep as others do, but let us be alert and sober." Paul is referring, of course, to the light of the Holy Spirit who indwells all true believers and who can enlighten us through our study of Scripture to know the season of the Lord's return (1 John 2:27).

The point is that we cannot know the date of the Lord's return but we can certainly know the season. The writer of Hebrews makes this clear when, speaking of the Lord's return, he writes that believers are to encourage one another "as you see the day drawing near" (Heb. 10:25). There is something we can see, something we can perceive, that will indicate to us that the Lord is about to return. Jesus himself made the same point in His Olivet Discourse when He said, "When these things [signs of the times] begin to take place, straighten up and lift up your heads, because your redemption is drawing near" (Luke 21:28).

❖ God's Lovingkindness ❖

As a matter of fact, God is obligated by His character to warn the world of the imminent return of His Son. The reason is that Jesus is returning in great wrath to "judge and wage war" (Rev. 19:11), and God never pours out His wrath without warning.

God does not wish that any should perish, but that all should be brought to repentance (2 Pet. 3:9). Therefore, God always warns before He executes His wrath. He warned the world through Noah for 120 years. He warned Sodom and Gomorrah through Abraham. He sent Jonah to warn the pagan city of Ninevah, and He sent Nahum to the same city 150 years later.

Likewise, God is warning the world today that His Son is about to return. He is calling the world to repentance through the "signs of the times." The Bible is full of these signs. There are about 500 prophecies in the Old Testament that relate to the second coming of the Messiah. In the New Testament, 1 out of every 25 verses is concerned with the return of Jesus.

In fact, there are so many signs that it is difficult to grasp all of them. The best way I have found to do this is to put them in categories.

❖ The Signs of Nature ❖

We are told to watch for earthquakes, famine, pestilence, and signs in the heavens (see Matt. 24:7 and Luke 21:11).

This is the least-respected category of signs for several reasons. For one thing, many people simply shrug their shoulders and say, "There have always been natural calamities, so what else is new?" Note that Jesus says these signs will be like "birth pangs" (Matt. 24:8) — that is, they will increase in frequency and intensity as the time draws near for His return. In other words, there will be more intense earthquakes and more frequent ones. That is exactly what is happening today.

Another reason these signs are given little respect is because most Christians are so rationalistic that they do not really believe in the supernatural, and they therefore find it difficult to believe that God speaks to the world through signs of nature. Yet, the Bible teaches this principle from start to finish.

God dealt with the world's sin through a great flood in the days of Noah (Gen. 6). He called the nation of Judah to repentance through a terrible locust invasion (Joel 1). In like manner, He called for the nation of Israel to repent by sending drought, wind storms, mildew, locusts, famine, and pestilence (Amos 4:6–10). The prophet Haggai pointed to a drought as evidence that God was calling the people to get their priorities in order (Hag. 1:10–11).

The New Testament begins with a special light in the heavens marking the birth of the Messiah (Matt. 2:2). On the day that Jesus was crucified, there was three hours of darkness and an earthquake (Matt. 27:45–51). When Jesus returns, the earth will experience the greatest earthquake in its history as every mountain is lowered, every valley is raised, and every island is moved (Rev. 16:17–21).

God has always spoken through signs of nature, and He continues to do so today. We had better pay close attention to them.

❖ The Signs of Society ❖

Jesus said that society will become increasingly lawless and immoral as the time approaches for His return. In fact, He said it would become as evil as it was in the days of Noah (Matt. 24:12, 37–39).

Paul paints a chilling picture of end-time society in 2 Timothy 3:1–5. He says it will be characterized by three loves — the love of self (humanism), the love of money (materialism), and the love of pleasure (hedonism). He then points out that the payoff of this carnal lifestyle will be what the philosophers call nihilism — that is, a society wallowing in despair. Men's minds will become depraved (Rom. 1:28), and people will call evil good and good evil (Isa. 5:20).

We are seeing these prophecies fulfilled before our eyes today as we watch our society reject its Christian heritage and descend into a hellish pit of lawlessness, immorality, and despair. Even worse, we are exporting our nihilism around the world through our immoral and violent movies and television programs.

❖ The Spiritual Signs ❖

There are both positive and negative spiritual signs that we are to watch for. The negative ones include the appearance of false Christs and their cults (Matt. 24:5,11,24), the apostasy of the professing church (2 Thess. 2:3), an outbreak of Satanism (1 Tim. 4:1), and the persecution of faithful Christians (Matt. 24:9).

These negative spiritual signs began to appear in the mid-19th century when Christian cults started forming. First came the Mormons, then the Jehovah's Witnesses, and then a great variety of spiritualist groups like the Church of Christ Scientists and the Unity Church.

The apostasy of the mainline Christian denominations began in the 1920s when the German School of Higher Criticism invaded American seminaries and undermined the authority of the Scriptures, teaching that the Bible is man's search for God rather than God's revelation to man.

During the 1960s Satanism exploded on the American scene and has since been exported worldwide through American movies, books, and television programs. Dabbling in the occult has become commonplace in the form of astrology, numerology, crystal gazing, transcendental meditation, and channeling. The whole trend has consummated in the appearance of the New Age movement with its teaching that man is God.

As society has secularized, true Christianity has come under increasing attack. Judeo-Christian values, once the foundation of Western Civilization, are now openly mocked, and those who still adhere to them are castigated as "intolerant fundamentalists" by the media.

The positive spiritual signs include the proclamation of the gospel to the whole world (Matt. 24:14), a great outpouring of the Holy Spirit (Joel 2:28–32), and spiritual illumination to understand prophecies that have been "sealed up" until the end times (Dan. 12:4, 9).

As with the negative signs, we are seeing these positive signs fulfilled in our day and time. Through the use of modern technology, the gospel has been proclaimed throughout the world in this century, and the Bible has been translated into all major languages.

The great end-time pouring out of the Holy Spirit that was prophesied by the prophet Joel has also begun. Joel called it "the latter rain" (Joel 2:23), and he said it would occur after the Jews had returned to their land. The state of Israel was re-established in 1948. In 1949 God anointed a ministry that would have a worldwide impact — the ministry of Billy Graham. Then, in the 1960s, came the Charismatic movement, which prompted renewal in worship and gave emphasis to the continuing validity of the gifts of the Spirit.

The acceleration in the understanding of Bible prophecy began in 1970 with the publication of Hal Lindsey's book *The Late Great Planet Earth.* It seemed to open up to popular understanding many prophecies that had been "sealed up" until the end times (Dan. 12:4, 9). Remarkably, it became the number one best seller in the world — with the sole exception of the Bible — for the next ten years![5]

❖ The Signs of World Politics ❖

The Bible prophesies that there will be a certain pattern of world politics that will characterize the end-time geopolitical map.

The focus will be the re-established state of Israel (Zech. 12:2–3). It will be besieged by a menacing nation from the "remote parts of the north," the nation of "Rosh" — or modern-day Russia (Ezek. 38:2, 6). There will also be a threatening nation to the east that will be capable of sending an army of 200 million — namely, China (Rev. 9:13–16 and Rev. 16:12–13). A third source of danger to Israel will be the Arab nations that immediately surround it. They will covet the land and will try to take it from the Jews (Ezek. 35:10 and 36:2).

Another key player on the world political scene in the end times will be a coalition of European nations that will form a confederation centered in the area of the old Roman Empire (Dan. 2:41–44, 7:7, 23–24, and Rev. 17:12–13). This confederation will serve as the political base for the rise of the Antichrist and the creation of his worldwide kingdom (Dan. 7:8).

Other international political signs include wars and rumors of wars (Matt. 24:6), civil wars (Matt. 24:7), and widespread international terrorism and lawlessness (Matt. 24:12).

❖ The Signs of Israel ❖

The signs related to the state of Israel are prolific and very important — more important, in fact, than all the rest of the signs put together.

The most frequently repeated prophecy in the Old Testament is the prediction that the Jewish people will be regathered from the "four corners of the earth" in the end times (Isa. 11:10–12). The Bible states that a consequence of this regathering will be the re-establishment of the state of Israel (Isa. 66:7–8). The Scriptures say that once the Jews are back in their land, the land itself will experience a miracle of reclamation (Isa. 35). The desert will bloom and people will exclaim, "This desolate land has become like the garden of Eden" (Ezek. 36:35).

Another end-time miracle will be the revival of the Hebrew language (Zeph. 3:9). Most people are not aware of the fact that when the Jews were dispersed from their land in A.D. 70, they ceased to speak the Hebrew language. The Jews who settled in Europe developed a new language called Yiddish — a combination of German and Hebrew. The Jews who migrated to the Mediterranean basin created a language called Ladino — a combination of Hebrew and Spanish.

Other significant signs of Israel that we are told to watch for in the end times include the re-occupation of Jerusalem (Luke 21:24), the resurgence of Israeli military strength (Zech. 12:6), and the re-focusing of world politics on Israel (Zech. 12:3).

All these signs have been fulfilled in this century. The nation has been re-established, the land has been reclaimed, the ancient language has been revived, the Jews are back in Jerusalem, and Israel is the focal point of world politics.

❖ The Key Signs ❖

As I said before, the most important signs are the ones that relate to Israel because God uses the Jews throughout the Scriptures as His prophetic time clock. By this I mean that very often when the Lord is revealing an important event that will take place in the future, He will point to the Jewish people and state that when a certain thing happens to them, the important event will also occur.

A good example of this principle can be found in Daniel 9 in the famous "Seventy Weeks of Years" prophecy. The prophet tells us to watch for a decree to be issued that will authorize the rebuilding of Jerusalem. He then says that the Messiah will come 69 weeks of years (483 years) after that decree is issued to the Jewish people.

There are two key prophecies which relate the return of Jesus to events that have occurred in Jewish history since 1948. These two events clearly established the period in which we are now living as the season of the Lords's return.

❖ The State of Israel ❖

The first is the re-establishment of the state of Israel, which occurred on May 14, 1948. Jesus singled out this event as the one that would signal His soon return.

His prophecy is contained in the fig tree parable (Matt. 24:32–35) which He presented in His Olivet Discourse. The day before He delivered this speech, He had put a curse on a barren fig tree, causing it to wither (Matt. 21:18–19). This was a symbolic prophecy that God would soon pour out His wrath upon the Jewish people because of their spiritual barrenness in rejecting His Son. The next day Jesus reminded His disciples of the fig tree. He said to watch for it to bloom again. In other words, He said watch for the rebirth of Israel. He indicated that when the fig tree blooms again, He would be at the gates of heaven, ready to return (Matt. 24:33).

Equally significant, He added an interesting observation: "Truly I say to you, this generation will not pass away until all these things take place" (Matt. 24:34). What generation? The generation that sees the fig tree blossom.

We are that generation. The fig tree has blossomed. Jesus is at the gates.

❖ The City of Jerusalem ❖

The second key event was prophesied by Jesus in the same speech, as recorded by Luke: "[The Jews] will fall by the edge of the sword, and will be led captive into all the nations; and Jerusalem will be trampled under foot by the Gentiles until the times of the Gentiles be fulfilled" (Luke 21:24).

The first half of this prophecy was fulfilled in A.D. 70, 40 years after Jesus spoke the words. In that year the Romans, under Titus, conquered Jerusalem and dispersed the Jews among the nations. Jerusalem remained under Gentile occupation for 1,897 years — until June 7, 1967, when Israel won the city back during the Six-Day War. The Jewish re-occupation of the city of Jerusalem is proof positive that we are living in the season of the Lord's return.

❖ A Provocative Challenge ❖

Whenever I present an overview of the signs of the times that point to the soon return of Jesus, I am often confronted by someone — often a professing Christian — who will say, "Come on David, these signs you are talking about have always existed in one degree or another, so what else is new?" They will then proceed to point out that there have always been wars and rumors of war, there have always been natural calamities, and throughout history Christians have always been persecuted. Then comes the inevitable challenge: "Show me something really new and unique that clearly points to our day and time as the season of the Lord's return."

The challenge is understandable, but it is not entirely legitimate. That's because Jesus said the end-time signs would be like "birth pangs" (Matt. 24:8). In other words, the signs would increase in frequency and intensity as the time draws near for Jesus to return. There would be more earthquakes, and more intense ones. Wars would be more frequent and more horrible in their degree of devastation. That, of course, is exactly what happened in the 20th century. All the signs increased exponentially in both frequency and intensity.

But still, it is legitimate to ask if there are any signs that are truly unique to our day and time — signs that have never existed before. Are there new signs that clearly point to this period of history as the time of the Lord's return? The answer is yes.

❖ A Key Prophecy ❖

A verse that immediately comes to mind in this regard is found in Daniel 12. Daniel was given many prophecies by the

Lord. Those relating to his day and time he clearly understood. He even seemed to understand prophecies that the Lord gave him relating to distant times, such as the succession of Gentile empires that would ultimately lead to the establishment of the Roman Empire. But when it came to prophecies about the end times, Daniel did not understand what was revealed to him.

He wrestled mightily with the prophecies and finally cried out to the Lord in despair. "I have heard," he said, "but I do not understand! What do these events mean?" (Dan. 12:8). The Lord, in effect, responded by saying, "Cool it, Daniel, because it is not for you to understand!" The Lord's actual words were, "Go your way, Daniel, for these words are concealed and sealed up until the end time" (Dan. 12:9). It was Daniel's responsibility to deliver the prophecies, not to understand them.

Note that Daniel was told the prophecies would not be understood "until the end time." In fact, in the very next verse the Lord told Daniel that at the proper time "those who have insight will understand" (Dan. 12:10).

Accordingly, there are many end-time prophecies that have never been understood until now, either because their understanding depended on historical events or because they were dependent upon technological developments. The fact that these prophecies have become understandable in recent years for the first time ever is proof positive that we are living in the end times. Let's look at some examples from the Book of Revelation.

❖ Revelation Examples ❖

The Tribulation Slaughter — Revelation 6 says that the Tribulation will begin with a series of judgments that will result in the death of one-fourth of mankind. The world's population is approaching six billion. That means one and a half billion people will die in the initial judgments, reducing the world's population to 4-1/2 billion. The next series of judgments, recorded in Revelation 8 and 9 will kill another third of mankind. One-third of 4-1/2 billion is another one and a half billion. Thus, in the first 3-1/2 years of the Tribulation, a total of 3 billion people will die. That's half the population of the world! Is this possible apart from the use of nuclear weapons? Only if it is a supernatural intervention of God. But God normally works through natural processes.

The unparalleled carnage of the Tribulation seems to me to point to nuclear weapons. Revelation 8 speaks of one-third of the earth being burned and one-third of the seas being polluted (Rev. 8:7–8). Later in the Tribulation, near the end, we are told that people will suffer from "loathsome and malignant sores" (Rev. 16:2). That sounds like one of the effects of radiation poisoning.

The advent of nuclear weapons makes possible for the first time the overwhelming Tribulation carnage portrayed in Revelation. I think nuclear power was what Jesus referred to in His Olivet Discourse when He said that the end times will be characterized by "men fainting from fear and with foreboding of what is coming on the world; *for the powers of the heavens will be shaken*" (Luke 21:26, emphasis added).[6]

The prophecies concerning the Tribulation carnage have clearly depended upon a major technological breakthrough for their understanding. That breakthrough occurred on July 16, 1945, when the first atomic bomb was exploded in New Mexico. When the first hydrogen bomb was exploded in 1952, we entered the era when, for the first time in human history, we could inflict upon ourselves the kind of carnage described in the Book of Revelation.

The Army of 200 Million — Chapters 9 and 16 of Revelation state that an army of 200 million soldiers will march "from the east" toward Israel. Daniel 11 indicates that this will be an army representing nations in revolt against the Antichrist.

Demographers estimate that the total population of the world at the time the apostle John wrote Revelation (A.D. 95) was only 200 million.[7] How could an army that size march out of the east? It made no sense. In fact, it took 1,650 years for the world's population to double to 400 million! At the beginning of the 20th century the total world population was only 1.6 billion, still too small for an army of 200 million to march from the east.

But the 20th century witnessed an exponential increase in population. The population count is now at 6 billion, and just one country to the east of Israel — namely, China — could field an army of 200 million.

Here we have a clear example of a prophecy about the end times that could never be understood apart from historical developments.

The Two Witnesses — Revelation 11 reveals that two great

witnesses of God will preach in the city of Jerusalem during the first 3-1/2 years of the Tribulation. Then, in the middle of that terrible period, the Antichrist will kill them.

We are further told that their dead bodies will lie in the streets of Jerusalem for 3-1/2 days and that all the people of the world will look upon them. How could that be? Prior to 1957 that prophecy was not understandable in natural terms. There was just no way that all the people of the world could look upon two dead bodies in the streets of Jerusalem.

All that changed on October 4, 1957, when the Russians sent up the first Sputnik satellite. Today, 43 years later, our planet has many man-made satellites circling it, making possible all sorts of instantaneous communication.

When those two prophets lie dead in the streets of Jerusalem, all someone will have to do is point a TV camera at them, send the signal up to a satellite, and all the world will be able to look upon them. Once again, modern technology has made an ancient prophecy understandable for the first time.

The Image of the Beast — Revelation 13 says that the Antichrist's religious leader, the false prophet, will make an image of the Antichrist that will appear to come alive and speak. This trickery will amaze most of the world's population and will cause many of them to give their allegiance to the Antichrist.

What is the explanation of this event? Many have concluded that Satan will empower the false prophet to give the image life. But Satan does not have the power to create life. Satan is a liar and a deceiver.

So, again, how can the false prophet give an image life? I don't see any way for him to do it apart from modern technology. The illusion can be created through the use of modern robotics.

In 1967 I took my family to Disneyland. We went into a theatre, and when the curtain opened, we saw a man who looked exactly like Abraham Lincoln sitting in a chair in the center of the stage. He stood up, walked to the edge of the stage, grabbed the lapels of his jacket, and proceeded to quote the Gettysburg Address. When he finished, a lady behind me exclaimed, "Wasn't he a good actor!" He was not an actor. The "actor" was a robot. That was 30 years ago. Think what could be done today with the advances that have been made in robotics and computer technology.

The Mark of the Beast — Another prophecy in Revelation 13 that is dependent on modern technology is the famous one that states the Antichrist will control the world's economy by requiring people to bear his mark or name on their hand or forehead in order to buy or sell anything.

Again, how could this be possible before the invention of laser and computer technology combined with the positioning of orbital satellites?

Such technology is already greatly advanced. I was recently in London and discovered that taxis in that city are being tracked by satellite. Semi-trucks here in America are being tracked in the same way. Veterinarians are advertising that they can implant microchips under your pet's skin. These chips can be read by a scanner in the event your dog or cat gets lost. It will only be a matter of time before a more advanced chip will enable your pet to be traced by satellite.

We have almost become a cashless society, with most purchases being made by credit card. The problem with the cards is that they can be lost or stolen. A good solution would be to use a laser to put your credit card number on your hand in such a way as to be capable of being read by a scanner.

The point is that for the first time ever the technological tools are in place for the Antichrist to exercise control over the world's population.

The Euphrates River — As I mentioned previously, in Revelation 9 and 16 we are told that an army of 200 million led by "the kings from the east" will march across Asia toward Israel during the Tribulation, most likely in revolt against the Antichrist. Revelation 16:12 indicates that this army will be held up at the Euphrates River until its water is suddenly dried up, enabling them to cross and proceed to the Valley of Armageddon.

Now, the Lord could miraculously dry up the water of the Euphrates River without any trouble at all, just as He parted the Red Sea for Moses and dried up the Jordan River for Joshua. But I think it is very interesting that this can now be accomplished overnight through natural means. In 1990 Turkey completed the construction of the massive Ataturk Dam on the Euphrates, and they in fact cut off the flow of the river in order to fill up the lake behind the dam. This action almost resulted in a war with Iraq.

❖ Other Contemporary Signs ❖

The list of modern-day signs given above is not an exhaustive one. They are simply some that I have pulled from the Book of Revelation. There are others that are unique to our day and time that can be found in prophetic Scriptures outside the Book of Revelation. Let me just mention a few.

The first that comes to mind is the acceleration of life. In Daniel 12:4 we are told that the speed of transportation and the volume of knowledge will vastly increase in the end times. We have witnessed the fulfillment of this prophecy in our lifetime. When the 20th century began, the vast majority of people were still traveling the same way they had been since the dawn of human history — namely, walking and riding a horse. Today we have autos, bullet trains, supersonic airplanes, and space ships. And all of this has developed in only 80 years.

Similarly, the growth of knowledge has been overwhelming. It is doubling every ten years. One Sunday edition of the *New York Times* contains more information than the average person in the 19th century was exposed to in a lifetime! Through the World Wide Web I can almost instantaneously access research resources all over the world. With the click of a computer key, I can go to the Vatican Library, and from there to the Library of Congress, and from there to the Jerusalem Museum.

The accelerator principle has also been evidenced in world evangelism, through the power of the Holy Spirit. Seventy percent of all the missions work done by the Church in its two thousand-year history has been accomplished since 1900. Seventy percent of that has been done since 1948, and 70 percent of that has been accomplished in the last ten years! In other words, the proclamation of the gospel is on an exponential curve.[8]

Much of the modern increase in missions outreach is due to technology, through the use of radio, television, movies, satellites, and the Internet. In April of 1996 Billy Graham preached a sermon that was broadcast to 200 countries in 40 different languages. It is estimated that 2.5 billion people heard or saw the message. The presentation was followed up with the distribution of 445 million pieces of literature in over a hundred languages.[9]

What we are witnessing in missions outreach is a fulfillment of Jesus' prophecy when He said, "This gospel of the kingdom shall be preached in the whole world as a testimony to all the nations, and then the end will come" (Matt. 24:14).

❖ The Uniqueness of Our Age ❖

After reviewing the prophecies listed above, I don't think we need any handwriting on the wall to indicate to us that we are living in a unique age. Historical developments and technological inventions are making it possible for us to understand many end-time prophecies for the first time. Even the phenomenal success of Hal Lindsay's book *The Late Great Planet Earth,* is a unique sign of the times. What was it that the Lord told Daniel? "These words are . . . sealed up until the end time. . . . but those who have insight will understand" (Dan. 12:9–10).

There is no way to escape the conclusion that we are living on borrowed time. The signs of the times are upon us, and they are shouting for our attention.

Endnotes

1 The Balfour Declaration is available in many sources. It can be found on the Internet at the following site: http://www.yale.edu/lawweb/avalon/balfour.htm.

2 Frederick A. Tatford, *The Midnight Cry: The Story of Fifty Years of Witness* (Eastbourne, Sussex: Bible and Advent Testimony Movement, 1967), p. 17.

3 Ibid., p. 35.

4 Ibid., p. 17–18.

5 Several years ago, *Time* certified that *The Late Great Planet Earth* was the number one best-selling book for the entire decade of the 1970s. The book has gone through 27 editions, has been printed in 50 languages, and has sold over 35 million copies worldwide.

6 *The Holy Bible,* Revised Standard Version (Grand Rapids, MI: Zondervan Bible Publishers, 1962).

7 United Nations, Population Division, Department for Economic and Social Information and Policy Analysis, "World Population Growth from Year 0 to Stabilization," available on the Internet at gopher://gopher.undp.org:70/00/ungophers/popin/wdtrends/histor.

8 *Generation,* a video production by Mars Hills productions (Stafford, TX: 1997), tape five, "The Final Frontier."

9 Billy Graham Evangelistic Association, P.O. Box 779, Minneapolis, MN, 55440.

Chapter 14

❖ ❖ ❖

Looking for Jesus

Are you living looking for Jesus? Do you yearn for His return? Do you pray daily, "Maranatha!"?

Paul told us in Titus 2:13 that we are to live "looking for the blessed hope and the appearing of the glory of our great God and Savior, Christ Jesus." In 2 Timothy 4:8 he said that there is a special reward — "a crown of righteousness" — that the Lord will give to any saint who lives their life with the love of the Lord appearing in their heart.

Have you ever stopped to wonder why this special reward is called a "crown of righteousness"? Why does Paul associate righteousness with devotion to the Lord's return?

It's because the two go hand in hand. This is a point that I constantly stress to pastors who do not understand the importance of preaching and teaching Bible prophecy.

❖ **The Practical Relevance of Prophecy** ❖

When I encounter such a pastor and ask him why he has ignored prophecy, his answer usually goes something like this: "Well, David, you don't understand because you are a traveling evangelist. If you were a pastor, you would understand. You see, I'm having to deal daily with every problem known to man. I have homosexuals and adulterers in my congregation, as well as gossips and slanderers. I have marriages on the rocks. I have parents at the throats of their teenagers. I have drug addicts and people addicted to credit cards. You name it and I'm dealing with it. The result is that I just don't have time to deal with esoteric, pie-in-the-sky subjects like Bible prophecy. After all, when you get right down to it, what difference does it make what a person knows about Bible prophecy?"

I understand where pastors like this are coming from. I sympathize with them, and I pray for them. There is no higher calling than that of a pastor, and there is no more difficult job on the face of the earth.

But any pastor who feels this way simply does not understand Bible prophecy. As I have already shown, a knowledge of Bible prophecy is essential to the development of a vibrant hope — and hope is desperately needed in these dark times.

Bible prophecy is also directly related to all the problems that pastors are battling in their congregations. The point about this that I try to drive home over and over is that Bible prophecy can have an overwhelming impact on the way people live here and now. If taught properly, it is not just pie-in-the-sky information relevant to a world that is yet to come. It can transform the way a person lives today, in this world.

❖ The Transforming Quality of Prophecy ❖

Let me put it succinctly. If a person can ever be convinced of two things related to Bible prophecy, his or her life will be transformed. Those two things are: 1) Jesus is coming back; and 2) His return is imminent — it can occur any moment.

Most Christians will respond to the question, "Do you believe Jesus is coming back?" by answering, "Yes." But their actions speak louder than their words. They don't live like they expect the Lord to return. Most are spiritual schizophrenics, walking with one foot in the church and the other in the world. They believe in the Lord's return in their minds, but not in their hearts. It is only when a belief moves from the mind to the heart that it begins to affect behavior.

Most Christians also seem to have no idea that Jesus could return any moment. Most are convinced that many prophecies must yet be fulfilled before the Lord can return. Well, there are many prophecies that must be fulfilled before Jesus returns to this earth to reign — a temple must be rebuilt in Jerusalem, the Antichrist must be revealed, and there must be seven years of Tribulation. But there is not one prophecy that has to be fulfilled for the

Lord to return for His Church in the Rapture. The Rapture is an event that can occur any moment.

❖ Two Returns of the Lord ❖

I attended a church faithfully for 30 years and never once even heard the word "rapture." I have since discovered that most Christians have had the same experience. The consequence is that most are not aware of the fact that there are going to be two future comings of the Lord.

One will be an appearing *for* His Church, to take the Church out of the world. The other will be a return to earth *with* His Church to reign for a thousand years.

The evidence of these two future comings of Jesus is very apparent when you study the only two detailed descriptions of the Lord's return that are contained in the New Testament. One is found in 1 Thessalonians 4:13–18, the other is in Revelation 19:11–16.

Table 3

The Two Future Returns of the Lord
Comparison and Contrast

The Rapture **1 Thessalonians 4:13–18**	**The Second Coming** **Revelation 19:11–15**
1. The Lord appears in the heavens	1. The Lord returns to earth
2. He appears for His Church	2. He returns with His Church
3. He appears as a Deliverer	3. He returns as a warrior
4. He appears in love	4. He returns in wrath
5. He appears as a Bridegroom	5. He returns as a King

In 1 Thessalonians 4 the Lord appears in the heavens. He does not return to earth. He appears for His Church. He is a Bridegroom coming for His bride. He appears in love as a deliverer to rescue His Church from the approaching wrath of God that will be poured out during the Tribulation.

In stark contrast, in Revelation 19 He is portrayed as returning to the earth with His Church, and He returns in great wrath as a warrior whose purpose is to judge and make war against the enemies of God. He also returns as a King to assert dominion over all the earth.

❖ How Signs Relate to the Rapture ❖

There are no signs for the Rapture because it is an event that can occur any moment. The signs relate only to the Tribulation and the Second Coming. But as we see the signs accumulating, we can be assured that the Rapture is near.

Tim LaHaye has explained the relationship between the Rapture and the signs of the times with a wonderful illustration. He tells about a friend of his who was walking through a shopping mall with his wife. He pointed out to her the fact that the merchants were putting up their Christmas decorations. She responded with what he thought was a curious question: "Do you know what those decorations mean?"

"Of course," he said, "they point to the soon coming of Christmas."

"Yes," she responded, "but they also mean that Thanksgiving is right around the corner!"[1]

❖ A Motivation to Holiness ❖

Now, let's return to my point. A person's life can be transformed if they ever come to believe two things: 1) Jesus is coming back and 2) His return can occur any moment. How can such beliefs change a person radically? Because they will motivate that person to holiness.

I know this is true from personal experience. I was a typical carnal Christian until I began studying and believing Bible prophecy. The moment I truly believed with all my heart that Jesus is coming back and may do so any moment, prophecy started to have a purifying affect upon my life. I didn't change overnight, but change was inevitable from that point on as the Holy Spirit began to convict me of areas of my life that were not ready for the Lord's return.

When a pastor starts preaching Bible prophecy, emphasizing the Lord's imminent return, he will discover that members of his congregation will start cleaning up their lives. They will put the booze and drugs aside. Marriages will begin to heal. Teenagers will be delivered from rebellion. There will be a rush to holiness.

❖ **Prophecy as a Purifier** ❖

The cleansing effect of prophecy is mentioned throughout the New Testament. Notice in the following Scripture quotations how the writer always relates the return of the Lord to righteousness and holiness:

> The night is almost gone, and the day is near. Therefore let us lay aside the deeds of darkness and put on the armor of light. Let us behave properly as in the day, not in carousing and drunkenness, not in sexual promiscuity and sensuality, not in strife and jealousy. But put on the Lord Jesus Christ, and make no provision for the flesh in regard to its lusts (Rom. 13:12–14).

> For the grace of God has appeared . . . instructing us to deny ungodliness and worldly desires and to live sensibly, righteously and godly in the present age, looking for the blessed hope and the appearing of the glory of our great God and Savior, Christ Jesus (Titus 2:11–13).

> Prepare your minds for action, keep sober in spirit, fix your hope completely on the grace to be brought to you at the revelation of Jesus Christ. As obedient children, do not be conformed to the former lusts which were yours in your ignorance, but like the Holy One who called you, be holy yourselves also in all your behavior; because it is written, "You shall be holy, for I am holy" (1 Pet. 1:13–16).

> The day of the Lord will come like a thief, in which the heavens will pass away with a roar and the elements will be destroyed with intense heat, and the earth and its works will be burned up. Since all these things are to be destroyed in this way, what sort of people ought you to be in holy conduct and godliness (2 Pet. 3:10–11).

> We know that when He appears, we will be like Him,

because we will see Him just as He is. And everyone who has this hope fixed on Him purifies himself, just as He is pure (1 John 3:2–3).

In every one of these passages the writer links the return of Jesus to a call for holiness.

❖ The Meaning of Holiness ❖

What is holiness? It sounds so theological. Let's try to get it down to earth. My practical definition is submitting to the lordship of Jesus. A commitment to holiness means allowing Jesus to control every aspect of your life through the indwelling presence of His Holy Spirit.

From time to time, you need to make an inventory of your life, asking the Holy Spirit to help you identify those areas that are not fully submitted to the lordship of Jesus. Ask yourself, "Is Jesus lord of my music and my reading material? Is He lord of what I eat and drink? Lord of my movies and TV programs? Is He lord of my job and my recreation? Is He really lord of anything in my life?" Ask the Holy Spirit to shine a spotlight on your heart to reveal the areas that need to be surrendered. He will do it.

The average Christian has made so many compromises with the world that he or she is often not even aware of many of them. This is partly due to being desensitized to sin by the paganism that surrounds us. It is also due to a famine of the Word in our lives. But even when we have been desensitized, the Word can convict us through its supernatural power.

❖ The Convicting Power of the Word ❖

That's what happened to King Josiah of Judah when he launched the greatest revival in the history of his nation. Even though he was a righteous person who earnestly sought the Lord, he was overcome with his sinfulness when the Word of God was read to him.

The story is a fascinating one that clearly shows the power of God's Word. Josiah felt led to purge the land of idols. In the process, he ordered that the temple be cleansed and repaired. As the priests were doing this, they discovered "the book of the law of the Lord given by Moses" (2 Chron. 34:14). It is no wonder the nation was in such sad shape. The Word of God had been lost! The book was taken to the king and read to him. As it was being read, Josiah became so convicted of his sins that he "tore his clothes" in repentance (2 Chron. 34:19). He then ordered that the Word of God be read to all the elders of Judah and Jerusalem (2 Chron. 34:29–30). This reading ignited a nationwide revival.

❖ Getting Serious about Holiness ❖

There is power in the Word, and we must feed on it daily if we are going to get serious about holiness. We need to get serious about holiness because I believe the message of the Holy Spirit to the end-time Church is, "Commit your lives to holiness."

Jesus is coming soon for His bride, the Church, and He wants a bride who is unspotted by the world. He is calling us out from the world. As He said in His final prayer with His disciples, we are to be "in the world" but not "of the world" (John 17:11, 16).

The message of the Lord's soon return is like a two-edged sword. It cuts one way for believers and another way for unbelievers. The message for unbelievers is, "Flee from the wrath that is to come!" The paradox is that Jesus is both the love of God (the cross) and the wrath of God (the second coming). The only way to flee from the wrath of Jesus is to run to the loving arms of Jesus, accepting Him as Lord and Savior. One of the best-kept secrets of the universe is that Jesus is returning in great wrath. Even most Christians are unaware of this fact.

❖ The Reality of God's Wrath ❖

Several years ago I reluctantly agreed to be the guest on a secular radio talk show in Oklahoma City. I say reluctantly because such programs usually end up with a lot of wrangling and shouting which I find unpleasant. I agreed to appear when the producer of the show told me that the host was on my ministry's mailing list and that he liked my writings. He assured me that the host would treat me fairly. I should have known, though, that I was headed for trouble when the producer said, "The host is a Christian, but none of his listeners know it."

I was interviewed over the telephone. The program began well with the host saying some nice things about my ministry and its publications. He then asked me to take five minutes to tell about my ministry before he opened the program to call-in questions. I didn't want to talk about the ministry. I wanted to talk about the Lord. So, I spent the five minutes talking about how the Lord had changed my life and how He could change anyone's life for the better if they would only submit to Him. When I finished, the host said, "That was very interesting, but it was not what I asked for. Please give us a word about your ministry. Could you sum up its message in one sentence?"

"Yes," I responded, "the purpose of the ministry is to proclaim the soon return of Jesus, calling believers to commit themselves to holiness and calling unbelievers to flee from the wrath that is to come."

"What do you mean by wrath?" he asked.

"I mean that the Lord is returning in vengeance to pour out the wrath of God upon the enemies of God."

"I've never heard such a bizarre thing," he snapped. "The Jesus I know wouldn't hurt a fly." Then he yelled, "Your God is a monster!" and he hung up on me. End of interview.

❖ Grace or Wrath? ❖

The truth is that the Creator of this universe is a righteous God who is very concerned about sin. The Bible teaches that He deals with sin in one of two ways — either grace or wrath. John the Baptist mentioned this in one of his sermons. He declared, "He who believes in the Son has eternal life; but he who does not obey the Son will not see life, but the wrath of God abides on him" (John 3:36).

Every person on planet earth is under either the grace of God or the wrath of God. For those under grace, the return of Jesus will be a blessed event. He will return as their "blessed hope." For those under wrath, the return of Jesus will be a terrifying event. He will come as their "Holy terror."

The principle is stated eloquently in the Book of Nahum. Of the righteous it says, "The Lord is good, A stronghold in the day of trouble, And He knows those who take refuge in Him" (Nah. 1:7). But with regard to the unrighteous, the message is stark and somber: "A jealous and avenging God is the Lord; The Lord is avenging and wrathful. The Lord takes vengeance on His adversaries, And He reserves wrath for His enemies. The Lord is slow to anger and great in power, And the Lord will by no means leave the guilty unpunished" (Nah. 1:2–3).

❖ The Prophets Speak of God's Wrath ❖

Isaiah says that on the day the Lord returns, His terror will be so great that people will crawl into holes in the ground and cry out for the rocks and mountains to fall upon them (Isa. 2:10–21). The prophet further states that "the earth will be completely laid waste" (Isa. 24:3), and the earth will be shaken so violently that it will reel "to and fro like a drunkard" (Isa. 24:19–20). He concludes by stating, "The Lord will come in fire . . . To render His anger with fury" (Isa. 66:15).

Jeremiah expressed a similar sentiment when he wrote, "The Lord will roar from on high. . . . A clamor has come to the end of the earth, because the Lord has a controversy with the nations. He is entering into judgment with all flesh; As for the wicked, He has given them to the sword" (Jer. 25:30–31).

The prophet Zephaniah devoted his entire book to the day of the Lord's return. He joined Isaiah and Jeremiah in speaking of the horrible nature of that day for unbelievers. He described it as "a day of wrath . . . A day of trouble and distress, A day of destruction and desolation, A day of darkness and gloom, A day of clouds and thick darkness" (Zephaniah 1:15). He said the Lord will pour out such wrath that men will stumble about as if they were blind, and "their blood will be poured out like dust" (Zeph. 1:17). He concluded by saying, "On the day of the Lord's wrath . . . all the earth will be devoured in the fire of His jealousy" (Zeph. 1:18). These are awesome words. They speak of a Holy God who will not tolerate unrepented sin.

❖ The Wrath of Jesus ❖

In the New Testament the Book of Revelation picks up the theme of the Hebrew prophets. It describes in detail the unparalleled wrath that will be poured out during the Tribulation, resulting in one-half the world's population dying in the first three and a half years (Rev. 6–9). It concludes with a portrayal of the Lord's return as a warrior of righteousness who comes to judge and wage war against unrepentant sinners (Rev. 19:11–15).

The humble Lamb who went to the Cross to die for mankind

returns as a roaring Lion. He does not return as some meek and mild wimp "who wouldn't hurt a fly."

Jesus takes sin just as seriously as His Father does. In Revelation 2 and 3 we have the closest thing in the New Testament to Scripture written directly by Jesus. These chapters consist of seven letters that He dictated to seven churches. Listen to what the one "who wouldn't hurt a fly" had to say to some of the churches:

> To the church at Pergamum: "Therefore repent; or else I am coming to you quickly, and I will make war against them [unrepentant sinners] with the sword of My mouth" (Rev. 2:16).

> To the church at Thyatira, speaking of a "Jezebel" in the church who was enticing people to commit acts of immorality: "I gave her time to repent, and she does not want to repent of her immorality. Behold, I will throw her on a bed of sickness, and those who commit adultery with her into great tribulation, unless they repent of her deeds" (Rev. 2:21–22).

> To the church at Laodicea: "I know your deeds, that you are neither cold nor hot; I wish that you were cold or hot. So because you are lukewarm, and neither hot nor cold, I will spit you out of My mouth" (Rev. 3:15–16).

❖ Withstanding God's Wrath ❖

The God of this universe is not a cosmic teddy bear who winks at sin. He is a God of holiness. He cannot be deceived. He is patient and long-suffering, not wishing that any should perish. But He is storing up His wrath for a day of terrible judgment.

The prophet Malachi asked, "Who can endure the day of His coming?" (Mal. 3:2). John echos those words when he speaks of "the wrath of the Lamb" and says that those who are subjected to that wrath will cry out, "Who is able to stand?" (Rev. 6:17).

The answer is simple. Anyone who puts their faith in Jesus as Lord and Savior will be moved from wrath to grace. Paul wrote, "Having now been justified by His blood, we shall be saved from the wrath of God through Him" (Rom. 5:9). Paul expressed the same idea in 1 Thessalonians 1:10 when he wrote that Christians are waiting "for His Son from heaven, whom He raised from the dead, that is Jesus, who delivers us from the wrath to come."

The choice between wrath and grace is yours. God made that choice possible through the gift of His Son who died on the cross for your sins so that you might be reconciled to the Father. God is so gracious. He sent His Son to die for us. He has delayed the return of His Son because He does not wish that any should perish, but that all should come to repentance (2 Pet. 3:9). Even during the Tribulation, the fundamental purpose of His wrath will not be to punish but to motivate people to repent so that they might be saved.

❖ Are You an Overcomer? ❖

If you have never received Jesus as your Lord and Savior, what are you waiting for? Time is limited. The only time you have guaranteed is this very moment. Life is fragile. It can be here one moment and gone the next. As I have said before, the Bible is full of gloom and doom for those who reject Jesus. But it has nothing but good news for those who have put their faith in Jesus. The Book of Revelation is full of glorious promises for "overcomers." Thirteen of these promises are contained in the seven letters Jesus wrote to the seven churches of Asia Minor (Rev. 2–3).

They are promises of eternal bliss. The Book of Revelation concludes with further promises to the "overcomer" — promises of eternal life on a new earth, living in the presence of the Creator. "There shall no longer be any death; there shall no longer be any mourning, or crying, or pain" (Rev. 21:4). John asserts, "He who overcomes will inherit these things" (Rev. 21:7).

Who is an overcomer? Jesus is the first and foremost overcomer. He overcame sin, the world, and death (John 16:33). Those who put their faith in Him become overcomers with Him. John put it in the form of a rhetorical question: "Who is the one who overcomes the world, but he who believes that Jesus is the Son of God?" (1 John 5:5).

❖ False Concepts of Salvation ❖

Perhaps you are thinking that you are saved because you were born into a Christian family. Salvation is not determined by natural birth. It is only spiritual birth that counts. Jesus said, "Unless one is born again he cannot see the kingdom of God" (John 3:3). It's amazing how many professing Christians sneer when asked if they are born again. Many proudly announce, "I'm not one of those 'born-again' types." That's a confession that they are really not a Christian.

Perhaps you are thinking that you are saved because you went through some sort of Christian rite like baptism. Religious rites do not save. You must willingly submit your heart to the Lord in repentance of your sins.

Perhaps you think you are saved because your name is on a church roll. Our churches are full of unsaved people, some of whom are Sunday school teachers, choir members, deacons, elders — and yes, even pastors. I've often said that the Sunday after the Rapture many churches will be filled with frightened people who will be seeking answers from unsaved pastors who have been left behind.

❖ The Nature of Salvation ❖

The essence of salvation is a relationship. Jesus did not say that eternal life results from baptism or church attendance or tithing. He said eternal life is to know the only true God and Jesus Christ whom He sent (John 17:3).

Perhaps you are a non-religious person or a person who has lived a life of willful sin. You may be thinking, *There is no hope for me. I have committed such terrible sins that God could never forgive me.* Not so. There is no sin so terrible that it can separate you from the love of God in Jesus Christ. That is what grace is all about — unmerited favor through the blood of Jesus. And the Bible says that when you place your faith in Jesus, God not only forgives your sins, He also forgets them in the sense that He will never hold them against you again (Heb. 8:12).

So, again, I ask, "Why are you delaying? What is holding you back? Is it foolish pride?" Isaiah says that on the day the Lord returns, "The proud look of man will be abased And the loftiness of man will be humbled" (Isa. 2:11).

❖ An Invitation ❖

I invite you to be born again and become an overcomer by praying this prayer:

Heavenly Father, I come to You, confessing that I am a sinner. I desire to accept Your Son, Jesus, as my Lord and Savior. Forgive me of my sins, indwell me with Your Holy Spirit, and seal me for redemption. Thank You, Lord. In Jesus' name, Amen.

If you just prayed that prayer, start seeking a church where the Bible is preached and Jesus is exalted as the only hope for the world. Seek an opportunity to confess your faith publicly before that congregation and then manifest your faith in Christian baptism. Get involved in a Bible study and prayer group, and start growing in the Lord.

❖ A Final Challenge ❖

We face dark days ahead as the forces of paganism intensify in these end times. But victory is coming. The Prince of Peace will soon arrive, and with Him will come the triumph of righteousness and holiness.

As we await the return of the Lord, we must —

> Stand on the Word
> Believe in God's power
> Rely on the Holy Spirit
> Practice tough faith
> Order our priorities
> Keep an eternal perspective
> Stand for righteousness
> Persist in prayer
> Surrender in worship
> Cling to hope
> And, live looking for Jesus

We are living in enemy territory. Let's never forget that. As C.S. Lewis urged us, let's conduct ourselves like commandos operating behind the enemy lines, preparing the way for the arrival of the Commander-in-Chief.[2] Equip yourself for combat and hold your ground, constantly praying, "*Maranatha!*" — Come quickly, Lord Jesus!

Endnotes

1 Tim LaHaye, *Rapture Under Attack* (Sisters, OR: Multnomah Publishers, 1998), p. 72– 73.

2 See footnote 5, chapter 8.

About the Author

Dr. David R. Reagan is the senior evangelist for Lamb & Lion Ministries, a prophetic ministry located in the Dallas, Texas, area.

Before founding the ministry in 1980, Dr. Reagan served for 20 years as a university professor, teaching international law and politics. Throughout that time he was an ardent student of the Bible.

Since 1980 Dr. Reagan has taught Bible prophecy in meetings and seminars held all across America and around the world.

His daily radio program, "Christ in Prophecy," is broadcast throughout the United States.

He has made many trips to Israel and is considered an expert on Middle East politics and Israel in Bible prophecy.

Dr. Reagan has been gifted with the skill to communicate complex ideas in simple, understandable terms. He is the author of several books, including the only children's book ever published about end-time Bible prophecy. It is entitled *Jesus Is Coming Again!* (Eugene, OR: Harvest House, 1992). His comprehensive book about Bible prophecy, entitled *The Master Plan* (Harvest House, 1993), has gone through many printings and has been published in many foreign languages.

Dr. Reagan and his wife, Ann, live in a Dallas suburb. They are the parents of two daughters and have four grandchildren.

For a catalog of Dr. Reagan's tapes and publications, write to Lamb & Lion Ministries, P.O. Box 919, McKinney, Texas 75070.